EPIC BIKE RIDES *of the* AMERICAS

Explore the Americas' most thrilling cycling routes on road, gravel and trails

HILLTOP

 Easy  Harder  Epic

CONTENTS

INTRODUCTION

Desert, forest, mountain, or urban jungle: the landscapes of the Americas are unparalleled in their diversity. So it followed that in order to create this book we approached a similarly motley crew of writers to contribute tales of their epic bike rides on these two continents. We asked hardy bike-packing adventurers such as Cass Gilbert, Lael Wilcox, Mark Beaumont and Sarah Swallow; road racers Keir Plaice, Andrew Bernstein and Riley Missel; the all-star editors and writers of Bicycling magazine Gloria Liu and Caitlin Giddings; and, of course, Lonely Planet's own group of globe-trotters.

That immense range of terrain means that whatever form of cycling you're into, it's not difficult to indulge it, or to try something totally new. For some of our contributors, biking was about escapism and involved nothing more complicated than packing some food, filling a water bottle, and meandering into the distance with the wind at their backs to explore industrial history or rural bliss. One or two went a lot further and, GPS unit in hand, ventured deep into the Andes of South America on laden bikes, powered by nothing more than their legs and a hunger to explore local cultures (and snacks). We've included several routes in the fast-growing field of bikepacking (like backpacking but on a bicycle!) that will hopefully inspire readers and riders to try something new.

Writers with families in tow recommended accessible rides along such rail trails as the Great Allegheny Passage and the Katy Trail. Other contributors pulled on skin-tight Spandex and sought out challenging climbs on vertiginous roads, whether in Colombia or California. Mountain bikers often preferred the descents, making pilgrimages to places like Whistler and Downieville to find their thrills and spills on rugged trails. Competitive types enjoyed the unique camaraderie of the new breed of gravel races. Our contributors crossed states (Iowa, Maine) and even entire countries (Ecuador, the USA two ways). And more than a few authors agreed that a good ride wasn't complete without a beer or two afterwards with old friends or new.

But what became indisputable – whatever your interpretation of 'epic' – is that an extraordinary range of cycling experiences is available in the Americas. You can have an epic adventure straight from your front door and be back before sundown. Or you can follow in the tire tracks of Sarah Swallow or Caitlin Giddings and pedal from the Atlantic to the Pacific oceans. We can't all take a sabbatical for cycling so this book also reflects varying levels of commitment. Some of these rides take just a couple of hours, others a day or two, a week, or several months. We've given a general indication of whether a ride is easy (in terms of terrain, distance, conditions or climate) or more challenging (steeper hills, longer distances, fewer snack stops). The goal of these stories is to inspire you to get your bike out (dusting it off and pumping up the tires first if need be) and explore somewhere new with the wind in your hair.

Cycling is the perfect mode of transport for the travel-lover, we cover more ground than if we were on foot, but without the barriers that a car imposes. We are immersed in our surroundings, self-powered, independent, and forever pondering the question 'I wonder what's over there?'. The bike rider is free to follow a whim, discover the limits of their endurance, or stop and settle for a while. Hopefully, this book will prove that there's no better way of experiencing a place, a culture and its people than by bicycle. And as some of these tales tell, arriving on a bicycle opens doors, literally and figuratively.

HOW TO USE THIS BOOK

This book is organized by country in alphabetical order. Each story features a first-hand account of a fantastic bike ride plus a toolkit to aid the planning of a trip – when is the best time of year, how to get there, where to stay. But beyond that, these stories should spark other ideas. We've started that process with the 'more like this' section following each story, which offers other ideas along a similar theme, not necessarily in the same country. Many of these ideas are well established routes or trails and we've suggested sources of detailed information. The index collects different types of ride for a variety of interests and locations.

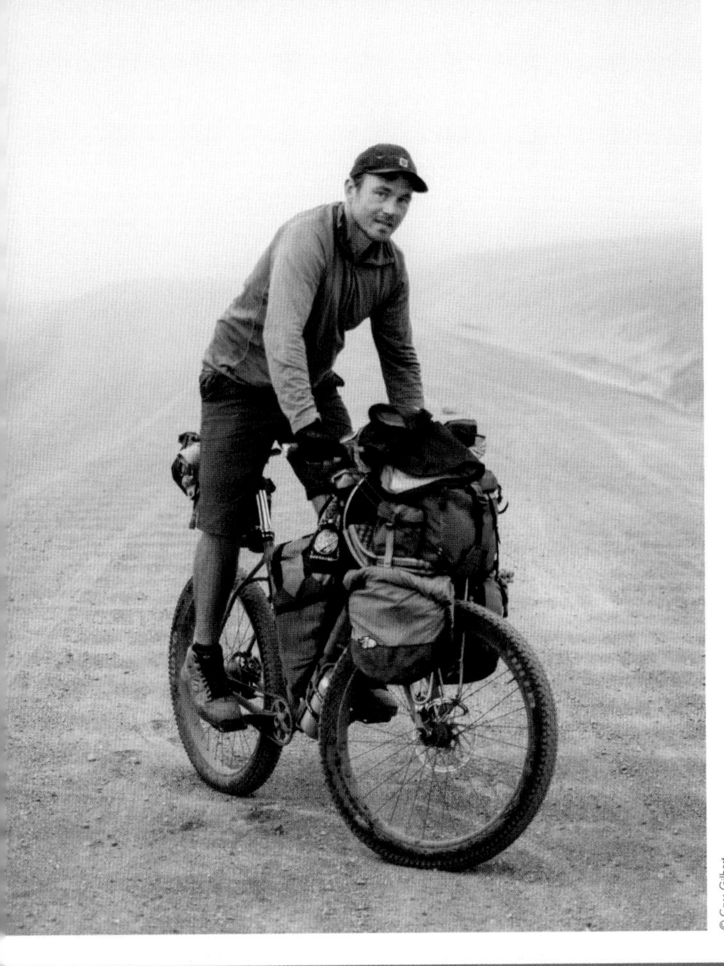

Clockwise from left: bikepacking across Ecuador; alpacas in Bolivia; the Golden Gate Bridge from Marin County, California. Previous page, clockwise from top: riding the Grinduro gravel race; mountain biking Downieville; exploring Oregon; a pitstop in Pennsylvania

© Cass Gilbert

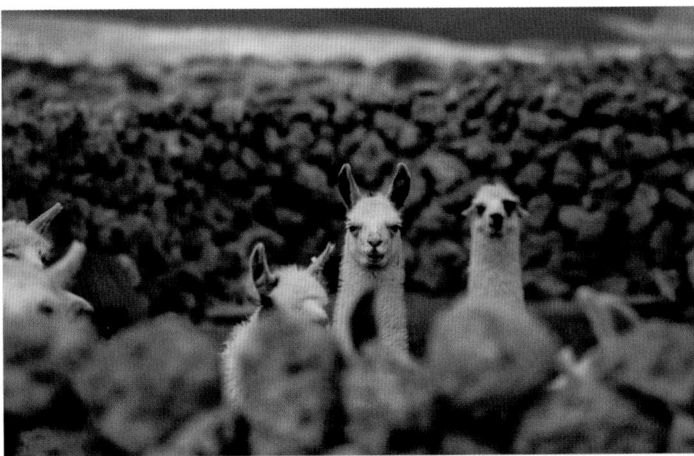

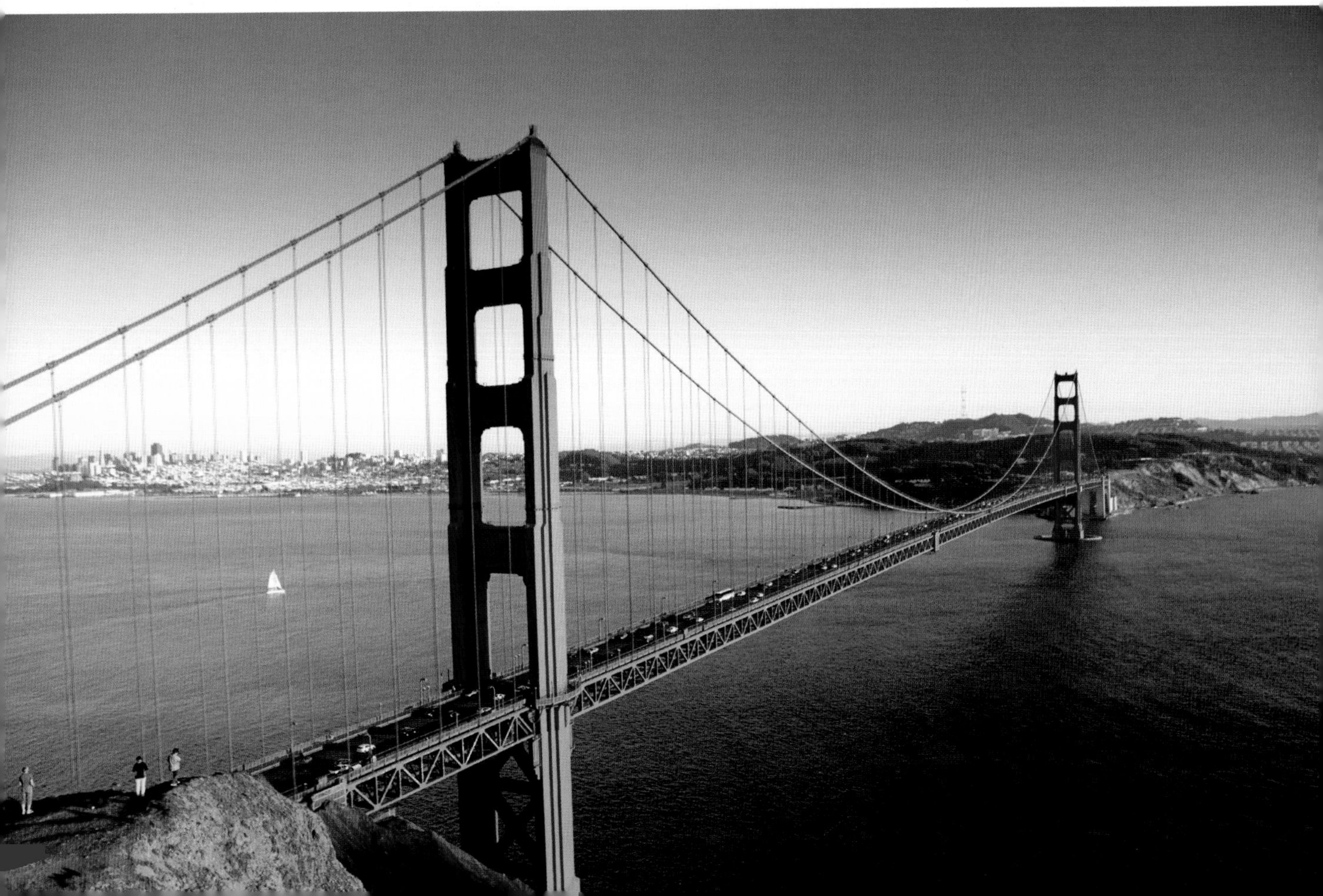

A WINE RIDE IN MENDOZA

Paved bike lanes lead from one vineyard to the next in Argentina's renowned Mendoza Valley, where you can swirl, sniff, sip and then spin onwards.

I don't normally drink wine for breakfast. Perhaps that's why I was grinning like a naughty kid when I found myself, just a few minutes after 10am one Wednesday morning, swirling a glass of malbec in Argentina's Mendoza Valley.

The enabler pouring me *vino* at Bodegas Lopez told me not to be ashamed: 'The morning is actually the best time to try wine because your palate is clean and alert,' she assured, before offering a second glass. It was a sweet wine this time with 'hints of pear and quince' – a healthy start, I supposed, for what was gearing up to be a full day of cycling through Argentina's preeminent wine region, which lies to the south of its namesake city along the country's western border.

Joining me at the saddle was Mendoza native Leo Garcia, an avid cyclist who was as eager as I was to pedal the sleepy, vine-lined roads. Before we set off on our journey, however, we opted for a quick tour of Bodegas Lopez to set the mood.

Opened in 1898, this was one of the first wineries built in the Mendoza Valley. It's now one of the largest in the country, producing mostly the regional specialty of malbec. The winery lies in a dusty satellite city of Mendoza called Maipú, which is prime real estate for the nation's top vineyards. With a new circuit of *ciclovias* (bike lanes), it's also a fantastic destination for hedonistic bike trips.

If there were no wines, there'd be no Maipú. Pedaling south from Bodegas Lopez on Ozamis St, in the direction of Maipú's main plaza, we saw dozens of historic buildings that had sprung up here in the late 19th century around a handful of brick-built *bodegas* (wineries). Many of these *bodegas* now lay in ruins beside our path.

One such relic was Antigua Bodega Giol, a once-majestic winemaking operation that was the largest in the world during its heyday in the 1910s. Garcia and I wandered through its three

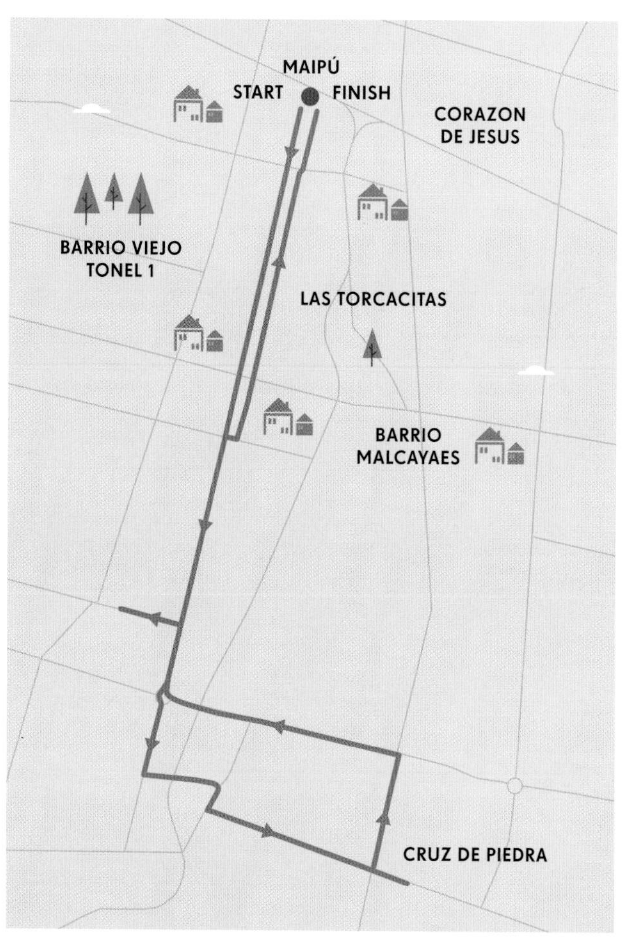

Clockwise from right: watch the grape harvest as you pedal past; relaxing at MAAL Wines after work; bottles ageing at Bodegas Lopez

subterranean tunnels – the old barrel rooms – where he told me, with no hint of irony, to be on the lookout for ghosts.

Like much of Argentina, Maipú gave off a distinct aura of faded grandeur. It was both unpolished and edgy – the kind of place where *campesinos* sold cheese and salami out of the back of trucks to accompany wine bottles labeled 'Rebellion.'

The grit of urban Maipú soon gave way to orchards of cherry and almond and, eventually, emerald-green olive groves. These spindly trees formed a patchwork grid beneath the snow-capped Andes, whose annual runoff is the reason this desert has metamorphosed into a green oasis. There were a half-dozen olive farms in the rural zone to the south of Maipú. We stopped for a break at 100-year-old Pasrai where there were generous tastings of olives, tapenades and extra-virgin oils. Our bellies sufficiently greased, Garcia and I pedaled onward beneath the parakeet-filled willow trees of Cruz Videla over to our next *bodega*, MAAL Wines.

Something of a playground for adults, MAAL Wines had everything from Frisbee golf to a foosball table and hammocks. It also had an open-air bar where we sampled some jammy malbecs and a highly hopped 'bohemian pale ale' called *Illegal* (so named because it's technically illegal to make beer at a winery).

With two wineries under our belts, it was time for a proper meal. For that, Garcia recommended we pedal 2 miles down Videla Aranda to visit his chef friend at La Cocina del Oso. Oso ('bear' in Spanish), was an appropriately named fellow with a lightning bolt of grey hair in his bushy brown beard. He'd adorned the walls of his rustic restaurant with poetry, antiques and local memorabilia, all of which rattled to the beat of Argentinean folk music. Oso brought out a pitcher of his silky homemade malbec while he cooked up beef empanadas (some *creole* style, others *Salteña* style). Then came the inevitable grilled meats. The meal ended two hours after it began with cheeses topped in a traditional jam of *cayote* (a fibrous squash) and Oso living up to his reputation as a spirited storyteller.

The afternoon sun was radiant by the time we rolled onward. It was so hot that even the once lively street dogs were now taking siestas.

I'd learned earlier how the intense sun concentrates juices in the wine grapes here. I began to feel as if it was sucking all humidity out of my skin, too, as we pedaled forward.

Now 7 miles from where we began, it was time to slowly work our way back to central Maipú, stopping along the way for short tastings at Trivento (a sophisticated, art-filled *bodega*) and Bodegas Familia Cecchin (a hippie-dippy organic vineyard). There were also craft breweries and liquor distilleries – neither of which we had time, nor the ever-fuzzying mental capacity, to visit.

Each of Mendoza's wineries had exuded a warmth and soul that's often missing in the Napas and Bordeauxs of the world. And because they cater to backpackers as much as jet-setters, we never felt out of place rolling up on two wheels. Those off the *ciclovias* even had bike-parking overseen by security guards. There was also something quite grounding about the whole experience. Not only did we consume wine at its origin; we arrived on our own steam. **MJ**

THE MALBECS OF MENDOZA

So powerful is the Mendoza brand that nearly two-thirds of all Argentinean wine comes from here. Most vineyards are located in the semi-arid desert along the eastern foothills of the Andes. Malbec is the region's signature varietal, with 75% of the world's stock produced here. Long known as an easy-drinking red with sweet tannins and silky textures, these days Mendoza malbec is often oaked longer for a more velvety punch.

Previous page: tracking true through vineyards in Mendoza

TOOLKIT

Start/End // Maipú
Distance // 14 miles (22km)
Getting there // There are a dozen daily flights between Buenos Aires and Mendoza, from where you can ride the Metrotranvía light rail to Estacion Gutierrez in Maipú.
Bike rental // Wine and Ride (www.wineandride.com.ar) is across the street from Estacion Gutierrez.
When to ride // Wineries are open year-round, though spring and fall offer the most agreeable climate for biking.
Where to stay // Sleep by the vines at Viña Maria, or in the old champagne cellar at Antigua Residencia.
More riding // You can tack on an additional day in the eastern part of Maipú, biking up the *ciclovia* alongside Urquiza, home to some of the most famous wineries in Mendoza.

Opposite: vines and mountains in the Elqui Valley of Chile

MORE LIKE THIS
WINE COUNTRY RIDES

FINGER LAKES, NEW YORK

Few Americans realize that the country's first bonded winery was not in California or Oregon but rather the spindly Finger Lakes of Upstate New York. More specifically, it was Pleasant Valley Wine at Keuka Lake. The modern-day wine trail around this Y-shaped lake is ideal for avid cyclists, who can tick off nearly a dozen wineries (and a half-dozen craft breweries) over one invigorating weekend. Start in Hammondsport, where you can taste the premium champagnes of Pleasant Valley and view eight stone buildings that are listed on the National Register of Historic Places. Be sure to try the region's signature dry rieslings and peppery cabernet francs as you stop at wineries on the route from here up to Penn Yan and back. With so many tempting vineyards, those with ambitious tasting goals may want to split the circuit up across two days.

Start/End // Hammondsport
Distance // 43 miles (69km)

ELQUI VALLEY, CHILE

Tucked away in the Andean foothills of northern Chile, on the southern edge of the world's driest non-polar desert, is a verdant oasis known as the Elqui Valley, where grapevines paint the desert green. Pedal from the coastal city of La Serena, Chile's second-oldest European settlement, following a rambling river valley away from the pounding Pacific and into the serene countryside. Soon after you reach the town of Vicuña (birthplace of Nobel Prize–winning poet Gabriela Mistral) you can stop at some of the highest wineries of the world, which produce rare-in-Chile grapes like garnacha and petite sirah at altitudes between 5900 and 7220ft. Elqui Valley is also the cradle of Chile's booming *pisco* (brandy) industry, with several distilleries where you can toss back a frothy pisco sour (the national drink). Pedal inland by day, and by nightfall, head to one of the valley's world-renowned stargazing facilities to watch as the inky sky fills with twinkling stars.

Start // La Serena
End // Alcohuaz
Distance // 68 miles (109km)

SONOMA VALLEY, CALIFORNIA

Far more bike-friendly (and friendly in general) than its snooty neighbor Napa, Sonoma Valley offers myriad ways for two-wheeling oenophiles to pedal through the pastoral countryside of Northern California. One of the more leisurely options, which will give you more time behind the glass than the wheel, is the 6-mile West County Regional Trail. This scenic route links the charming Sonoma Valley towns of Sebastopol and Forestville via a former railway line. It's paved almost the entire way, though you will pedal over an elevated boardwalk as you pass through the Atascadero Creek Ecological Reserve, an important local wetland. Wineries along the trail specialize in earthy pinot noirs and chardonnays that are more balanced than the creamier style found elsewhere in the state.

Start // Forestville
End // Sebastopol
Distance // 6 miles (9.6km)

BUENOS AIRES' BIKE PATHS

The chaos, colour and character of the Argentinian capital's barrios is best viewed from two wheels, as you ride through its past to its present.

From Jorge Luis Borges' short stories of knife fighters and tango dancers who owned the street corners of the old city, to the elegant tree-lined avenues that hark back to the capital's golden age, street life is central to Buenos Aires' lore and legend.

It's no different today – sidewalk cafes where the city's handsome citizens while away hours, vendors selling everything from feather dusters to hammocks, and the city's famous dog walkers wrangling hounds of every shape and size: it all happens on the street. You don't even need to venture inside a museum to see some of the city's best art – a thriving street art scene means you can enjoy contemporary masterpieces without ever dismounting your bike.

I'd lived in Buenos Aires before the bike paths were laid, and was used to traveling by taxi, bus or on foot. But when I returned on a recent visit I was delighted to find a new way to enjoy the city, cycling swiftly and safely through the cobbled streets of Palermo, sneezing at the plane trees that drop their fine fluff during the springtime, and admiring the purple blooms of jacaranda along Avenida del Libertador.

My favourite ride takes you from La Boca to Parque de la Memoria, an easy 5.5 miles if you go direct, but you'll want to meander through the city's cycleway network, taking in the sights and sounds of several *barrios* (neighborhoods), each one very distinct.

La Boca is the logical place to start, because while it may not be the spot where the city was first founded by the Spanish (that honour belongs to Parque Lezama, which you'll ride past soon enough), it represents Argentina's birthplace as a polyglot,

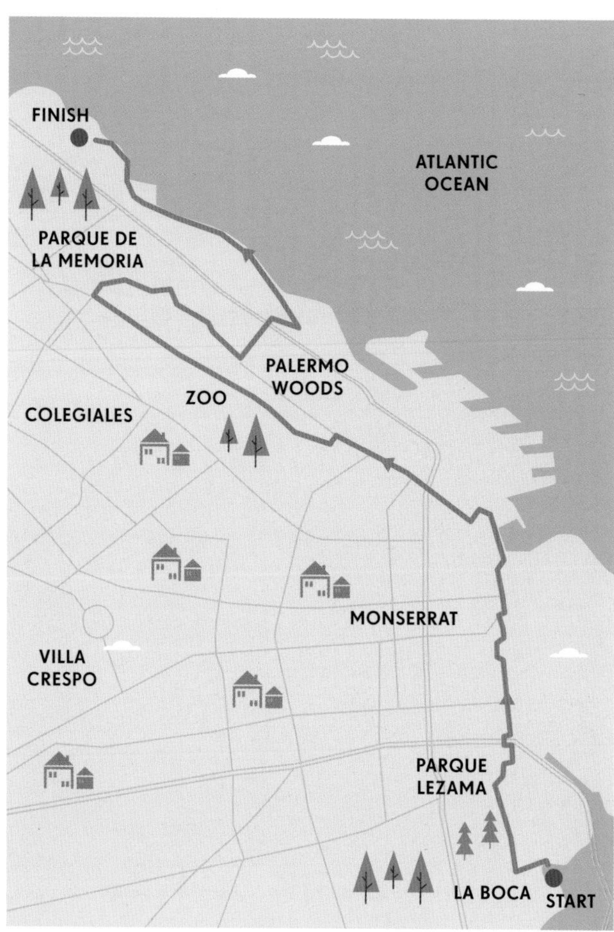

immigrant nation. It's here that hundreds and thousands of migrants poured off their ships and into the boarding houses and poor neighborhoods of the city's south. 'The history of Buenos Aires is written in its telephone directory,' penned English writer Bruce Chatwin, and more than half those names are Italian, mixed up with German, Welsh, Irish, French and Spanish.

The backbone of your ride is El Bajo – the wide multi-laned thoroughfares of Paseo Colón and Avenidas Libertador and Figueroa Alcorta. The *porteños* (locals or people of the port) refer to it as El Bajo (meaning 'low') because it's the low-lying land sloping down toward what was once the banks of the wide brown waters of the Río de la Plata. The city has turned its back on the river, blocking the view with high-rises – you'll not catch a glimpse of the water at this end of town unless you choose a detour through the swanky remodeled docklands of Puerto Madero, or take a ride through the leafy Parque Ecológico.

From La Boca, the next neighborhood heading northward is San Telmo. Once the home of the well-heeled, a yellow-fever epidemic saw them abandon their now-crumbling mansions for the northern end of town. On Sundays, San Telmo's Calle Defensa is taken over by street stalls selling handicrafts and bohemian fashion. There's usually a grungy young tango band or two, while Plaza Dorrego

"A thriving street art scene means you can enjoy contemporary masterpieces without dismounting your bike"

hosts an afternoon open-air *milonga* (tango party). For a bit of literary history, take a ride up Calle México to the old Biblioteca Nacional, the National Library where Borges was director for years, and wrote many of his most celebrated stories.

Just a little further along Defensa, you'll hit the Casa Rosada, or Pink House – Argentina's seat of government. Famous as the place from which Eva Perón made her stirring, strident speeches, it looks over Plaza de Mayo, the political heart of the country, which is usually filled with protesters of various stripes. Up Avenida de Mayo you can get a feel for Buenos Aires' more opulent past, with the ornate facades of once-elegant buildings now dark with soot.

Back on the Bajo, you'll head further north to Recoleta, and then on to Palermo. It's worth ducking up into the heart of each *barrio* and along its smaller streets. You'll find plenty of bars and restaurants with outdoor tables where you can eat while keeping

SHOPPING IN THE MARKETS

You can even shop on two wheels in Buenos Aires, especially if you hit the city's famous markets. There's San Telmo on Sundays and Plaza Francia, Recoleta from Friday to Sunday. But the loveliest is the Mercado de las Pulgas – the Flea Market – on Avenida Dorrego and Avenida Álvarez Thomas, where you'll find everything from priceless antiques to kitsch urban trash. The market is open from Tuesday to Sunday.

Left to right: an impromptu tango demonstration in La Boca; the Plaza de la República and its Alberto Prebisch-designed obelsik; an EcoBici bike-share rack; refreshments at San Telmo market. Previous page: a bikeway lined by jacaranda trees

an eye on your bike – a good idea in this city.

The end of your ride takes you along the beautiful Avenida del Libertador, through the Palermo Woods with their artificial lakes and exquisite rose garden. The place to rest after cycling this wonderful city is at one of its newest parks, Parque de la Memoria. Here you'll finally come face to face with the river; its *dulce de leche* waters lap against this quiet green space, dotted with sculptures. A wall bears the names of the thousands of Argentines who disappeared during its Dirty War, when the military government attempted to cleanse society of any political dissidents by murdering them or driving them into exile. It's a solemn but picturesque spot, and its sadness doesn't inhibit the young lovers who go there to smooch between classes at the nearby university. Irrepressible Argentines.

Any time of day is a good time to cycle, as this is a city that truly never sleeps. On a recent evening ride, I stopped for refreshment on Libertador to find an elderly woman and her pooch rendezvousing with her middle-aged daughters and their own canine companions for coffee and cake. It was midnight, and we shared a joke as joggers padded past and the cars racing by helped light the summer evening. Porteños love their city, and know how to enjoy its beauty and its chaos. **SG**

TOOLKIT

Start // La Boca
End // Parque de la Memoria
Distance // 5.5 miles (9km), but detours recommended.
Getting there // International travellers arrive at Ministro Pistarini Airport at Ezeiza. Flights from nearby countries land at Palermo's convenient Jorge Newbery Airport.
Bike rental // Some hotels have free bikes for guests: try Casasur Bellini in Palermo. Biking Buenos Aires (www.bikingbuenosaires.com) rents bikes by the hour and day.
Bike share // See www.turismo.buenosaires.gob.ar/en/article/cycling for a downloadable map.
Tours // Biking Buenos Aires (www.bikingbuenosaires.com) has a good selection, including one dedicated to street art.
When to ride // Spring, from mid-October to December.
Bike purchases/repairs // Try Canaglia Bicicletas.

Opposite: the annual Bike the Drive event in Chicago sees Lake Shore Drive closed to motorized traffic for a day

MORE LIKE THIS
CITY RIDES

CHICAGO, USA

Few serious cyclists would go to the Windy City specifically to ride their bikes. There's that relentless wind for one thing. And the place is as flat as the city's calorie-laden pizzas. But if you are in Chicago – whether for business, pleasure or both – a bicycle is a surprisingly good way of getting about. In 2018 the city spent more than $50m on cycling infrastructure and now has more than 200 miles (322km) of protected, buffered or shared bike lanes, and its bike share program, Divvy, has more than 600 stations. The Lakefront Trail, arguably the country's busiest mixed-use route, stretches for 18 miles (29km) along the shore of Lake Michigan. To test your legs, try the 60-mile (96km) North Shore Loop from Wicker Park to Fort Sheridan and back – grab details and a coffee from the city's Rapha Clubhouse on N Milwaukee Ave.

Start/End // Wicker Park
Distance // 60 miles (96km)
Info // www.rapha.cc

MONTRÉAL, CANADA

With its savagely hilly topographical profile and harsh seasonal weather conditions, Montréal has been described as an unlikely cycling city, yet that's exactly what it has become, with well over 373 miles (600km) of bike trails slithering around town – almost 155 miles (250km) of them separate to road traffic – and more than 5000 public-use bikes available for rent. Each summer, some 30,000 people rock up in Jeanne-Mance Park for the Tour de l'Île de Montréal, a road-riding challenge that has several distance options (the 15-mile/25km or 31-mile/50km classic, and the 40-mile/65km or 62-mile/100km Découverte). The routes – which roll around the Island of Montréal and span the St Lawrence River across Jacques Cartier and Champlain bridges, stream over Île Sainte Hélène and through Parc Jean-Drapeau, exploring Longueuil and Parc Michel-Chartrand before returning to the start – can be ridden at any time, but roads are closed to traffic during the event.

Start // Parc Ave
End // Jeanne-Mance Park
Distance // Ranges from 15 miles to 62 miles (25km–100km)
Info // www.velo.qc.ca

SEATTLE, USA

To win the no.1 spot in *Bicycling* magazine's annual list of America's best cities for cyclists, a city needs to bring its A game. That's what Seattle (the 2018 champion) has done: bike lanes are protected by concrete buffers, traffic signals have been re-timed to turn red for people driving more than 25mph (40km/h) on certain roads, and there are 60 miles (96km) of greenways underway. The result for this fast-growing city has been more cycle commuters, fewer single-occupancy vehicle journeys, an engaged cycling community and more female riders. And this is all in a city noted for the high H_2O content of its weather. Cycle the 30-mile (48km) Urban Loop to see some of Seattle's sights, including the waterfront or for a tougher challenge try the annual fund-raising Seattle to Portland ride organized by the Cascade Bicycle Club. It's big in participants (8000) and distance (206 miles/330km).

Start // Seattle
End // Portland
Distance // 206 miles (330km)
Info // www.cascade.org

PRAIRIE

TO THE TIP OF PATAGONIA

Cyclists rub shoulders with gauchos and guanacos in southern Argentina, braving howling wind to reach the tip of the South American continent.

Out on the bolt-straight roads of the Argentinian *pampa* (plains) my handlebars stay true, but my mind wanders. The open expanse of Southern Patagonia is a pensive place, a vast and empty land that stirs memories and emotion, like a calling to fill its void.

As my legs spin, I hum along to the buzz of knobbly tyres on smooth asphalt. I listen to the snap of my open shirt, which flaps behind me like a cape. I try and clear my head. But like any meditation, I become stuck on certain thoughts, clanking around like coins in a washing machine. Before long, an ostrich-like rhea waddles out of the camouflage of the plains. I smile, my spirits lifted. Then, a guanaco, the camelid native to these parts, breaks rank and jumps daintily over the endless fence line I've been following. It makes a chuckling sound as I pass, as if remarking on the ridiculousness of my toils.

It's a sentiment that seems to be echoed by others. Once, I see the blur of a passenger photographing me from a minivan that hurtles past. What must they be thinking? I guess I must look a little crazy, bearded and unkempt, out here in the emptiness. Later, a couple flag me down to quiz me about my bike. We talk a while by the roadside. I've noticed a distinct soulfulness in Argentinians, perhaps intensified by the thought-stirring sparseness of their land. 'Que lindo este viaje,' the man says, gesturing to his heart, and shaking my hand warmly. 'What a beautiful journey.'

A beautiful journey indeed, and one that captures Patagonia's contemplative character, its windswept isolation and its spectacular vistas. Indeed, the ride down from El Chaltén showcases one its finest moments; the granite silhouette of Mt Fitz Roy is the stuff of picture postcards and mountaineering legends.

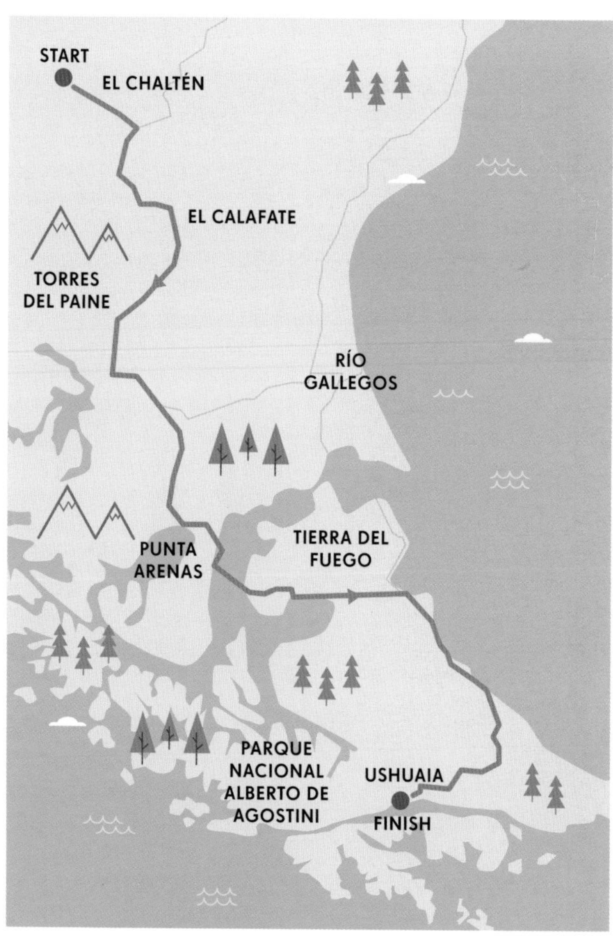

I pedal on. As asphalt peters out, I plough my way through deep, corrugated *ripio* (gravel), gliding from one side to the other in search of the truest line. In this light, it's hard to even tell what time of day it is. It could be just before sunset, but in fact it's early afternoon. Scale plays games on the *pampa*, and distance takes on a different quality; perhaps a more mysterious form of measurement, like leagues, is appropriate. Only roadside shrines mark the passing of time, and drainage culverts, into which cyclists sometimes burrow to escape the howling winds.

And those winds! They're incessant. Thankfully, my southerly trajectory means they're in my favour much of the time. But when they're not, it's like slamming against a steel wall. A particular tactic is thus required: strategic hops from one wind-free or rain-sheltered enclave to another. Most are abandoned buildings, skeletal husks that resonate with former lives. Like hallowed secrets, the exact locations of these sanctuaries are swapped around a carton of wine at a campsite, or scrawled onto a crumpled map out on the road.

Among the most popular is the so-called Pink Hotel on Ruta 40, the legendary road that spans the entire length of this country. An abandoned complex set on a solitary stretch of *pampa*, the Pink Hotel has long shielded a migration of riders from the howling, tent-crushing wind that gathers with gusto each afternoon. On the night I pass through, it's a surprisingly social premises. I'm one of five riders heading south, joined by a French-Canadian couple braving the elements north. We roll out our mats on the hotel's parquet floor and sign the guestbook: the canvas of a graffitied wall, onto which cyclists scrawl their names and a précis of their journeys.

PENGUIN COLONIES

No visit to Patagonia is complete without an encounter with its most characterful residents. Of the two penguin colonies en route, one involves a ferry ride to Isla Magdalena, home to 60,000 pairs of Magellanic penguins. Like drunkards dressed up for a ball, they stagger around in the high winds. The other is at Parque Pingüino Rey in Bahia Inútil, where cyclists can camp near a group of majestic King Penguins that stand up to 3ft tall.

Clockwise from top: King penguins at Parque Pingüino Rey; riding a fully-loaded fat bike; icebergs calving at the Perito Moreno glacier

Other such places of calm come and go. At a lonely outpost near Tapi Aike, Fabien the police officer ushers me in, as he has done to so many cyclists before me. He feeds me a hearty dinner, and together we watch dubbed movies late into the night. And there's Panadería La Union, about which I hear stories months before I actually arrive. Its location is triple-ringed excitedly on my dog-eared map, and a note scrawled to the side: 'Bakery. Delicious empanadas and cakes. Hosts cyclists for free.'

Breaking the monosyllabic mood of Southern Patagonia, there are also moments of startling eloquence. Sometimes, it's as simple as a lenticular cloud, or a team of muscular horses watching me ride by. At other times, it's raw geology. In El Calafate, I head out to Perito Moreno Glacier. Spanning 2.5 miles in width, the sight itself is as impressive as the sound it emits: a non-stop soundtrack of gurgles and murmurs, of deep, resonant rumbles and thunderous crunches.

I ride on, away from Ruta 40, forging my way closer to the coastline, until finally I cross the Strait of Magellan to Tierra del Fuego, the Chilean and Argentinian archipelago that lies off the southernmost tip of the South American continent. It's named after the myriad of fires once kept by the indigenous Yámana – a hardy folk who walked barefoot through snow. By now, I'm a member of my own impromptu cycling collective, pilgrims drawn from around the globe, pedaling by day and sharing stories by night.

For many, riding to the very tip of the South American continent is the end of long, arduous and undoubtedly beautiful journey; adventures that have unfolded from Colombia, Mexico or even Alaska. And now here we are. Together, we cycle through the gates of Ushuaia. Connected by a rush of similar emotions, we high-five. We hug. We look round in slight disbelief. Yes, we've arrived. Ahead, the road has finally run out. **CG**

"Together we cycle through the gates of Ushuaia. Connected by a rush of similar emotions, we high-five"

TOOLKIT

Start // El Chaltén
End // Ushuaia
Distance // 714.5 miles (1150km)
Getting there // Fly or bus into El Calafate, and out of Ushuaia.
When to ride // The best time to visit the area is during Patagonian summer – from November to March.
How to ride // Head north to south, or face a soul-destroying headwind much of the way.
Where to stay // Bring a stout tent, and keep your eyes peeled for abandoned houses!
What to take // Weather can be notoriously mixed; pack plenty of layers and reliable waterproofs.
Detours // Allow time to day hike in Argentina's world class Los Glaciares National Park, explore Torres del Paine in Chile, or connect this route with the 621-mile (1000km) Carretera Austral.

Opposite: a volcanic backdrop to bike riding in Bolivia

MORE LIKE THIS
REMOTE RIDES

SALAR DE UYUNI, BOLIVIA

Cycling atop the salt crust of Bolivia's Salar de Uyuni – and the more petite but perfectly formed Salar de Coipasa – is an undisputed highlight of many a South America journey. It's a high-altitude ride that takes five or six days, segmented by an opportunity to resupply with water and food at the midway settlement of Llica. As the largest salt flat in the world, cycling here provides an otherworldly experience. There's nothing quite like pitching your tent on a bleached white canvas, seasoning your dinner with the salty ground on which you're sitting, and awakening in the morning to a glow of ethereal, lavender light. This journey can only be undertaken in Bolivia's winter, as during summer the salt lakes are inundated by seasonal rain. See p26 for a story about the Salar.
Start // Uyuni
End // Sabaya
Distance // 186 miles (300km)

RUTA DE LAS VICUNAS, CHILE

If you wish to continue your South American adventures, this route explores the Bolivian borderlands and the altiplano of northern Chile by connecting three areas of protected land: Lauca National Park, Isluga National Park and the Reserva Nacional las Vicunas. The latter takes it name from the wild cousins of the llama that roam this *pampa*. Look out too for flamingos and rhea, flightless ostrich-like birds that are known as *suri* in the indigenous Aymara language. When not watching for wildlife, you can focus your attention on the feast of geographical features – the Salar de Surire salt lake, Volcan Guallatire and several hot springs along the way. The route uses unpaved roads that are relatively straightforward to navigate but beware cold nights, the lofty altitude, strong winds and limited food resupply stops. The dirt roads tend to be in better riding condition in the winter if you can cope with the cold.
Start // Putre
End // Lago de Coipasa
Distance // 182 miles (293km)
Info // www.bikepacking.com/routes/ruta-de-las-vicunas-northern-chile/

MAAH DAAH HEY, NORTH DAKOTA

In the language of the Mandan Native American tribe, Maah Daah Hey means 'an area that will be around for a long time,' but this 144-mile (231km) bikepacking trail has only recently been revitalised, thanks to the efforts of volunteers and the Forest Service (see info below). Today, the route offers a full immersion into the badlands of North Dakota, crossing the Little Missouri River twice, where another immersion is a risk if the water is high. The terrain ranges from clay buttes, layered with color, to grass plains. Numerous access points and 11 campgrounds mean that it's possible to bike just a section of the trail or the whole thing – not to be underestimated, this is rugged country. Wildlife you'll spot along the way ranges from prairie dogs and coyotes to the bison that roam nearby Theodore Roosevelt National Park. Roosevelt himself described the region as 'a place of grim beauty.'
Start / End // The northern trailhead is 15 miles south of Watford City; the southern trailhead is at the Burning Coal Vein campground
Distance // 144 miles (231km)
Info // www.mdhta.com

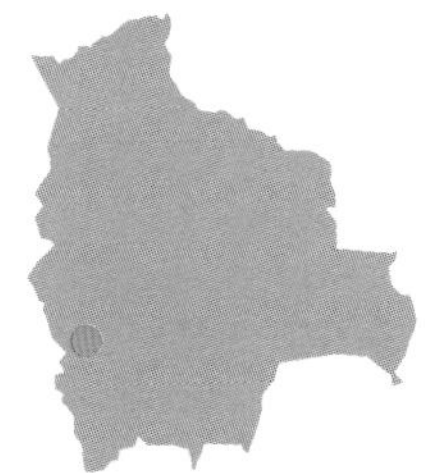

THE SALAR DE UYUNI

A cycle-touring pilgrimage, the Salar de Uyuni and neighboring Coipasa have drawn two-wheeled travelers to Bolivia for years. With bleached white canvases and lavender-tinted sunrises, there's nowhere in the world quite like them.

In the dusty village of Vichaya, a fiesta builds in momentum as drunken revelry charges the air. Hired in from La Paz, a sharp-looking band plays tirelessly, trumpets and tubas glinting in the midday sun. Bowler-hatted women swirl their skirts and petticoats in perfect synchronicity. Their masked husbands, dressed in the shimmering Morenada costumes of the Bolivian Andes, launch into an elaborate dance inspired by the suffering of African slaves, brought to work in the silver mines of Potosí.

The mood is generous and upbeat; luckily, full inebriation has yet to be reached. Plastic cups of beer are pressed into our hands. I make the mistake of sipping mine without first offering due thanks to Pachamama – Mother Earth. 'We must respect Pachamama and give back to her,' reprimands an elderly *campesina* with intensity. 'Pachamama is the earth on which we walk.' She looks over at our grubby, battle-scarred bikes, fresh from crossing the country's beautiful and solitary Salar de Coipasa and the surrounding altiplano.

'She's the earth along which you ride your bikes,' adds the lady for the sake of clarity. Her drunken husband, hair matted and eyes glassy, nods in solemn agreement. I try again, this time dutifully waving my cup skywards, sploshing beer onto the ground as custom dictates, before taking a generous swig. They smile, appeased.

For almost as long as I can recall, traversing Bolivia's Salar de Uyuni had been my cycle-touring dream, sparked by images I once saw of a tribe of bearded, ragtag bike travelers pedaling across its open, featureless breadth. For many, riding atop the thick crust of this salt lake, and the more petite but perfectly formed Salar de Coipasa, are undisputed highlights of a trip to South America.

It is, however, a trip you'll need to time just right. Only during

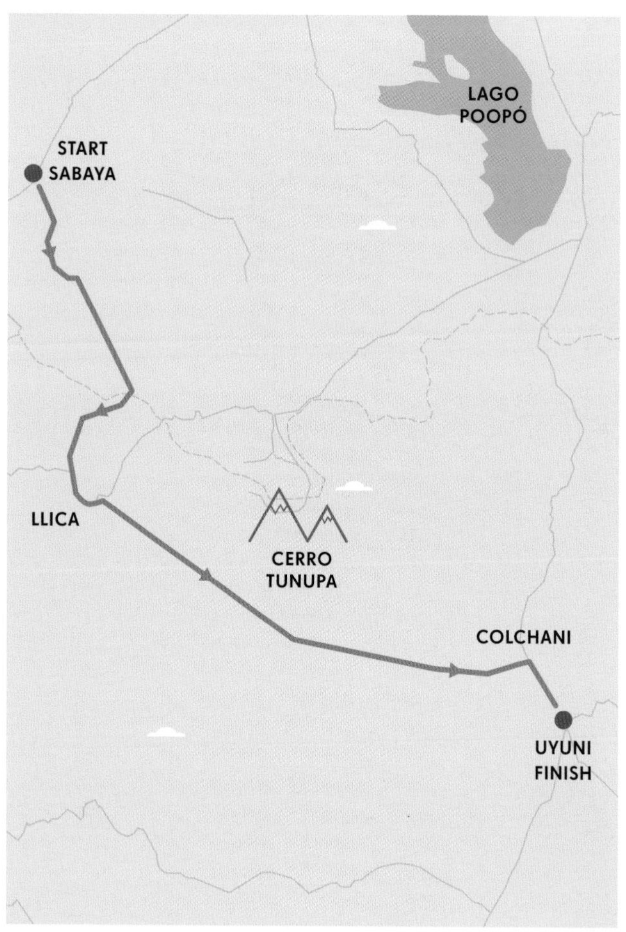

Left to right: traditional dances in Vichaya; a pause for the laden riders in Challacollo; an alpaca

"Bereft of tracks and traffic, a cyclist is free to sail any which way, like a ship out at sea, if the wind is blowing kindly"

the winter, when the nighttime temperatures plummet and the monsoon rains have long passed, are the salt lakes dry enough to cross. And even then the shallower edges will likely have a spongy crunchiness to them, because beneath these crusts hide reservoirs of brine. It's said that close to half the world's lithium deposits are found here.

Faint tracks crisscross its expanse. Which one you choose is up to you. Wherever you point your handlebars, perspective plays tricks in the mind and distances lose meaning. In every direction, islands of rock rise out of the shimmering distance. The closest looks to be half an hour's ride away... but perhaps it's half a day. Bereft of tracks and traffic, a cyclist is free to sail in any direction, like a ship out at sea, especially if the wind is blowing kindly. In fact, I even closed my eyes and dared myself to pedal for a minute or more at a time, knowing there was nothing to bump into.

Like those before me, my own crossing was segmented by a resupply of food and water in the small settlement of Llica. Deep sand and corrugation mine the roads that cross this finger of terra firma, one that divides the Salar de Uyuni with that of Coipasa. Aside from a chance to fill water bottles and feed, Llica brought with it yet another typically spirited and drunken festival. Such is the dichotomy of Bolivia. Empty desert silence one moment, rambunctious partying the next. A brass band prowled the streets, kids in traditional costumes danced and elderly women gossiped, all of them unflinching and impervious to the cold. No one even seemed to know when the party had actually started, or indeed, with habitual Latin American ambiguity, how long it might go on for. Three days? Five days? 'It will end tomorrow,' said one lady. 'It has to. We need to sleep...'

I didn't feel like waiting to find out, as the promise of a more restful silence called us towards the *salar* once more. Encircled by distant volcanoes, the Salar de Coipasa glittered in the afternoon sun, salt crystals paving our way like roughly cut diamonds. It was a precious realm we had all to ourselves and we even stopped to camp for the night, for no other reason than to bide our time and soak up every moment of this otherworldly experience.

Bolivia's altiplano and its salt lakes will forever remain a highlight of all my travels on two wheels. My strongest memories? Squinting into the blinding, midday light. Feeling my own crispy skin crinkle, ever so dry. Pitching my tent on a bleached white canvas. Seasoning my dinner with the ground I slept on. Awakening in the morning to a glow of lavender light. And above all, just closing my eyes, and riding. **CG**

GHOST TRAINS

Located a short bike ride outside of Uyuni, the train cemetery is a must-visit (best timed at midday to avoid the jeep tour groups). It's a surreal experience to poke around these rusted, stripped-out carcasses – like a scene from a post-apocalyptic movie – which are remnants of a railroad project that fell through in the 1940s, when the mining industry collapsed. Most of the steam trains herald from the UK and date back to the early 20th century.

Previous page and overleaf: sailing across the salt flats of Salar de Coipasa and setting camp for the night

TOOLKIT

Start // Sabaya

End // Uyuni (or the other way round)

Distance // 110 miles (180km)

Getting there // La Paz International Airport is the best place to fly into.

When to ride // Bolivia's winter (May–October) is the only season to complete this ride; the nights can drop below freezing but the days are sunny and dry. During the summer, monsoon rains make the salt flats impassable by bike.

Where to stay // The ride across both salars takes four days. Grab a rock to drive stakes into the ground if you want to pitch your tent in the middle of nowhere. Llica offers the perfect spot to resupply between Uyuni and Sabaya, and to rest up; spend several days at altitude before setting out.

What to take // The riding is straightforward, aside from the sandy, bumpy tracks in and out of Llica. Bring sunglasses!

Opposite: catch your breath on a high pass on the Ruta de las Seis Miles between Argentina and Chile

MORE LIKE THIS
SALTY ADVENTURES

SALAR DE SURIRE, CHILE

Although there's nowhere quite like the Salar de Uyuni, the Salar de Surire in neighboring Chile has a similar vibe, albeit with more life. In fact, you can extend your ride across the Bolivian altiplano to include the Parque Nacional Lauca too. The area is teeming with wildlife, from leggy pink flamingos, fleet-footed vicuñas (the wild relative of the llama) and ostrich-like birds called suri, generally to be seen bounding across the open *pampa*. The same advice applies here as in Uyuni; the *salar* can only be ridden in winter (May to October) and be sure to acclimatise thoroughly beforehand and carry plenty of warm layers. As a sequel to Coipasa, allow five more days for this ride to Putre, resupplying on the border at Colchani/Pisiga, where food and fresh produce is available. Just be very careful about acclimatization.

Start // Colchani/Pisiga border
End // Putre
Distance // 180 miles (290km)

RUTA DE LAS SEIS MILES NORTE, ARGENTINA/CHILE

The Argentinian Puna also offers a very barren, windswept feel with a salty theme. It comes complete with dream-like panoramas of mineral-streaked mountains, as well as lava flows and salt fields. Skirting the border between Chile and Argentina, it's lined by some of the highest volcanoes in the world and is far removed from any evidence of human activity, bar occasional mining. The altitude hovers at 11,500ft (3500m), adding to its ethereal feel. If you want an extremely remote and physically demanding challenge here, consider the Ruta de las Seis Miles Norte. It's best ridden between November and January to avoid potential rains and electric storms. Prep your bike with large volume tyres to help tackle soft surfaces, and allow room in your panniers for several days of food and water, which is generally scarce.

Start // Fiambala, Argentina
End // San Pedro de Atacama, Chile
Distance // 487 miles (784km)

BADWATER BASIN LOOP, CALIFORNIA

In the US, Death Valley, the largest national park in the Lower 48s, offers more salt-tinged remoteness, but at much lower altitudes. In fact, the salt flats in Badwater Basin lie at a mere 282ft (86m) below sea level. This area can only be explored by bike in the winter, as temperatures in the summer reach 115°F (45°C) or more, though beware of frigid nights, short days and a general lack of water. As a taster, a loop can be made out of Saline Valley Rd, over Lippincott Pass, along Lippincott Rd, Racetrack Valley Rd and back over Hunter Mountain Rd; such a ride includes 4900ft (1500m) in elevation gain. Pack plenty of water and expect mixed surfaces, including rough corrugated (washboard) roads. Allow time for a detour to Racetrack Playa to experience the mysteries of its 'sailing rocks,' slabs of dolomite and syenite that leave long, visible tracks as they slide ever-so-slowly across the playa surface.

Start/End // Saline Valley and Hunter Pass Road
Distance // 52 miles (84km)

RIDE THE WHITEHORSE TRAILS

Just under the curve of the Arctic Circle, in Canada's ultra-remote Yukon Territory, Whitehorse possesses magical mountain-bike trails beneath the midnight sun.

Studying a guide to Whitehorse's mountain-bike tracks is like eyeballing a plate of spaghetti dished up by an excessively flamboyant and generous chef. Some 700km (435 miles) of rideable trails have been mapped within the city limits of the Yukon Territory's capital – 300km (186 miles) of sensational singletrack, and 400km (248.5 miles) of delicious doubletrack and dirt roads.

I can't think of another metropolis in the world that offers an off-road feast comparable to the bikers' banquet served up here. But this tasty tangle of tracks also makes it difficult to decide where to start. Or finish. Or go in the middle. You could potentially pedal for days – weeks even – and not cycle over the same bit of dirt within this maze of interconnecting spruce-fringed paths.

It's possible to splice several trails together into one epic continuous ride, instead of doing little circuits, but it definitely helps if you know the lay of the land – or roll with someone who does. Which is why I'm grateful to be following the flowing lines

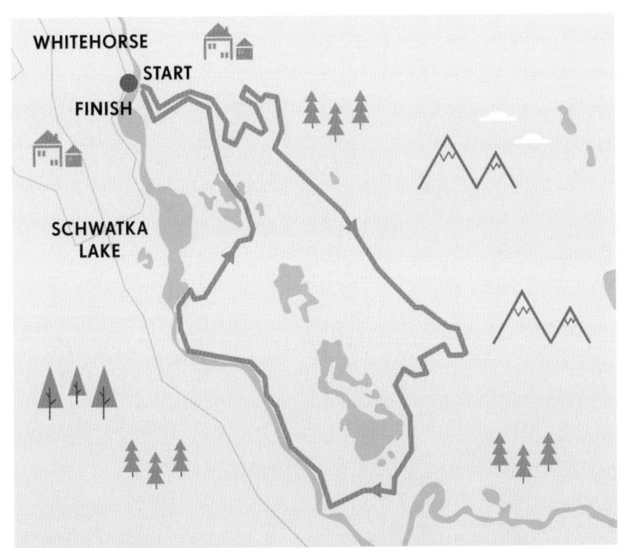

© Dan Barham

being etched in the earth in front of me by local guru, Sylvain Turcotte, owner of Whitehorse MTB base Boréale Explorers, and a pro trail hound.

We're riding around a super scenic combination route on the outskirts of Whitehorse, on the Grey Mountain side of the mighty Yukon River – an emerald waterway that elbows right through this enigmatic territory, before crossing the border into Alaska.

You can reach the trailheads directly from the CBD, with the wilderness beginning as soon as you leave the city streets, pass through Rotary Peace Park, cross the bridge and set off up Grey Mountain Rd. Our route – one of myriad options – begins with a gentle ascent to the Upper Riverdale Trail, which quickly delivers a cracking vista back across Whitehorse city and the great green Yukon.

Crossing Grey Mountain Rd, we follow the Yellow Brick Rd, a trail that leads (via several short connecting tracks) not to a wizard, but to the next best thing: the brilliant blue Boogaloo Trail system, which is every bit the 'buffed out, fast-flowing and glorious piece of singletrack' that David, another local guide, had promised it would be.

Although this isn't like Vancouver's notoriously gnarly North Shore scene, the trails do boast plenty of technical features. There are chicken runs alongside some of the scarier obstacles, in case you veer onto a track that's beyond your skill level, but routes are clearly signed and graded according to International Mountain Bike Association (IMBA) standards: green circle routes are easy, blue square trails more challenging, black diamond tracks demand technical skill (or blind bravery) and double black diamond runs are only for highly experienced and/or pain-impervious riders.

"The Southern Tutchone – First Nation people of the Whitehorse region – used the banks of the Yukon as a trading route"

Other clues to how tricky a trail might be can be found in the extra colorful vernacular employed in the name – SFD (Straight Fucking Down) being a prime example of a track that delivers exactly what it swears it will.

Leaving Boogaloo behind we venture further up the flanks of Grey Mountain and tie together a bunch of blue and black tracks – including Payback, SFD, Girlfriend and Juicy – for a long, flowing (and occasionally eye-wateringly rapid) descent around Chadburn Lake to the start of the iconic Yukon River Trail.

This open and undulating trail traces the east bank of the Yukon River for 4 miles, rolling spectacularly along the steep ridge and occasionally ducking and diving into the forest. The loose-dirt path isn't overly technical, but it is narrow and demands full focus, because one lapse of concentration or ill-timed gaze at the lovely views might result in a high-speed tumble all the way into the freezing embrace of the river.

This path is steeped in history. For centuries before the arrival of Europeans, the Southern Tutchone – First Nation people of the Whitehorse region – used the banks of the Yukon as a hunting and trading route. And in the late 1890s, prospectors (including the

author Jack London) with heads and hearts running hot with gold fever, rushed this way, in a desperate scramble to reach Dawson City and the Klondike to stake their claim. What they would have given for a sturdy dual-suspension steed I can only imagine.

The route rages on, clinging to cliffs and sidestepping bluffs, right through the historic ruins of an old boom town, Canyon City, an important stop-off during the 1898 Klondike Gold Rush – stampeders would stop here before nervously negotiating potentially lethal rapids just downstream.

It's not a bad spot for riders to calm their own nerves before pedaling the precipitous Rim Trail, which tiptoes along the edge of Miles Canyon and ultimately leads down to the shores of Schwatka Lake, where glacial waters await those courageous enough to make the plunge.

And then there's a decision to be made. Head back to Whitehorse or explore more trails around the Hidden Lakes? The day is getting old, but that scarcely matters. It's midsummer, a time when the Yukon lives up to its nickname as the land of the midnight sun.

Whitehorse occupies a position on the globe so far north that the sun barely sets for several weeks around the summer solstice, and the sky never gets properly dark. There's even a 24-hour mountain-bike race held here, where using lights is against the rules. As Robert W Service, the bard of the Yukon, once observed: 'There are strange things done in the midnight sun.'

We ride on towards the Hidden Lakes. To pass up the opportunity of finding more cycling gold in these hills really would be strange. **PK**

CARCROSS

Canada's newest mountain-bike mecca is in Carcross, home to the Tagish First Nation. Around Montana Mountain, a trail network of 46.5 miles (75km) – including 22 miles (35km) of singletrack – has been developed from old mining paths in a groundbreaking project involving local indigenous youth groups and cyclists. 'Mountain Hero,' the star route, is an IMBA epic-rated trail featuring 12.5 miles (20km) of climbing and a 5-mile (8km) descent to Nares Lake.

Left to right: taking a break by the lake near Carcross, Yukon; shredding forest singletrack in Whitehorse, Yukon. Previous page: cornering in Carcross, south of Whitehorse

TOOLKIT

Start/End // Whitehorse

Distance // 31 miles (50km)

Tour // You can ride independently (free) or with a local operator such as Boréale Explorers (www.be-yukon.com), which provides good-quality bikes, expert guidance and yurt-based accommodation in the midst of the trails.

What to take // A decent dual-suspension mountain bike, along with a helmet, some armour and all the usual spares and tools. Carry bear spray (seriously) and insect repellent.

When to ride // Unless you have a fat bike (a mountain bike with supersized tyres) tracks are only rideable May to October. Check out June's 24 Hours of Light MTB festival.

More info // See www.yukonbiking.ca. Printed waterproof maps can be purchased in Whitehorse's two local bike shops, Cadence Cycle and Icycle Sport.

Opposite: riding the Benchlands Trail near Canmore

MORE LIKE THIS
CANADIAN BIKE TOWNS

CUMBERLAND, BRITISH COLUMBIA

There's a reason Darren Berrecloth, Canadian freeride mountain biker and all-round fat-tire legend, lives on Vancouver Island: the place is packed with trails for riders of all abilities (though skewing to the more experienced mountain biker – this is British Columbia after all). And the town of Cumberland, midway up the island, is at the center of a motherlode of cross-country trails that take riders up into the forested mountains or down to the storm-tossed west coast. Because this is BC, expect big trees, lots of difficult, damp twists and turns, and a sense of having accessed a higher state of consciousness. The trail guardians are the UROC (United Riders of Cumberland), who provide maps to the 170 or more trails, host such events as the Twelve Hours of Cumberland, and support women and youth riders. Venture further by hopping on a ferry to Hornby Island for yet more magical mountain biking.
Distance // Variable
Info // www.unitedridersofcumberland.com

CANMORE, ALBERTA

A great concentration of trails surrounds Canmore in Alberta, as you'd expect of a town just west of Calgary and in the shadow of the Rockies in Banff National Park. There are routes for all abilities, from wide, scenic dirt roads to more technical challenges such as the 5-mile (8km) Highline Trail. Local guiding companies can show visiting riders the ropes. Canmore Nordic Centre Provincial Park has more than 100km of mapped trails, plus rentals, lessons, tours and a skills park. Cox Hill in the Kananaskis area is another hotspot – although remember that you're a long way north here and snow can be present all year round. Canmore itself has dozens of places in which to eat and drink. Then explore further trails in the region around Fernie, 124 miles (200km) to the south (see p62).
Distance // Variable
Info // www.albertaparks.ca

COLLINGWOOD, ONTARIO

Representing the east, on the shore of Lake Huron, Collingwood mixes parties and mountain biking much like Whistler on the west coast, if on a smaller scale. Just a couple of hours from Toronto, Collingwood makes for an exciting weekend escape if you enjoy life-accessed downhill tracks, forested singletrack, beaches, and late-night drinking and dancing. Which is all of us, right? The downhill tracks are in Blue Mountain Bike Park, which offers rentals, lessons and carefully maintained trails.
A maze of the best cross-country trails in the province radiates across the Niagara Escarpment from Collingwood (guides are advised) to test your lungs and legs. Or you can head further out to the Kolapore Highlands for 30 miles (50km) of rooty trails. Finish the day with a bracing dip in Georgian Bay before exploring the town's bars and brews (Collingwood has not one but three microbreweries).
Distance // Variable
Info // www.kolaporetrails.org; www.bluemountain.ca

THE CABOT TRAIL

Around the rugged northern shore of Cape Breton in Canada lies a beautiful 186-mile loop that circumnavigates Nova Scotia's storied past.

'Do it in a day, and we'll give you honorary Nova Scotian citizenship,' an old racing buddy told me. That was not something I was going to take lightly. Considerate and polite, he might be 135lbs soaking wet, but he would be the first guy at your side if you got into an argument at the bar.

I remember one of my first big races; I said I'd cover the breaks, but once the peloton got going, my heart was in my throat. He pulled me aside before the team meeting the next morning.

'Man. What happened?'

I had done alright, I thought. I had made it to the end.

'You have to cover the attacks.'

A couple of hours later, I was in my first professional breakaway.

After that, riding 186 miles around Cape Breton should have been nothing.

But there I was on North Mountain, watching the September sun sink over the trees, as the road wound like a ribbon of grey kelp over mossy stone. The Atlantic glinted in the distance, crashing on to the rocky beach in Chéticamp, which I had left at dawn. I wanted to be there before nightfall. But first, I had to make it to the top of that damned hill.

Why did I have to do it the hard way? Most start the Cabot Trail in Baddeck, a tidy collection of clapboard houses and shops on the northern shore of Bras d'Or. From the town's harbour, they set off with plans to be back in a few days – couples on hybrids, solo tourers with overstuffed panniers. Most were going clockwise. I went anti-clockwise. I was staying in a cottage up on the northwest coast, and I did not want to ride into the wind on the flat for 60 miles at the end. The climbs would give me

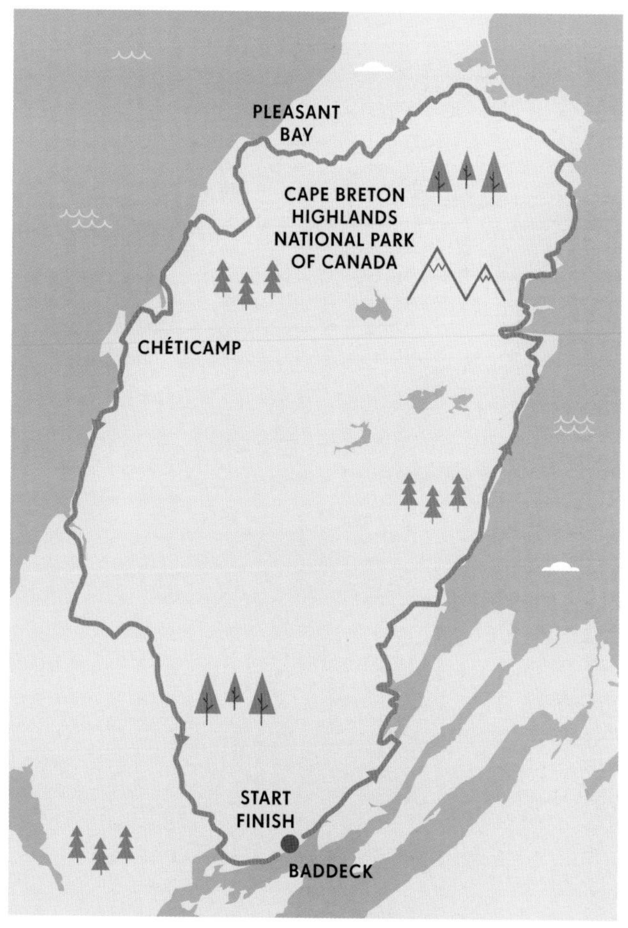

"During the Highland Clearances in the first half of the 19th century, tens of thousands of Gaels fled Scotland for Nova Scotia"

something to look forward to. Descending French Mountain as the sun dropped below the most distant swell would be a magnificent finale, I'd thought.

My shoulders tensed. Every turn of the pedals promised to be my last. I ground on. It was a glorious day in an Indian summer; a hint of salty chill blew off the sea. There were too many miles to go. And I had had all the time in the world.

Heading south, with the early mists, my chain whirred, as the road rolled through grassy fields. Below, waves crashed on to the rocks. Fishing boats chugged away from the docks. The Acadian *tricolore*, with its bright yellow star, flapped above every white-, red-, or blue-washed house.

I stopped at a gas station. A group of men sat inside drinking coffee between racks of chocolate bars and cigarettes. They greeted me in their French, quite distinct from Québécois, descended from settlers who moved to *L'Acadie*, a separate colony of New France, in the 17th and 18th centuries. Long persecuted by the British after France's American defeat, many were expelled to the southern colonies or Europe. It was years before the British allowed them to return to their old territory.

On the road further south, the fields turned to forest and the route got hillier. French signs gave way to English with Gaelic subtitles, promoting *céilidhs* – house parties with folk music and dancing – among other events. During the Highland Clearances in the first half of the 19th century, tens of thousands of Gaels fled Scotland for Nova Scotia, eventually to work the island's coal mines and fish its shores.

A barn was painted with white lettering: 'This is unceded Mi'kmaq territory.' I struggled on, understanding better, perhaps, the idea that the Mi'kmaq had lived by for more than 10,000 years. Those fishing villages I'd passed, sheltered by a natural cove, the beaches, the few patches of fertile soil – they were there by the island's grace. For someone else to own the wild and rugged land that you love, the land that has provided for your family's living for as long as anyone can remember, is absurd. The Highlanders knew that. So did the Acadians. So, for that matter, did the United Empire Loyalists forced out of the United States for their fealty to the British Crown. Their lives were hard, and their relations were often fraught, but together they made Cape Breton their home.

The road flattened. The bush thinned to scraggly pines. The descent to Pleasant Bay left me breathless. I climbed MacKenzie Mountain as the sun was setting. It was just as tough, but I had the wind at my back.

Up in the Highlands, I saw seven moose in the dusk – all mothers and their young. I descended French Mountain in the dark. I was empty. Spray from the sea blew onto the road. In the light of the stars and the headlights behind me, the cliffs towered ahead. It was another hour before I made it to Chéticamp.

An honorary citizen? That's not for me to decide. But I was hardier and humbler. At the bar that night, there were chansons and fiddle music and dancing in moccasins. **KP**

MUSIC

Cape Breton is famous for its fiddle music. Brought over by Scots who escaped the Highland Clearances during the 19th century, the traditional dance rhythms that Scottish music lost when it was transferred into concert halls were preserved in Cape Breton's taverns and homes. A *céilidh* is an unforgettable experience. The islanders' fast, powerful playing is bound to get you tapping your toes.

Clockwise, left to right: Cape Breton remains a fishing community; the French influences are inescapable and delicious; fuel up for the arduous climbs. Previous page: the Cabot Trail highway hugs the coast

TOOLKIT

Start/End // Baddeck

Distance // 186 miles (300km)

Getting there // From the international airport in Halifax, it is a 3.5-hour drive to Baddeck; or fly on to Sydney, from where it is an hour by car to Baddeck.

Where to stay // Rental cottages and bed and breakfasts abound along the Cabot Trail. Cape Breton Highlands National Park has excellent camping facilities. There is also a wide range of hotels on the island, from luxury resorts to roadside motels.

When to ride // The weather is best from June until October. In July and August, the road can be busy.

What to take // Bikepack the Cabot Trail over several days, ride from cottage to cottage with a change of clothes and a credit card, or do the loop in a day. Take a good jacket with you, as it can get wet and windy quickly.

Opposite: live music, here at the annual South by Southwest festival, defines Austin

MORE LIKE THIS NOTE-PERFECT RIDES

DIRT ROAD WORLD CHAMPIONSHIPS OF THE WORLD ROUTE, ATHENS, GEORGIA

The music scene in Athens, Georgia, is legendary. A quirky jumble of neoclassical homes, tumbledown bungalows, and frat houses set around a charming old centre, the otherwise quiet southern college town is home to a bevy of iconic rock clubs, clubs and cafes. REM got its start playing house parties in Athens. Countless others have followed their lead, moving on to 40 Watt and the Georgia Theatre, before topping charts all over the world. The many local roads, paved and unpaved, are good, too, rolling through the surrounding forests (try riding the route of the cutely named Dirt Road World Championships of the World). In the off-season, the Winter Bike League is one of the best group rides in America. In the summer, the Athens Twilight Criterium is about as rock and roll as cycling gets.
Start/End // Athens
Distance // 95 miles (153km)
Info // www.ridewithgps.com/routes/18816978

MJ 100K, AUSTIN, TEXAS

Lance Armstrong may have once been based near Austin but the city is better known as one of the world's best locations for live music. Home to South by Southwest and the Austin City Limits festivals, it hosts up to 100 shows in its bars and cafes every night. Jazz, blues, rock – you name it. Austin is known for its eclectic sounds, including the 'progressive country' that Willie Nelson founded there during the 1970s. The riding around Austin is darn good, too. Roads snake off into Texas Hill Country, where you'll find all sorts of riders, from competitive racers to mountain bikers in cut-off jeans. Drop by Armstrong-owned Mellow Johnny's bike shop on Saturdays at 8am for the MJ 100k, a spirited loop with a few town-sign sprints.
Start/End // Mellow Johnny's
Distance // 62 miles (100km)
Info // www.mapmyride.com/us/austin-tx/mj-100km-route-306329931

MEDELLÍN CIRCUIT, COLOMBIA

Known as 'the land of a thousand rhythms', Colombia is home to a medley of musical cultures. Blending indigenous and African beats with European influences and hypermodern sounds, its artists create songs that are all their own and appeal all over the world. Medellín – the country's second largest city and a UNESCO City of Music – is home to a huge number of clubs that are open all night and play everything from tango to reggaeton. Nestled in the middle of the Andes, the city's cycling culture is world class too. The pros take on nearby mountains such as Santa Elena, La Ceja, and La Unión in the Tour of Colombia. You don't even need a racing bike to ride a stage of the race though. The peloton has competed on a 8-mile (14km) circuit in the centre of Medellín. Riding that route on a townie bike is an excellent way to see the city. There is one steep climb to get your heart racing, before you head out for another night on the town.
Start/End // Medellín
Distance // 8 miles (14km)

VANCOUVER'S NORTH SHORE

Steep, slippery and technical, Vancouver's North Shore trails set trends that the rest of the mountain biking world followed, and they remain a challenge for every rider.

'Follow me,' said my guide, Johnny Smoke. We pedaled past a chain-link fence to the top of a trail called CBC. It's named after the Canadian Broadcasting Corporation's TV mast at the top of Mt Seymour, and it was to be my first taste of North Shore mountain biking.

On first inspection, the North Shore of Vancouver is a sedate suburb of this west coast city, backed immediately by three densely forested 4000ft mountains: Cypress, Fromme and Seymour. But for mountain bikers of a certain age, the North Shore has a mystique that can make their local trails seem mundane. It's an aura caused not only by the Pacific mists that envelop these slopes but the skein of slippery, steep and scary trails through the trees that the mist obscures. So, before my pilgrimage to the Shore, I approached Canadian pro mountain biker Richie Schley for some advice.

'Without question, this is the most difficult riding in the world,' he told me. Which wasn't much comfort.

The story of the Shore starts much further back. In the 19th century, 300ft cypress trees thrived in these mountains. Their timber was of such quality – strong, hard and durable – that settlers soon set about chopping the trees down during the next century. Younger trees began to grow back eventually: hemlock, cedar, maple and fir. But littering the forest floor were the colossal stumps

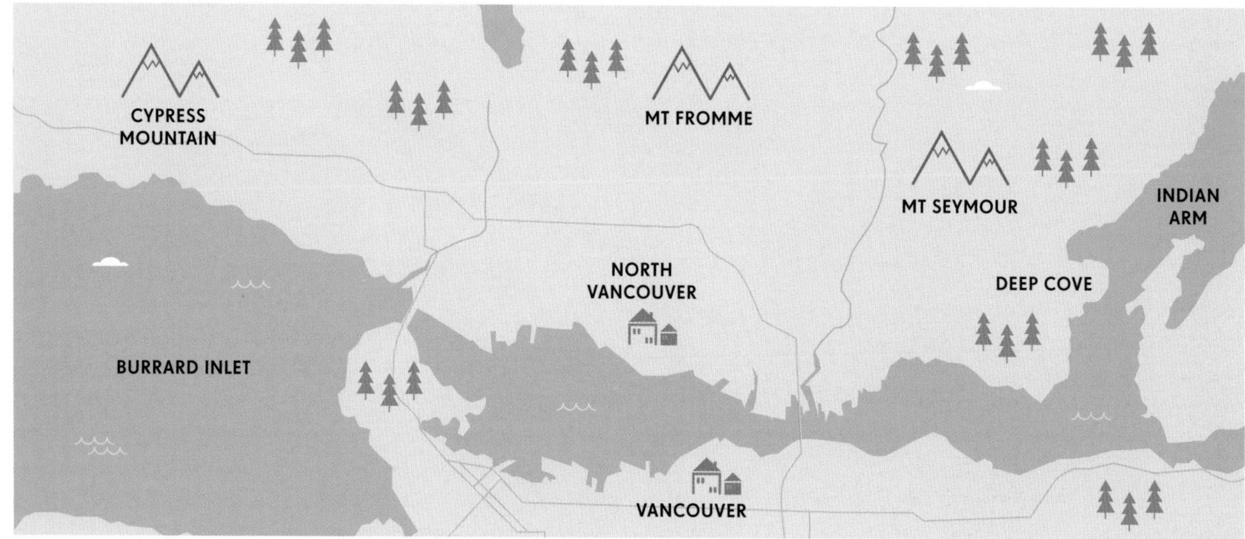

and trunks of some of the original cypress giants.

Fast forward to the late 1970s and early 1980s and groups of long-haired outdoorsy types living in small North Vancouver communities such as Deep Cove, on the edge of Indian Arm inlet, started exploring the logging tracks of the surrouding mountains on cruiser bicycles. Much as the Northern Californians were doing during the same era, they modified their bikes to have better brakes, knobblier tires, stronger components. Come the 1990s, these pioneers, including a young Johnny Smoke, were building trails to descend through the forest rather than staying on the gravel tracks. Trail builders, most famously 'Dangerous' Dan Cowan and Todd 'Digger' Flander, built their way over and around natural obstacles. Bogs were bridged and huge tree stumps breached by log ladders – they were fortunate in that cypress logs split effortlessly, making ladder building that much easier. Steep granite slabs, of which there are many, became trail features to be conquered, not avoided.

Of course, none of this activity was officially sanctioned and the trails remained the preserve of this group of in-the-know local riders: entrances were disguised and the cryptic names of the earliest trails, such as 7th Secret and Ladies Only, added to the North Shore cult. As builders constructed ever more outrageous stunts, video producers came to film local bikers riding higher and narrower ladders and plummeting off ever-larger drops for series such as *Kranked* and *North Shore Xtreme*. The trails' names gave some clue of what to expect: Flying Circus was a terrifying network of fist-wide ladders suspended by Dan Cowan 16ft high in the trees. Even in those pre-internet days, word spread through the world's mountain biking community: suddenly, this corner of Vancouver was a global influencer, hosting magazine shoots and fostering the sport's new superstars, riders like Wade Simmons and Richie Schley.

Today, every trail network, from Scotland to New Zealand, has North Shore–style features, whether that's woodwork ladders, skinny planks or teeter-totters to balance along, and log rides. And on the North Shore, things have changed too. Trails are no longer for twenty-something rebels, they're a playground for all ages, genders and demographics. There are now about 125 mapped trails across the three North Shore mountains, mostly signposted and graded from greens and blues to black diamonds and double-black diamonds. The love that has gone into constructing trails like Expresso, Ladies Only and Upper Oil Can on Mt Fromme is apparent every foot of the way.

But it takes joining a trail day organized by the North Shore Mountain Bike Association (NSMBA) to find out how the trails are maintained. Thirty bikers, with picks, shovels and gloves, head to the top of one of the beginner-level trails, Bottletop. In Vancouver's wet climate, poor drainage means erosion, so channels are cut for water to run across the trail. A discussion develops about a tight turn around a tree stump: 'If you dumb it down, how will people learn how to ride?'

The modern North Shore trails tend to be faster and wider with more flow thanks to berms and jumps. Older trails fall in and out of

"The North Shore's trails are a playground for everybody and the love that has gone into them is obvious"

favor, with some favorites – such as CBC – in a state of disrepair until it's their turn for attention from the volunteer maintenance crews of the NSMBA.

If the traffic is light you can drive from downtown Vancouver into the mountains in 30 minutes. It doesn't take a lot longer to ride. Come 5pm and convoys of cars and pick-ups bearing $5000 bikes converge on the logging roads heading up to Seymour and Fromme. Bikes are checked, armour strapped on and then, after a hard day at the office, it's play time.

For my first taste of the North Shore, all those years ago, Johnny and I segued from trail to trail, threading our way down Mt Seymour; Pangor was a carefully crafted highlight. We detoured to see the climax of Boogieman, a double-black diamond trail. The ride finishes down a long, steep rock slab – at the end a ladder reaches out into nothingness. Look ahead when you drop off the end because there are trees inches away from your landing spot. And then you have to make a jump over a 6ft gap.

We bursted out of the forest onto a suburban street and rolled, wide-eyed, back to Johnny's house. Clearly, it would take a few more descents before I could follow Richie Schley's advice for riding the Shore: 'Never hesitate.' **RB**

ENDLESS BIKING

Endless Biking is a North Vancouver mountain bike guiding business started in 2004 by former pro riders Darren Butler and Kelly Sherbinin. Together with their team of instructors, they offer a taste of the Shore to groups and individuals with confidence-building tuition to help first-timers with the steep learning curve. Whether you're a beginner or a gravity-oriented rider looking for gnarlier experiences, Darren and Kelly love sharing the Shore's wealth.

Left to right: boardwalk on Mt Fromme's Ladies Only trail; riding Lower Griffin on Mt Fromme; eerie mountain mist at Deep Cove, conquering logs on Cypress. Previous page: rolling the rock face on Dale's Trail on Mt Seymour

TOOLKIT

Start/End // Trailheads on Fromme, Seymour and Cypress
Distance // Various, typically less than 2 miles (1.5km)
Getting there // Vancouver International Airport is south of downtown Vancouver.
What to take // There are several shops and outfitters (including Endless Biking) that offer good quality rental mountain bikes if you don't want to use your own. But bring your preferred helmet (full-face or with extended coverage), pads, shoes and pedals, gloves and backpack.
Where to stay // Your best bet is to book private bike-friendly accommodation in North Vancouver neighborhoods.
When to ride // Although the ocean moderates Vancouver's climate, expect snow in winter, although lower trails may be rideable.
More info // The NSMBA (nsmba.ca) offers trail maps.

Opposite: a Tyax Adventures float plane shuttles riders to the trailhead in the South Chilcotins

MORE LIKE THIS
BUCKET LIST BRITISH COLUMBIA

THE KOOTENAYS

Whump, whump, whump. The helicopter drops you, your crew, and your bikes at the top of Texas Peak and the start of a 5,500ft descent on epic trails all the way back to your base, Retallack Lodge. Heli-biking in British Columbia's backcountry is true bucket-list biking and Retallack Lodge, 12,000 acres of wilderness deep in the Selkirk Mountains of the Kootenay region east of Vancouver, has got the experience dialled. An expansive network of trails is accessed from the lodge by either helicopter or all-terrain van. There's no doubt that the trails are challenging for the beginner, and suited to the keen intermediate and advanced riders due to a variety of carefully maintained and low traffic enduro-style descents from alpine peaks to deep within the tree canopy. Highly experienced guides, including Johnny Smoke, ensure guests make it safely back to the timber-framed lodge where gourmet dining and drinks await. Three days of guided riding and a heli-drop costs about $2000 per person.

Distance // various

Info // www.retallack.com

THE CHILCOTINS

Swap the helicopter for a float plane with Tyax Adventures' two-, three- or four-day backcountry mountain bike trips through the South Chilcotins, north of Vancouver. The multi-day adventures see Tyax guides shepherding riders through flower-filled alpine meadows, past glacier-fed lakes and over mountain passes, overnighting in camps and cabins. Flying to the trailheads in a de Havilland Beaver float plane is an option for most of the trips – a four-day tour of the Chilcotin's classic trails costs $1700 per person with a flight. The outfitter's extended backcountry tour covers around 90 miles (140km) over seven days – don't underestimate the physical demands of two-hour, off-road climbs. Three-day women-only bike camps are also available. The Chilcotin range is famed for its single-track trails and independent bike-packing is also possible for experienced riders prepared for river crossings and grizzly bears.

Distance // various

Info // www.tyaxadventures.com

THE SEVEN SUMMITS

This is a trail not a mountain range but it's one of four Canadian trails that have been certified 'epic' by the International Mountain Bike Association (IMBA). The Seven Summits is a 22-mile (35km) point-to-point route in an eastern region of British Columbia called Rossland. The trail was completed in 2004 by the Kootenay Columbia Trails Society (KCTS) and is just as much of a challenge now as it was then. It consists of thrilling singletrack descents and tough climbs through some remote high-country landscapes: riding north to south, super-fit racers can do it three hours, the average for an experienced mountain biker is five hours but plan on a full day in the saddle. There are more than 50 other trails, of varying degrees of technical difficulty, to explore around this former gold-mining settlement.

Start // Nancy Green Pass

End // Paterson

Distance // 22 miles (35km)

Info // www.kcts.ca

WHITEFISH TO BANFF

Don't have the time (or legs) for all 2700 miles of the Great Divide Mountain Bike Route? Fear not. This wild 350 miles into Canada packs in its greatest hits.

The Great Divide Mountain Bike Route (GDMBR) is a legendary 2700-mile route from Banff, Alberta to Antelope Wells, New Mexico along the Continental Divide. But if I had to choose just one leg, it would be the wild 350 miles up from Whitefish, Montana to Banff. Renowned for its passage through vast wilderness, commanding views of the Canadian Rocky Mountains, glacial lakes, wildlife sightings, and technical terrain, the ride from Whitefish to Banff guarantees to deliver all the adventure of the GDMBR in a fraction of the distance. (In case you're wondering how the Continental Divide gets its name, rivers arising here either drain into the Pacific or, far to the east, into the Atlantic.)

Crisscrossing the Continental Divide through northern Montana and southern Canada you'll climb 24,000ft along surfaces that range from pavement to good gravel, 4WD roads and singletrack. The native wildlife is as impressive as the landscape: in the densely wooded and rugged terrain live grizzly bears, wolverines, mountain lions, bighorn sheep, elk and moose.

Most of the GDMBR through-bikers travel from north to south, but since the route can get busy with cyclists during the peak summer season, I prefer to ride against the tide, south to north. This way, I still encounter other inspiring through-bikers but maintain my own rhythm – it also means that, come the ride's end, I'm rewarded with the grand scenery of Banff National Park.

The ride begins as it goes on: with a leg-draining climb concluding in a high-altitude reward. From the adventure hub and historic logging town of Whitefish, Montana my partner and I make our way up the 30 miles to Red Meadow Pass, where we cool off in a small, pristine alpine lake with mountain views. Refreshed,

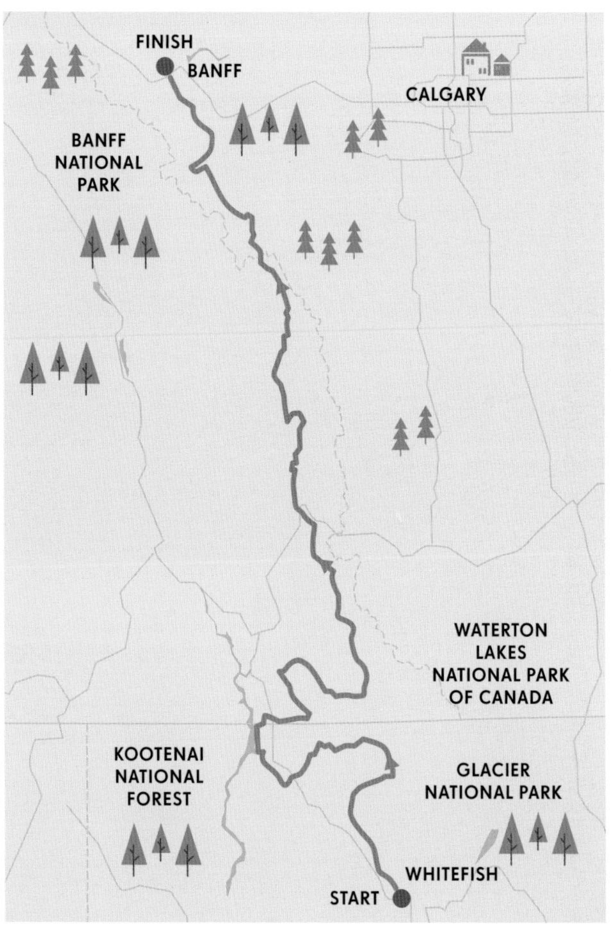

we descend to the North Fork Road, watched over by the nearby peaks of the Rocky Mountains as we wind our way north to the final pass in the US to climb. More gradual than Red Meadow, the meandering Whitefish Pass delivers us to Eureka for resupplies and the official border crossing.

Here in Canada the ride takes a turn for the wild. The terrain is much more remote and challenging, and almost immediately a tough climb, our steepest and longest climb yet, requires frequent dismounting and walking (at least we get the opportunity to snack on roadside thimbleberries). The pay-off, though, is worth the effort – a descent, via a short but very steep hike-a-bike, into the last undeveloped valley of British Columbia. The Flathead River Valley is 110 miles of unbridled wilderness, and is known as the 'Serengeti of North America' by biologists for its abundant wildlife populations.

The valley lives up to its reputation. It's raining and eerily quiet, the terrain varying from doubletrack to washed out rocky roads with rushing water and granite all around. Some call this stretch of the Flathead River Valley the 'Grizzly Bear Highway' so we make sure to be very 'bear aware.' In the event, we encounter only moose, towering along the roadsides and plowing through the dense woods as we startle them – and more rain. So we take refuge in Butt's Cabin, a forest service patrol shelter, drying our clothes before the wood stove. By mid-morning the sun is out and we are revitalized for the final, strenuous challenge that the Flathead River Valley has in store us: a bridge is down so it's off the bike and into the river water to reach the far bank.

BE 'BEAR AWARE'

This route travels through bear and mountain lion country. While riding, make a lot of noise and carry a can of bear spray that is easily accessible. Hang your food and toiletries away from your camp. In the rare event that you encounter a grizzly bear or mountain lion, stop what you are doing, ready your bear spray, speak calmly to reveal your presence, and slowly back away. Do not turn your back on the animal. See www.bearsmart.com and www.mountainlion.org

Clockwise from top: lakeside riding; deer in the Flathead River Valley; gravel roads cross parks and forests. Previous page: meadows, waterfalls and mountains in Kootenay National Park

Reaching the small towns of Sparwood and then Elkford, we once more embrace civilization, reveling in proper lodging and meals, and taverns where we meet locals who live in these remote regions for the rich coal mining and logging industries. They are big business in every sense: prominently on display in the center of Sparwood is the 23ft-tall 'Terex Titan', at one point the world's largest truck, now a local tourist attraction.

Even more impressive are the mountains, mantled here and there (for now) with glaciers, that herald entry into Banff National Park via a long, gradual climb from Elkford. Civilization has its downsides too, alas. To protect our lungs from the dust kicked up by the traffic on the busy dirt roads of the park, we cover our mouths with bandannas and turn off onto a hiker-biker only trail that takes us along the west side of Spray Lake. The trail is fun and flowing, the air is crisp and clear, and the setting of rocky, pyramidal peaks emerging from glacial turquoise lakes is awe-inspiring. We spend the night along the shores of Spray Lake to explore nearby waterfalls and to take in the remote and quiet part of an otherwise busy National Park. The echoing, doleful call of loons – Canada's iconic, aquatic birds – wakes us in the morning for our final day of cycling.

We continue the ride on an old railroad grade that runs along the lakefront, stopping now and then to sunbathe, swim, and to soak up the grand surroundings we have called home for the last few days. Reluctantly, we saddle up for the last time, and follow the dirt bike trails through the park to the end of the route, just outside of the town of Banff. The contrast between our wilderness solitude and the tourist crowds of Banff poses our final psychological challenge. But if you can't beat them, join them – so we mingle with the day-trippers for one final swim in the blue waters of Bow Falls. **SS**

TOOLKIT

Start // Whitefish, Montana, US

End // Banff, Alberta, Canada

Distance // 350 miles (563 km)

Getting there // Kalispell Airport (35 minutes' drive) or Amtrak train to Whitefish.

Getting away // A bus service leaves every two hours from Banff to Calgary Airport. Shuttles back to Whitefish are available for rent through the Whitefish Bike Retreat.

What to take // An up-to-date passport for entry into and departure from Canada, GPS device, camping equipment, water filter, cookware, smell-proof bags, a battery charger, swimsuit, camera, bug and bear spray!

When to ride // Mid-June through mid-October.

Where to stay // In Whitefish – the Whitefish Hostel and the Whitefish Bike Retreat, which offers a comfortable lodge and a campground owned by a seven-time rider of the GDMBR. There are budget motels in Eureka, Sparwood and Elkford along the route. Banff lodging can be busy and expensive; stay in one of the campgrounds outside town.

More info // www.adventurecycling.org/routes-and-maps/adventure-cycling-route-network/great-divide-mountain-bike-route

Opposite: aspens, sunshine and dirt trails in Colorado

MORE LIKE THIS GREATEST HITS OF THE GREAT DIVIDE MOUNTAIN BIKE ROUTE

WIND RIVER

The Wind River Range is home to some of America's most beautiful alpine, high desert. This 215-mile (346km) section of the GDMBR takes you to the best of it, crisscrossing the Continental Divide among aspen stands and craggy mountain faces, before dropping down to the wide-open high desert valleys of sage, and perfect backcountry camping with vistas as wide as they are long plus great sunsets. After a refreshing resupply in the bustling town of Pinedale, the route follows a picturesque section of high desert doubletrack along the Lander cutoff (an historic westward wagon route) and ends in the ghost town of Atlantic City. Conditions are best July through late September, but mosquitoes are notoriously bad during the summer – bring plenty of bug repellent. Water can be scarce so carry plenty and refill when you can. Shuttling to and from the start and finish can be difficult, so research in Pinedale or hire a ride through Craigslist.

Start // Moran, Wyoming
End // Atlantic City, Wyoming
Distance // 215 miles (346km)
Info // www.ridewithgps.com/routes/28880111

COLORADO'S ROCKIES

The section of the GDMBR that travels through the Colorado Rocky Mountains is not to be missed, taking in scenic mountains, aspen stands, alpine meadows, historic (and hip) mountain towns. Most days will be spent ascending one long mountainous climb after another at elevations from 7000ft to nearly 12,000ft. The long descents will open new valleys and landscapes to enjoy and deliver you to an ideal camp spot along a cold stream. Bike-friendly mountain towns are frequent and offer many natural health food stores, good bakeries, hostels, bike shops, and opportunities to fuel up on espresso. July through early October is the best time to ride this route to avoid snowfall, but be prepared for afternoon thunderstorms and cool nighttime temperatures. The section ends by climbing to the highest elevation along the entire GDMBR, Indiana Pass, before the chunky descent to Pagosa Springs where you can soak your sore legs in hot springs before coordinating your shuttle (the nearest airports are in Durango and Denver).

Start // Breckenridge, Colorado
End // Pagosa Springs, Colorado
Distance // 320 miles (515km)
Info // www.ridewithgps.com/routes/28880220

GILA NATIONAL FOREST

Don't underestimate this southerly stretch of the GDMBR. The Gila National Forest may be understated compared to the Rockies but its highlights – mellow terrain, historical significance, remoteness and accessible hot springs – are as memorable as any on the route. You'll spin along quiet dirt roads through unspoiled pine forests, rugged mountains, deep canyons, flat mesas and along flowing streams (a rarity in southwest New Mexico). This area has a rich history of Ancestral Puebloans, Spanish colonizers, prospectors, conflict (during Apache Wars the Battle of Pino Altos took place a few miles north of Silver City), and even criminals (Billy the Kid and Butch Cassidy were known regulars in these parts). The route is best ridden during the summer and fall from Silver City, north to Pie Town so that you can end your ride with well-deserved dried apple pie, and enjoy the company of the locals while you wait for your shuttle.

Start // Pie Town, New Mexico
End // Silver City, New Mexico
Distance // 173 miles (278km)
Info // www.ridewithgps.com/routes/28880122

WHISTLER MOUNTAIN BIKE PARK

The world's greatest mountain-biking playground is on every shredder's bucket list – so stop making excuses and go full send in British Columbia.

The idea came about in the middle of a dreary, relentlessly grey Northeast winter. My friend Rob Fatz and I were on yet another frigid trail ride, all bundled up, when I said, 'We should go to Whistler.'

People say this kind of stuff a lot. For mountain bikers, Whistler, British Columbia is a bucket list trip, a place that is the source of the Instagram photos you dreamily scroll through while eating lunch at your desk: near-vertical rock slabs, brown ribbons dancing through leggy pine forests, dirt so dark and crumbly you can practically smell the decomposing organic material right through the screen.

The problem with bucket list trips, though, is that you tend to think you have years to do them. I'd always assumed I'd go to Whistler one day, when I lived closer than Pennsylvania, when work was less hectic. But later, Rob texted: 'Tickets to Whistler are only $400.' And I thought, 'What am I waiting for?' Winter was crushing our souls. We all needed to do something that felt fun and impulsive. When we looped in our friends, Rob Bekesy and Aaron Fry, they replied immediately: 'In.'

Whistler is home to over 300 miles of singletrack. But at the heart of the adrenaline-soaked town is the Whistler Mountain Bike Park, with over 56 miles of singletrack for every level of rider.

On our first morning (of three), we walked past shops featuring rental fleets of carbon full-suspension dream bikes, and squeezed past riders in pads and full-face helmets. It was like Disneyland for mountain bikers.

The goals: 1. Have fun. 2. Don't die. At Whistler, the trails are not only coded by color – green circles for beginners, blue squares for intermediate riders, black diamonds denoting

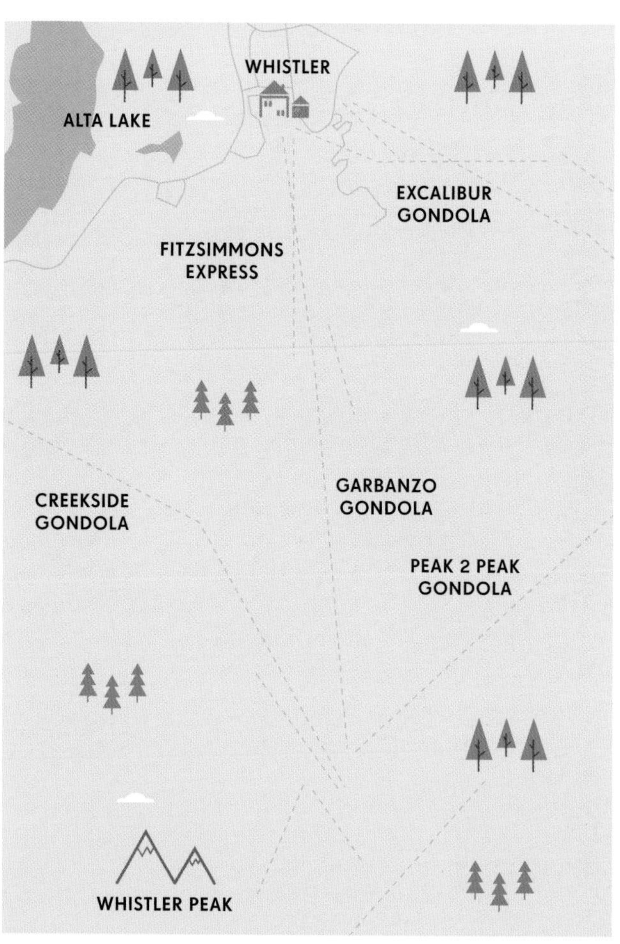

advanced terrain, and double-black diamonds for experts only – but are also marked 'flow' trails, which are mostly smooth and machine-cut, or 'technical,' for more natural terrain with rocks, roots, and chutes. We started the green flow trail, EZ Does It, which featured lovingly shaped berms connected by rolling dirt sidewalks. Enticing options beckoned off to the side: a dark, mysterious, blue technical trail here, a black flow trail there. The sheer number of choices was intoxicating.

Over the next few days, we explored nearly every blue and black trail at the park. Whistler Bike Park's trails are so class-leading that its principal trail builder, Tom Prochazka, now owns a company called Gravity Logic that has done trail work for over 130 parks worldwide. Gravity Logic features are built to allow riders to progress their skills safely. On blue flow trails like C-More and Crank it Up, I sailed over jumps with deftly sloped landings that wouldn't buck me off my bike if I came up short. As I grew to trust the jumps, my index fingers stayed glued to the grips longer instead of reaching for the brakes. At the end of the first day, we approached a section that exited the woods via a 4ft wooden drop, followed by a medium-sized tabletop. I soared off the drop, went over the tabletop at full speed – and caught enough air to overshoot the landing. 'I've never seen you go so big!' Aaron whooped.

On black-diamond technical terrain, we met sections that would test the riding limits of even very skilled cyclists, like a boulder section as tall as a house on the trail Original Sin. A group of riders was standing at the precipice, camera phones out – the international signal for 'Something Scary Ahead.' Two glacial

GO TO BIKE SCHOOL

Whistler goes big on everything bike-related, and its mountain bike instruction program is no exception. With everything from group lessons for kids and 'summer gravity camp,' to women's only, private clinics and guided tours, Whistler offers coaching for riders at every level. A friend who was an expert cross-country racer but struggled with getting off the ground attended a clinic, and was soon flying off features.

Clockwise from above: Whistler's lifts usually reopen in May; the Top of the World is a backcountry descent from the mountain's highest point; practise your airborne skills in the bike park. Previous page: descending the Top of the World trail

boulders formed a sheer chute rippled with step-downs and deep fissures. Aaron and Fatz rattled down – Bekesy and I chose to scrabble along the side. On Duffman (another black technical trail), steep, dusty chutes laden with rooty step-downs were interspersed with wooden bridges that reminded us to use the brakes judiciously. Each time I cleared a tricky section, a sense of achievement (and relief) washed over me.

The bike park boasts 4900 vertical feet from the base to the highest lift-accessed point. Which means that runs from top to bottom, with a few rests thrown in, can last 45 minutes. The gondola rides back up climb fast enough to make your ears pop, but count on 25 minutes per ascent.

It's not easy to get four working professionals together for an adventure like this – we knew our trip was special. But it was easy to feel celebratory in this town. With some lifts in the bike park open until 8pm, we could stop for leisurely, midday lunches (including, of course, poutine – chips, gravy and cheese curd). At the end of each day, caked with dust and sweat, we'd roll up to one of many outdoor bars, order cold, local beers, and toast the day.

On our final morning, we took the Peak Chair to the highest point on the mountain, called the Top of the World, at just over 7000ft. As the lift whisked us above the tree line, our feet dangled above piles of glacial rock and unmelted snow, and the expansiveness of the scenery had a dizzying effect. From the Top of the World, we descended, winding our way through a tundra-like landscape: fuzzy green lichen, chunky rocks, blue mountains layered in the distance, under a sky so big it dwarfed us, our worries, in fact any thought beyond exactly what we were doing right at this moment. Our 13-mile backcountry descent, exploring well beyond the bike-park boundary, ended up taking us two hours, with stops. But we'll remember it for a lifetime. **GL**

"We descended under a sky so big it dwarfed us, our worries, and any thought beyond what we were doing"

TOOLKIT

Start/End // Whistler Mountain Bike Park, Whistler, BC
Distance // 125 miles (200km) of trails, with 56 miles (90km) of singletrack.
Getting there // Two hours from Vancouver International Airport, or 4½ hours from Seattle-Tacoma International Airport.
Where to stay // Hotels, condo rentals, and Airbnbs abound, but for a quieter experience, stay at the end of the Village that's near the Whistler Olympic Plaza.
When to ride // The park opens from mid-May to mid-September, but go early before the trails get too beaten up.
What to ride // A downhill mountain bike, but long-travel trail or enduro bikes also work. There are countless rental shops in the Village offering top-of-the-line full-suspension bikes, at about $80 to $120 a day during peak season. Don't count on shipping a bike from the US – it can get delayed in customs.
What to take // A full-face helmet, goggles (the trails are dusty) and, at minimum, kneepads.

Opposite: twists and turns at Sun Peaks Bike Park

MORE LIKE THIS
THREE CANADIAN BIKE PARKS TO DROP IN ON

FERNIE ALPINE RESORT

Bordering Alberta, Montana, and Idaho, the Kootenay Rockies of British Columbia provide a backdrop to many of the high-alpine rides in this region. Fernie is one of eight towns that cater to mountain bikers, known as the Kootenay Dirt 8 – which also includes other famed BC riding destinations like Revelstoke, Golden, and Nelson – and hosts one of the three lift-accessed bike parks in the area. Fernie Alpine Resort has a more rugged feel than Whistler Bike Park, with old-school wooden features like skinnies (elevated wooden bridges that test your balance) and wall rides, and a strong, bike-crazy local community.

Start/End // Fernie, British Columbia
Distance // 22 miles (35km) of lift-accessed trails
Info // www.skifernie.com/purchase/mountain-biking

MONT-SAINTE-ANNE

In the town of Beaupré, Québec, on the east coast of Canada, the resort of Mont-Sainte-Anne awaits. Even its cross-country (XC) trails, all 81 miles (130km) of them, are known for being rocky and rooty: the mountain was the only North American stop for a UCI World Cup in 2018, and features one of the most technical XC racecourses on the circuit, which hits gradients of 48% on some of the descents. And among the 19 miles (30km) of downhill trails, there's not a green run to be found. Plus, it's often wet, making the rocks and roots even slicker. But the park also has some machine-built blue trails, like the flowy La Grisante, with its poppy rock features and rollers; and La Boutteaboutte, with its long, wooden bridges – meaning that not every ride down has to be a test of your mettle.

Start/End // Beaupré, Québec
Distance // 19 miles (30km) of downhill trails; 81 miles (130km) of XC trails
Info // mont-sainte-anne.com/en/summer/mountain-biking

SUN PEAKS RESORT

Canada's second-largest ski area lies 35 miles (56km) northeast of Kamloops, BC and each summer transforms into a bike park with over 2000ft of lift-accessed vertical. Sun Peaks was home to the Canadian Downhill National Championship from 2014 to 2016, and still hosts the prestigious BC Downhill Championship. It's known for its natural-feeling trails, and is making an effort to be more family-friendly. A Bike Skills Park with a 'magic carpet' lift, kid-size berms, rollable drops, and jumps opened in 2018. Also new for 2018 was a 5.5 mile (9km) green trail from top to bottom. For the shredders, the newly rebuilt XL jump line, Steam Shovel, offers seemingly endless series of tabletop jumps with dreamy lips. And for a backcountry riding experience, don't miss the lift-accessed, 5-mile (8km) Altitude XC trail, which winds past wildflower meadows and alpine lakes.

Start/End // Sun Peaks, British Columbia
Distance // 38 trails (Sun Peaks does not have an official distance count for its trails)
Info // www.sunpeaksresort.com/bike-hike/bike/bike-park

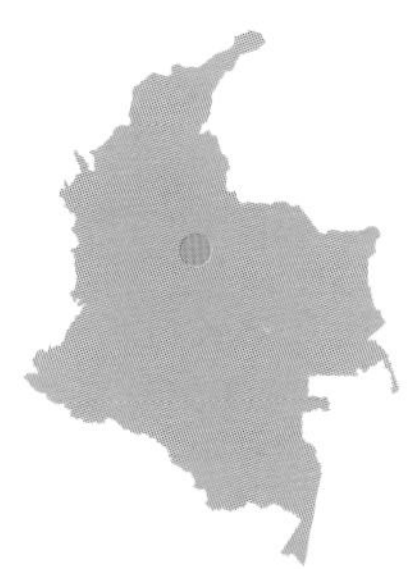

NAIRO'S NEIGHBORHOOD

Colombia is at peace, at last. How better to celebrate than with a ride to the mountainous birthplace of its latest cycling hero?

A dozen routes (and 3600 vertical feet) lie between Villa de Leyva and the giant murals and statues of cycling star Nairo Quintana that adorn the side of a small store outside the town of Cómbita, where the latest in the line of the country's great cyclists was born and raised. If you're not familiar with the successes of Quintana and his illustrious peers and forebears, you will be before long. Colombians are cycling mad, and proud of their homegrown professionals and their achievements.

For our pilgrimage to 'la casa de Nairo', rather than take one of the paved routes, we – myself, my wife and two friends – head around the southern bow of the ship-shaped mountain that stands over Leyva's east side, turn up a canyon, and on to gravel roads toward Chiquiza and then San Pedro de Iguaque and up and over toward Cómbita. We will climb over 7000ft during the day, almost entirely on dirt and gravel, up slopes designed for horses and trucks, from valley heat to high-altitude cold, past *campesinos* (agricultural workers) bent over potato plots, laden donkeys, and

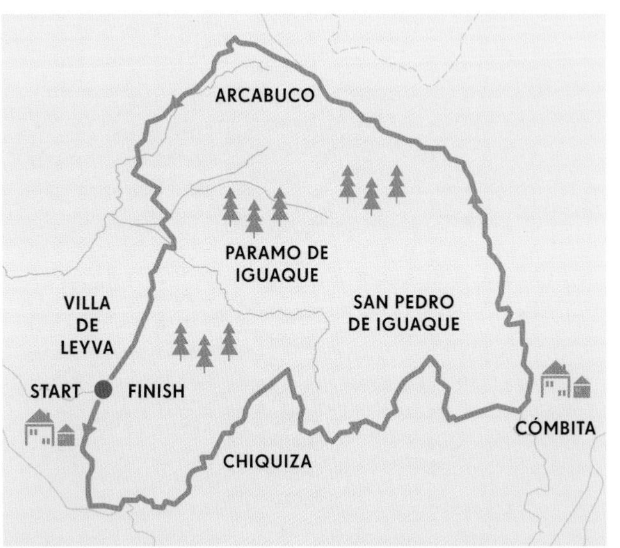

tiny towns with tiny squares. We'll top out at 10,700ft and begin whistling back toward Leyva on the paved road through Arcabuco.

At the route's furthest point lies a larger-than-life shrine to national hero Nairo Quintana, next to a little store down the hill from the home of Nairo's parents. It's not actually Nairo's house, we find out, but we don't really care. The Nairo Pilgrimage is just an excuse to go on a really good bike ride.

Heat presses into our backs on the lower slopes. We've left the pavement behind us, mostly, though some of the switchbacks and ramps are so steep that they've been concreted (the gradient makes it feel like you're on a stair-stepper machine). Pleasingly, this is one of those mountains that allows you to see exactly how far you've come, snaking up its flank. A quick glance over the shoulder: 'We started down there?'

The road surface is crushed rock and dirt, decently maintained and easily covered on 32mm semi-slicks. The road curves back and forth through farm fields tended by *campesinos*. A man in his sixties is bent over a potato patch, pulling small red orbs out of the earth and tossing them in a white canvas bag. He unfolds as we approach and throws a wave. A million chickens run about and dozens of dogs look up briefly from their naps. A llama chews at us.

We've climbed 2000 feet on dirt, which somehow took two hours, and it's time for the first stop for water in Chiquiza. We rattle across a miniature cobblestone square toward a little store, where a woman seems annoyed that we're interrupting her viewing of a soap opera.

The middle of a long ride is often the most difficult passage, mentally if not physically. The road after Chiquiza rolls and then ramps up again, along a ridge to San Pedro de Iguaque. Another hour and we have climbed 3500 of our 7000ft but have done so

PEACE

For decades civil conflict consumed Colombia, as governments waged war against a long-running insurgency. To travel for discovery and enjoyment was to take your life in your hands. As a local guide told us: 'Driving was really dangerous. Around 5pm, the guerrillas come to the main roads and kidnap everyone. We did not know our own country.' One joyful result of peace coming to Colombia is that parts of the country, long a mystery to all but guerrilla groups, are being rediscovered.

Clockwise from above: the ride to Nairo's house; paying respects to the Colombian star; expect hummingbirds wherever you are in Colombia; taking the high road. Previous page: climbing the dirt road to Nairo's house

in 15 miles, which means that more than 45 miles remain. We're averaging a brisk trotting pace. It's best not to think in terms of distance on the way up.

Three hours into our Nairo Pilgrimage, we climb on new pavement out of San Pedro de Iguaque to a rolling plateau at 10,000ft – a sea of pastureland cut by dirt roads. A bite to the air reminds you of the elevation. We're higher than Cómbita and Nairo's house. Far higher than the highest paved roads in Europe. A storm brews in the direction we're heading. Temperatures have dropped into the 50s.

A descent to the main road ends our quiet hours on dirt. Since leaving the road out of Leyva we have encountered perhaps a dozen motorcycles, half-a-dozen small trucks, and a handful of loaded horses and donkeys. It's why we chose this way, even though it's meant we've traveled 32 miles in five hours.

Nairo's house – or at least, that of his parents – is easy to spot. It sits off to the left on a sweeping right bend and out front are a pair of 10ft-tall Nairo Quintana statues on bikes, one of which has mechanical legs that spin when it's turned on, and wall-sized murals of the local-boy-made-good in various states of stone-faced victory. A massive grin on the larger of the figures feels slightly inappropriate for a rider notorious for his poker face, but it fits the mood.

The place is an adorable little truck stop, basically. Except it doesn't sell gas, it sells Nairo. There are shirts in yellow, the color of Colombia's soccer team, and pink, the color of the Giro d'Italia (which he won in 2014). The parking lot in front of the building is a rotating carousel of pilgrims like us, on motorbikes, in cars. A truck pulls up. The driver jumps out, grabs a selfie with the Nairo statue, then jumps back in the cab and roars off in a cloud of smoke. **CF**

TOOLKIT

Start/End // Villa de Leyva
Distance // 57 miles (91km)
Getting there // Fly into Bogotá, then, ideally, hire a driver and van for baggage transfers while you ride (the Pure! Colombia guide service organized this for us).
Where to stay // Lodging is relatively cheap. We stayed in the lovely B3 Hotel in Bogotá at the end of our stay for $50 a night and used Airbnb to find a fantastic spot in Villa de Leyva.
When to ride // Colombia is equatorial, the driest months being December to March, and July and August.
What to take // A road/gravel bike with clearance for up to 40mm tires. Colombian hills are long and steep so gear as you see fit. It's hot and muggy down low, often cold up top – bring layers, decent gloves and a good rain jacket.
Altitude // The good riding will take you up to 10,000ft and beyond, so acclimatize for a few days – altitude sickness is serious.

All images © Caley Fretz

Opposite: Colombian pro cyclist Egan Bernal races to the finish line at the top of Alto de las Palmas on stage six of the 2019 Tour of Colombia

MORE LIKE THIS COLOMBIAN CLIMBS

ALTO DE LETRAS

'Start early,' everyone says of Letras, first and foremost because it takes a long time to ride 50 miles (80km) uphill and, second, because if you don't get up and out of the lowlands before mid-morning you might just melt. Mariquita, at the base of Letras, has the feel of a crossroads town. The climb starts no more than a two-minute ride from its center. It points around a left-hand curve and won't stop climbing for the full 50 miles (80km). The hardest sections are the first 15 miles (25km), up to the town of Fresno, and the last 9 miles (15km), because by then you've been climbing for four to six hours and it's relentless. The altimeter tops out at 12,100ft but you climb more than 13,000ft – blame the dips. Eventually you'll break through the clouds and see a statue of the Virgin Mary that marks the top of the pass.
Start // Mariquita
End // Letras
Distance // 50 miles (80km)

ALTO DE LAS PALMAS

This climb out of party-mad Medellín is perhaps the city's favorite cycling route, and guaranteed to grow in popularity after the heroics of the trio of Colombians who contested the epic finale of the 2019 Tour of Colombia's queen stage. The riders – Nairo Quintana, Miguel Ángel López and Iván Sosa – slugged it out over the final three miles (5km) of this 11-mile (18km) ascent as if they were track cyclists and not riding at an altitude of over 8000ft. The average gradient is 7% and it tilts up to 9% at the top. Unlike the multi-lane highways elsewhere, this is a single-lane road that rewards riders with views over the city and then highland villages with green pastures. Catch your breath at the top before descending the way you came.
Start // Medellín
End // Alto de las Palmas
Distance // 50 miles (80km)

ALTO DE MINAS

Another classic climb out of Medellín – to Alto de Minas – features an altitude gain of 4000ft with a maximum gradient of more than 11% (but an average of 4%). It starts from the suburbs south of the city and you'll have to first cross over 'Little Minas' before descending back into the steamy jungle lowlands in preparation for the ascent proper on a road that hugs the contours of Minas. The temperature drops the higher you go and you'll usually experience clouds and mist higher up Colombia's hills. The return trip is 30 miles (48km) or you can combine it with a ride up Las Palmas for a 70-mile (113km) route with more than 8000ft of climbing.
Start // Medellín
End // Alto de Minas
Distance // 15 miles (24km)

sky
sky
sky
sky

CUBA'S SOUTHERN ROLLER COASTER

Pounded by surf, overshadowed by mountains and deeply imbued with revolutionary history, this lonely ride along Cuba's Caribbean coast pulsates with natural and historical drama.

Cuba is full of dichotomies and its roads are no exception. Take Carretera N20, for instance, 106 miles (170km) of potholed asphalt that runs along the south coast between Santiago de Cuba and the rustic village of Marea del Portillo, a spectacularly battered thoroughfare that could quite conceivably be described as the nation's best and worst highway. Shielded by purple-hued mountains that tumble down to meet the iridescent Caribbean, it scores 10 out of 10 for craggy magnificence. But, lashed by hurricanes and beset by a severe lack of maintenance, it can be purgatory for aspiring drivers. Not surprisingly, few cars attempt it, leaving the road the preserve of goats, *vaqueros* (cowboys) and the occasional two-wheeled adventurer.

During nearly 20 years of travel in Cuba, I have traversed this epic highway in numerous ways, most notoriously on a protracted hitchhiking trip involving at least a dozen changes of vehicle, from a terminally ill Fiat Uno to a truck where the only other passenger was a dead pig. But my preference, if time and weather allow, is to tackle it on a bicycle. As visceral experiences go, this is Cuba at its most candid. The salty air, hidden coves, and erstwhile revolutionary history conspire to form a proverbial Columbian voyage of discovery that becomes more magical the further you pedal.

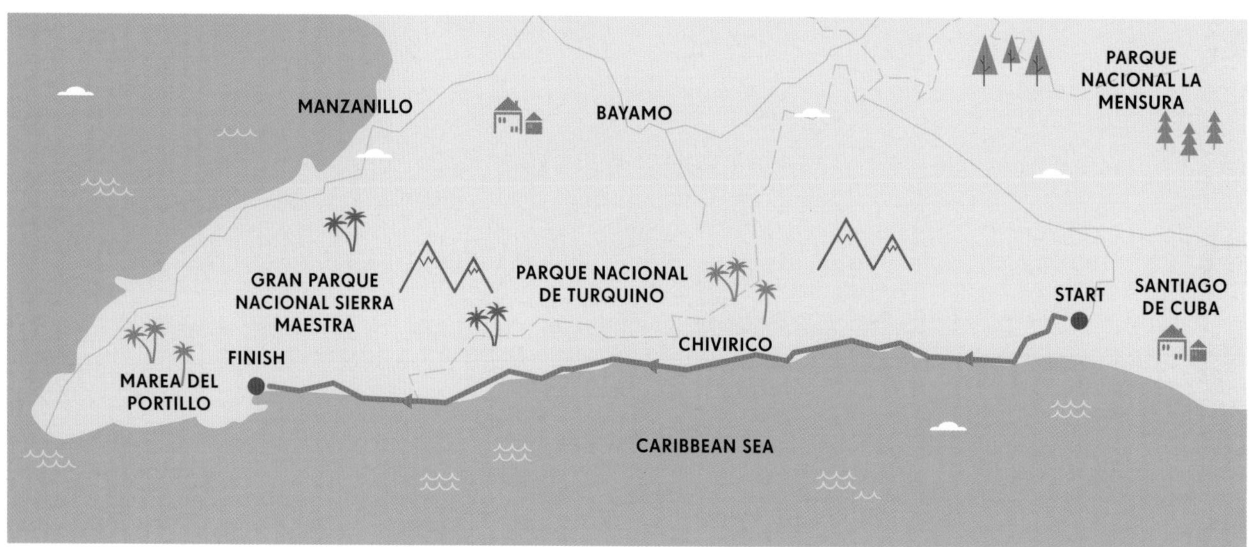

Fidel Castro and his band of bearded guerrillas lived as fugitives in these mountains for over two years in the late 1950s and the sense of eerie isolation prevails. Indeed, so deserted is the road that, in the handful of bucolic hamlets en route, farmers use it to air-dry their coffee beans, kids hijack it for baseball games, and cows parade boldly down the middle of the sun-bleached thoroughfare as if the motor car had never been invented.

Base camp for anyone attempting the ride is Santiago de Cuba, the nation's second largest city and, in many respects, its cultural capital. Heading west from here, the journey is best split into three stages. While route-finding is easy, the ups and downs of the highway as it curls around numerous headlands present a significant physical challenge. Be prepared. Roadside facilities range from scant to non-existent.

The first time I ventured out on a borrowed bike, I carried inadequate provisions and ended up knocking on the doors of isolated rural homesteads to 'beg' for water. Sure, I met some very obliging *campesinos* (country dwellers) offering liquid refreshment (including rum!), but the head-lightening effects of the dehydration probably weren't worth it. To avoid a similar fate, arm yourself with a robust bike and carry plenty of food and water.

The first, recently repaired section from Santiago to the small town of Chivirico sees a modest trickle of traffic. Look out for growling *camiones particulares*, the noisy trucks that act as public transport in these parts. Around Chivirico you might spy another unique Cuban-ism, the *amarillos*, government-sponsored transit officials named for their mustard yellow uniforms; their job is to stand by the side of the road and flag down passing vehicles for hitchhikers.

"This remote region has remained utterly unspoiled, a glorious ribbon of driftwood-littered beaches"

Chivirico also has one of the route's strangest epiphanies, the Brisas Sierra Mar, an unpretentious all-inclusive hotel that springs seemingly out of nowhere 40 miles (65km) west of Santiago. Treat yourself: there is precious little accommodation for the next 62 miles (100km).

West of Chivirico, traffic dwindles to virtually nothing, while the eroded state of the road can make the going ponderous, even for cyclists. Fortunately, the magnificence of the scenery makes slow travel highly desirable.

This remote southeastern region has remained unspoiled, a glorious ribbon of driftwood-littered beaches and surf backed by Cuba's two highest peaks, Turquino (6476ft) and Bayamesa (5256ft). Such settlements that exist are tiny and etched in revolutionary folklore. El Uvero at the 60-mile (97km) point has a monument guarded by two rows of royal palms commemorating a battle audaciously won by Castro's rebels in 1957. Further west, La Plata, the site of another successful guerrilla attack, maintains a tiny museum. Just off the coast, vestiges of an earlier war lie underwater

© Pierre Logwin | Alamy Stock Photo, © M G Therin Weise | Getty Images, © Mark Read

CLIMBING PICO TURQUINO

Cuba's highest mountain, Pico Turquino (6476ft), is regularly climbed from Hwy 20, starting from a trailhead at Las Cuevas just west of El Uvero. It's a steep and gruelling 10-hour grunt to the top and back, but no specific mountaineering skills are required. The ascent must be made with a guide, but can be split over two days, with a night spent in a basic mountain shelter.

Left to right: a coast road in the Sierra Maestra; Catedral de Nuestra Señora de la Asunción in Santiago de Cuba; street scene with a 1951 Plymouth in Santiago de Cuba; the Sierra Maestra. Previous page: a rural church in Santiago de Cuba

in the wreck of *Cristóbal Colón*, a Spanish destroyer sunk in the 1898 Spanish-American war. Today it's a chillingly atmospheric dive site.

By now the steep headlands and tropical temperatures will have turned your legs the consistency of overcooked spaghetti. La Mula, around 6 miles (10km) west of El Uvero, is a rustic *campismo* with basic bungalows where you can recuperate just moments from the ocean.

On day three, as the road crosses from Santiago de Cuba province into Granma, I like to pull over at one of the wild, Robinson Crusoe–like beaches and admire the increasingly dry terrain. Dwarf foliage including cacti is common, a result of the rain shadow effect of the Sierra Maestra. Aside from sporadic ramshackle villages, civilization is confined to occasional *bohios* (thatched huts) dotting the mountain foothills. Sometimes, you'll inexplicably spy a lone sombrero-wearing local pacing alongside the roadside, miles from anywhere, clutching a machete.

The tiny fishing village of Marea del Portillo is equipped with two low-key resorts that guard a glowering dark-sand beach framed by broccoli-green peaks. Don't be deceived by the home comforts. You've just arrived in one of the most cut-off corners of Cuba. To the north, crenellated mountain ridges shrug off clusters of bruised clouds. To the west sits Desembarco del Granma National Park, famed for its ecologically rich marine terraces. For me, this is paradise personified, a chance to resuscitate my bike-legs, carb-load at the hotel buffet and go off into the wilderness to explore some more. **BS**

TOOLKIT

Start // Santiago de Cuba
End // Marea del Portillo
Distance // 106 miles (170km) along a rutted but easy-to-follow road.
Getting there // The nearest airport is Aeropuerto Antonio Maceo, 4 miles (6km) south of Santiago de Cuba. From here, there are daily flights to Havana (with US connections), and direct flights to Canada.
Bike rental // This is rare and unreliable in Cuba. Most serious cyclists bring their own bikes with them.
Where to stay // Club Amigo Marea del Portillo (+53 23-59-70-08; www.hotelescubanacan.com); Campismo La Mula (+53 22-32-62-62; www.campismopopular.cu); Brisas Sierra Mar (+53 22-32-91-10; www.hotelescubanacan.com)
When to ride // The best time is mid-November to late March. However, the road is prone to flooding and closures. Check ahead in Santiago.

Opposite: a Cuban cigar roller in the Valle de Viñales

MORE LIKE THIS
CUBAN RIDES

LA FAROLA

Hailed as one of the seven modern engineering marvels of Cuba, La Farola (the lighthouse road) links the beach hamlet of Cajobabo on the arid Caribbean coast with the nation's beguiling oldest city, Baracoa. Measuring 34 miles (55km) in length, the road traverses the steep-sided Sierra del Puril, snaking its way precipitously through a landscape of granite cliffs and pine-scented cloud forest before falling, with eerie suddenness, upon the lush tropical paradise of the Atlantic coastline. For cyclists, it offers a classic Tour de France–style challenge with tough climbs, invigorating descents and relatively smooth roads. La Farola starts 124 miles (200km) east of Santiago de Cuba and is thus best incorporated into a wider Cuban cycling excursion. You could also charter a taxi to drop you off at the start point.
Start // Cajobabo
End // Baracoa
Distance // 34 miles (55km)

GUADALAVACA TO BANES

Talk to savvy repeat visitors in Guadalavaca's popular resort strip and you'll discover that one of the region's most memorable activities is to procure a bicycle and pedal it through undulating rural terrain to the fiercely traditional town of Banes 21 miles (34km) to the east. This beautifully bucolic ride transports you from the resort-heavy north coast to a gritty slice of the real Cuba in a matter of hours along a road where you're more likely to encounter a horse and cart than a traffic jam. Some of the resorts lend out bikes but pedaling these basic machines can be hard work; in-the-know visitors often fly in with their own bikes (Holguín's Frank País international airport receives direct flights from the UK, Canada and Italy).
Start // Guadalavaca
End // Banes
Distance // 21 miles (34km)

VALLE DE VIÑALES

Viñales is a small farming community that does a lucrative side-business in tourism. It sits nestled among craggy *mogotes* (steep, haystack-shaped hills) in Cuba's primary tobacco-growing region. With about as much traffic on its roads as 1940s Britain, the region – which is protected as both a Unesco World Heritage site and National Park – is ideal for cycling. Various loops can be plotted around the valley's multifarious sights, which include caves, tobacco plantations, climbing routes and snippets of rural Cuban life. Riders can hire from the Bike Rental Point in Viñales' main plaza. Or your *casa particular* (private homestay, of which there are dozens in the village) may have bicycles available to rent.
Getting there // Viñales is easily reached from Havana by bus
Distance // Whatever you feel like

AN UPHILL PURSUIT OF ECUADORIAN BLACK GOLD

On a nine-month expedition from Alaska to Tierra del Fuego, Mark Beaumont tackled an arduous ascent through agricultural heartlands to find fine coffee and even better company.

I was now south of the equator, having crossed it on the Pacific Ocean aboard the *Crown Opal*. My voyage through the Panama Canal had been a welcome break after many months cycling south from Alaska. My legs felt very fresh, albeit wobbly after three days at sea.

Guayaquil in Ecuador is positioned 40 miles up the estuary of the Guayas River. My slow arrival to South America gave me hours to soak up the geography of this new continent. After riding through North and Central America, I was excited to head into the Andes.

I was the first public passenger the Russian crew had ever allowed onboard. No wonder they weren't practiced hosts. But they certainly gave me a great send-off, lining the bows as I clipped my bags back on the bike and pedaled away. My cycling clothes were brilliantly white again, my hair oddly sun-bleached now it was clean. It felt like a fresh start, with just six weeks to reach Aconcagua in time to climb.

The first couple of days riding in Ecuador, across the very flat agricultural plateau until I reached the town of Santa Rosa, started to lull me into a false sense of confidence. Out of the tropics, I was keen to start camping again, but Ecuador is the biggest banana producer in the world, and I was lost in a world of Dole and Del Monte plantations, so there was nowhere obvious and I spent my first night in the town of Naranjal. A room cost $12 and I was intrigued to see the receptionist working on a typewriter.

Tap, tap, tap, tap, slide... ting.

For a few more dollars I bought myself half a cooked chicken and managed to find my way to the flat roof of the hotel. Looking across a sea of rooftops, aerials and drying washing, as the sun went down, I reflected on a good start to South America.

I woke at 5.30am the following morning to the sound of torrential

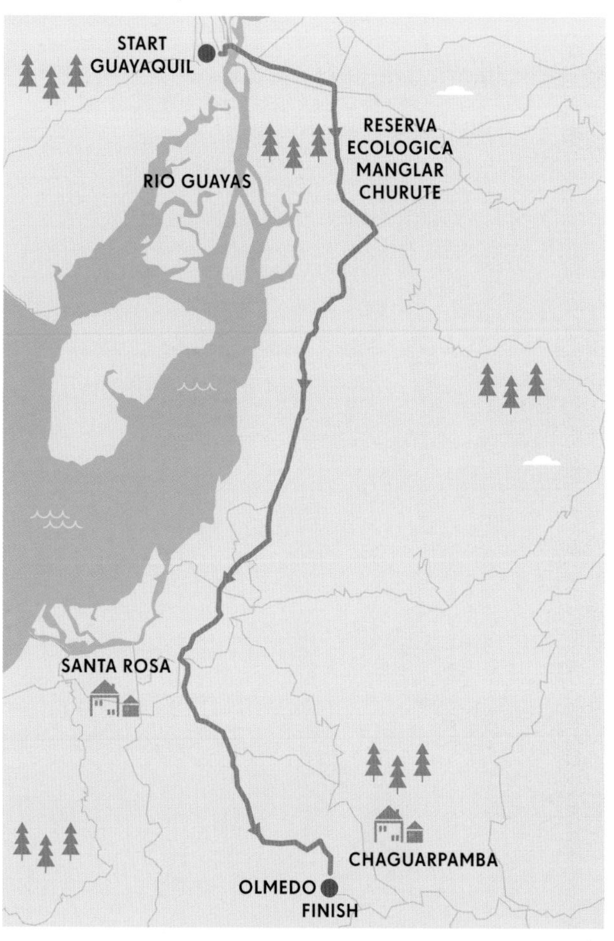

rain on the window, so reset my alarm for 7.30am. I thought I had left the rainy season behind in Central America. Sunrise was at 6am and being near the '*ecuador*', sunset was predictably 12 hours later, so I was keen to get early starts, just not in heavy rain.

The road soon started climbing into the Andes. My target was to reach the village of Olmedo at about 4000ft to visit a coffee plantation. I knew it wouldn't be a simple climb, but I never expected it to be as tough as it was. I finished my second breakfast at 10.30am and by 2pm I had covered 28 miles, a new slow record. Then I slowed further. The road soon steepened so that the average gradient was from 8 to 12%. Before long, the sun burned through the cloud and it was hot work, pedaling uphill at walking pace.

As I climbed, the tarmac started getting patchier so I cycled down the middle of the road where possible. There were soon long sections of gravel, which were often ridged from where water had run. Then the tarmac ran out and I spent the rest of the day on dirt.

The climb was beautiful and took regular and long switchbacks. These weren't alpine-style hairpins but detours of many miles as the road found a reasonable route upwards. It's one thing knowing you will be climbing all day, it's another actually looking up to see the road that you will be cycling on in a few hours' time, as long as you keep that leg-sapping rhythm going. The bike and I weren't enjoying the loose gravel and relentless gradient. This time I was carrying even more than your average trekking bike setup, laden with filming and communication gear.

I had meant to be in Olmedo by lunchtime, yet it was mid-afternoon by the time I reached Chaguarpamba, still 9 miles short. The road continued upwards until sunset, by which time I was wondering where this elusive coffee plantation was. The reward for this long climb eventually came as the sun slowly sank – the view across the mountains was utterly breathtaking. I was caked in dust

COFFEE AT ALTITUDE

Café Altura, or mountain-grown coffee, earns a premium price because the beans mature more slowly at higher altitudes, so they become harder, denser and more intense. Angelino still hand picks the beans, de-shells them using a 4ft mortar and pestle, before slow roasting over an open fire and hand grinding them.

"It's one thing knowing you'll be climbing all day, it's another looking up to see the road you'll still be riding in a few hours"

Clockwise from above: a local iguana; the ride's starting point of Guayaquil; Mark Beaumont sifting and roasting beans; raw coffee beans. Previous page: a coffee plantation in Ecuador

from passing trucks and exhausted when I came across a track down to my left. This was very steep indeed, and I struggled with the heavy bike on the loose dirt. Eventually, in the growing dark, I found myself in the tiny village centre of Olmedo.

I had been communicating with my host Angelino by phone in very broken Spanish. He had been getting worried. It transpired that the road to Olmedo was directly along the flat valley bottom. Nobody had told me this, and it turned out that the road I had followed was new, not shown on my map – hence my confusion why it had taken so much longer than I had planned.

Angelino had a wonderfully welcoming home. The kitchen/living room was lined down one side with large hessian bags of coffee beans, the coffee filter on the table was replenished regularly and bottles of coffee liquor sat at the side. Eight of Angelino's friends and neighbors were there and spent most of the evening with us. His wife was the local primary school teacher and he proudly proclaimed that she taught English. Maybe so, but we soon gave up and stuck to Spanish. I was the only person not drinking coffee, although I did try some coffee wine, which was surprisingly good. Even his two young teenage daughters sat at the dinner table drinking straight black coffee. I do love coffee but was ready to sleep and didn't want anything to spoil that.

In the days ahead there would be a lot more tough roads as I headed for Peru, so I looked forward to taking the following morning off, enjoying some good company and exploring the *café altura* plantation to learn more about this prized black gold. **MB**

TOOLKIT

Start // Guayaquil
End // Olmedo
Distance // 200 miles (320km)
Getting there // Guayaquil is a major city with an international airport. Once in the highland of Ecuador you can carry on south towards Peru, where the next town is Piura, or continue on an anticlockwise loop in Ecuador to Cuenca and back to Guayaquil. Public transport is basic, but reliable, so catching a bus back to the coast is also an option.
What to ride // There are numerous bike/outdoor shops in Guayaquil, but don't expect them to have the same range of equipment as in North America. For any cycling trip in South America, unless working with a local tour operator, it's worth bringing your own bike and equipment. Heading south, the roads are good quality, flat and wide, with regular supply stops. Once climbing into the Andes, the roads deteriorate, with fewer towns, so using wider and grippier tyres is recommended – 35mm or more for touring.

Opposite: Hatcher Pass in Alaska

MORE LIKE THIS
METTLE-TESTING CLIMBS

HATCHER PASS, ALASKA

This stunning day ride is a little under 100 miles (160km) long and should only be tried in the middle of summer as Hatcher Pass is closed with snow for most of the year. From Anchorage, Palmer is less than an hour's drive, or a morning's ride, and from there you can start this loop in either direction. There is a good hard shoulder and sections of cycle lane on route 3, which heads north up to Talkeetna, but once past the Willow or Farm Loop turnoffs make sure you are stocked up with food as there are no supplies on the pass. Don't worry about water, however, as you follow Willow Creek for a lot of the way. Remote farmsteads and a sublime climb take you from the valley floor through the snowline, before a fast switchback descent to Matanuska River, from where Hwy 1 takes you south and back to Palmer.

Start/End // Palmer, Alaska
Distance // 91 miles (146km)

THE MENDOZA PASS, CHILE/ARGENTINA

This classic route over the Andes is best tackled in two days. Following the lush vineyards from Los Andes, the roaring Aconcagua River offers a clue as to what comes next – a staggering switchback ascent through the ski resort of Portillo to the border post. If you're riding a gravel bike then you can get your passport stamped at Chilean immigration and cut onto a 5-mile (8km) dirt track over the Paso Internacional Los Libertadores, at 10,500ft. If you are on a road bike then you will need to jump in an escort vehicle through the short tunnel to the Argentinian side, where you can find a bed and basic services in Puente del Inca. The main town on the long and very gradual descent all the way to Mendoza is Uspallata, where there's camping, a supermarket and a bank, before the touristy village of Potrerillos heralds a drop into the vineyards of the malbec capital of the world.

Start // Los Andes, Chile
End // Mendoza, Argentina
Distance // 173 miles (278km)

THE ALASKA HIGHWAY

Best tackled over a week, this route forms the mid-section of what used to be called the Alcan (Alaska–Canada) Highway, connecting the US state with the Yukon Territory and British Columbia. This stretch takes in the grandeur of the Northern Rockies, exploring Stone Mountain Provincial Park and Muncho Lake Park, promising glimpses of wildlife such as bears, wood bison, moose and bald eagles. Watson Lake is one of several small communities along the route well stocked for stopovers or day trips into the wilderness. Although this is a major trunk road for Alaska, traffic is generally light and there is a generous hard shoulder for cyclists throughout. Because of the harsh winters and permafrost under the northern stretches, there are roadworks each summer, so you'll come across some stretches of gravel. From fully laden touring bikes to carbon race bikes with no luggage, all cycling setups are suitable for this route.

Start // Whitehorse, Yukon
End // Fort Nelson, British Columbia
Distance // 594 miles (956km)

TRANS-ECUADOR MOUNTAIN BIKE ROUTE

The Trans-Ecuador Mountain Bike Route is a three-week, off-road ride that runs the length of the country's volcanic corridor, from the Colombian border to the fringes of Peru.

In 2012, I undertook my first bike trip to Ecuador, with the intention of unearthing as many dirt roads as I could. Little did I know that this petite, rugged land would draw me back, again and again, enticing me into a more formal project: to map a route that runs the length of the Ecuadorian Andes, via the road less travelled. We launched the Trans Ecuador Mountain Bike Route, or TEMBR, as it has become known, in 2016. It's almost 860 miles, a circuitous ride that traces the country's Avenue of the Volcanoes – as coined by the 19th-century Prussian naturalist, Alexander von Humboldt – from the northern border with Colombia to the edge of Peru. Reflecting Ecuador's beauty and diversity, it's a ride that strikes a balance between spots of touristic interest with remote backcountry riding, namely the tracks and trails that cross its tufty *páramo*, the high altitude, alpine tundra so particular to the tropical Andes.

To ride it, I teamed up with three Ecuadorian siblings. As organic farmers, accomplished climbers and outdoorsmen to the fingertips, the *hermanos* Dammers shared an understanding of the interconnectivity of the land; to them, the Ecuadorian Highlands are as much a source of work and sustenance as they are a place of adventure.

Over the weeks spent researching the ride, we navigated through the mountains using methods both modern and traditional: paper maps, Google Earth, a GPS and smartphones all played their part. But it was local insight that lent the route its particular flavor; on one occasion we questioned a horse rider, his braided ponytail jet black under his traditional fedora, his shoes resting in stirrups carved from wood. '*Préstame paso, compañero?*' one of the brothers asked politely, requesting passage along an

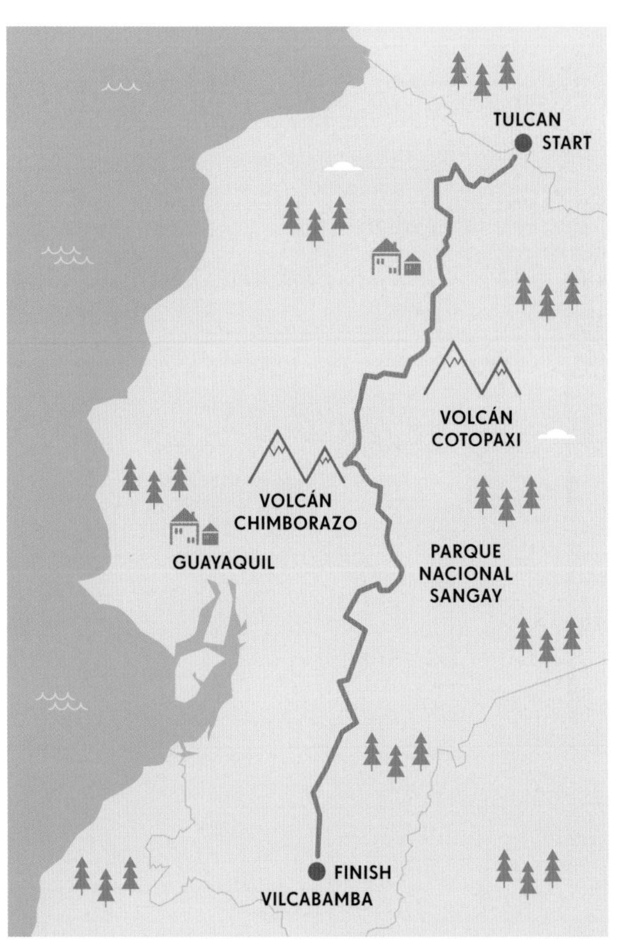

unconventional trail we were investigating. '*Sigue, sigue*' (keep going), came the reply, with a smile. He pointed us towards a faint footpath that dropped steeply through a series of switchbacks and crossed a fast-flowing river by way of a tree trunk. There, we stopped to camp, requesting fresh milk and eggs from a passing farmer. Truly, this was the good life, Ecuadorian style.

The route itself, however, begins with a lonesome meander through the Reserva Ecológica El Ángel, on Ecuador's border with Colombia, where a legion of velvet-leafed *frailejón* plants appear and disappear in the *páramo* mist, rising and receding across the tundra like the tide. Specific to just a handful of humid, high altitude regions, *frailejón* are intrinsic to Ecuador's water cycle. As tall as humans, they only start to grow at elevations above 7500ft, their hairy leaves catching moisture in the air and feeding it into the earth. Riding through their congregation is a particular feeling; as if you're observed by thousands of beings from another planet.

Descending back down to the Inter Andean Valley, our R&R takes the form of a stopover in Otovalo, home to Ecuador's biggest textile and handicraft market. A classic, cobbled climb leads onwards to windswept Lago Mojanda, from where riders are drawn to Guayllabamba, source of delicious, succulent *chirimoya*, an exotic fruit of these parts.

A network of typically Ecuadorian backroads – unpaved, sometimes grassy, sometimes cobbled – then has us gaining altitude once more in search of the perfectly conical Cotopaxi volcano, its National Park speckled with delicate, miniature, mossy flora, particular to its tundra, as well as high-altitude *Polylepis*, with its distinctive, dark and flaky bark.

Almost every day begins with what we've come to call an 'Ecuadorian Breakfast': a long, protracted, heavenwards climb. When we strike into the fertile highlands around Quilotoa, however, the landscape takes on a different character. Here, steep-sided hills are home to shepherds herding sheep and llamas, as well as patchworks of quinoa and potato fields, staples of the Quechuan diet. Beyond, Salinas de la Guaranda is home to a thriving, grassroots tourism and local business infrastructure; among its many projects, this small settlement even has a chocolate factory. This is a place where you're just as likely to see men in handwoven ponchos galloping across the horizon as you are to see alpaca farmers bouncing along dirt roads on old motorbikes.

No visit would be complete without taking in the grandeur of Volcán Chimborazo, the loftiest volcano in the country, in a park that shelters highland owls, Andean condors and vicuña. Ahead lies the push to Cuenca, reached via the noted Incan ruins of Ingapirca. Cuenca itself is Ecuador's most appealing city, with its rich display of colonial architecture, as well as a strong artistic and musical vibe.

Finally, we had a route we could be pleased with. One that strived to encourage bicycle tourists to escape the hectic traffic of the Panamerican Highway and delve deep into Ecuador's

ECUADOR'S WARES

Set aside rest time in the mountain town of Salinas de Guaranda. This settlement, in the shadow of Chimborazo, has a thriving network of cooperatives, including a chocolate factory and suppliers of dehydrated mushrooms. Tie in your visit with Ecuador's markets, often held on a Wednesday or a Saturday. There's no better place to re-supply with wholesome, locally grown and package-free produce.

Left to right: gentian flowers are part of the páramo's ecosystem; fresh, cheese-filled corn cakes; a baby vicuña in the Chimborazo National Park; always expect four seasons in one day. Previous page and overleaf: the high traverse between Angamarca and Simiatug is often lost in a swirl of clouds

> *"Cuenca itself is Ecuador's most appealing city, with its rich display of colonial architecture, as well as a strong artistic and musical vibe."*

backcountry, without missing some of its classic sights. Staying high in the Andes for much of the time, it's a showcase of remarkable variety: patchwork fields in its rural settlements, the technicolored hubbub of its markets, the beautiful city of Cuenca and, of course, the majestic volcanic backdrop for which Ecuador is known.

TEMBR was never meant to be the easiest crossing; rather, one that would help visitors appreciate the fabric of Ecuador's culture and lend a deeper insight into its mountain communities, via the very contours of the land. Most importantly, it's a ride that seeks to remind us all of the importance of the quiet and ethereal *páramo*, as a source of inspiration, of water, and of life.

With every year that has passed, the Trans Ecuador Mountain Bike Route has become increasingly established. I'm thrilled that bicycle tyre tracks are now imprinted across the country's backroads. Yet still I find myself returning. I tell myself it's to 'improve the route' but, in reality, it's because I've become at home in the Ecuadorian highlands. The land may not be my own, but I'm proud to show it off to other cyclists. **CG**

TOOLKIT

Start // Tulcan
End // Vilcabamba
Distance // 858 miles (1381km). The ride takes three to four weeks to complete.
Getting there // The easiest access point is via Quito's international airport. Ecuador is well served by affordable, bike-friendly public transportation, including pickup trucks that can whisk you up many of its climbs for a few dollars.
When to ride // Embark on this trip during the dry season, between May and September, though quality waterproofs are still recommended.
What to ride // Given the route's cobbled surfaces and often mixed off-road conditions, a 'plus-sized' tyre makes sense. That said, any mountain bike will suit the ride, ideally with front suspension for added comfort. A key requisite is to pack light, to make easier work of the country's many climbs.
More info // A complete gpx file can be found at www.bikepacking.com/tembr

Opposite: the Ruta Maya de los Cuchumatanes passes through such towns as Concepción Huista

MORE LIKE THIS
LATIN AMERICAN CLIMBS

LAS TRES VOLCANES, ECUADOR

Also in Ecuador, and ideal if time is limited, the Ruta de las Tres Volcanes zooms in on three of the country's iconic volcanoes. It connects Cotopaxi to Chimborazo – the latter's peak actually marks the Earth's closest point to the sun – via the turquoise waters of Quilotoa's crater lake. Compared with the dirt-road medley of TEMBR, this route features more in the way of rugged singletrack and open *páramo* riding, so it's best undertaken on a mountain bike. Be warned that there are a few stout hike-a-bikes to contend with, so packing light is advised. Cycling between these three volcanoes is a wonderful way of unearthing some true Ecuadorian backcountry riding in a jam-packed five days, plus time beforehand to acclimatize. It is sometimes hard fought and muddy, but always worthwhile, with the added bonus that the route ends in Salinas de Guaranda, home to those locally produced chocolates...

Start // Pintag
End // Salinas de Guaranda
Distance // 258 miles (415km)

BOYACÁ, COLOMBIA

Further to the north, and similar in topography in places, the Boyacá region of Colombia's Eastern Cordillera makes a great multi-day route. San Gil, the country's adventure capital, and Villa de Leyva, a picture-perfect heritage town, make great start and end points. In between, a series of unpaved roads strike east towards the Cocuy National Park, creating a route that can be tackled over a couple of weeks. Like Ecuador, this region is abundant in the high-altitude *frailejón* plant. This part of the Andes is also unfeasibly hilly. No wonder many of Colombia's top road climbers are plucked from these mountains and nurtured into world-class athletes. December to March and July to August are the recommended times to travel, though being so close to the equator, expect rainfall nonetheless.

Start // San Gil
End // Villa de Leyva
Distance // 375 miles (604km)

RUTA MAYA DE LOS CUCHUMATANES, GUATEMALA

For those who prefer their mountainous epics to be a little lower in elevation, consider a tour of the Guatemalan Highlands; specifically, the Sierra de los Cuchumatanes, a range that's sometimes called the Peru of Guatemala. If you have 10 days available, the Ruta Maya de los Cuchumatanes promises a thorough exploration of the area by way of both remote riding and more established tourist sights. Highlights include a visit to the intricately painted church in San Andrés Xecul and an amble around Chichicastenango's famous Sunday market. English is rarely spoken away from the Gringo Trail, so consider preluding your trip with a few days studying Spanish in nearby San Pedro La Laguna. Guatemalan hills can be ferociously steep; thankfully, omnipresent 'chicken buses' can generally take bikes on their roofs, should your legs run out of steam. The country's dry season is between November and April. Affordable flights into the capital, Guatemala City, are easy to source.

Start // Quetzaltenango
End // Chichicastenango
Distance // 330 miles (530km)

C 526BCB

FAMILY BIKEPACKING IN ECUADOR

Picturesque Quilotoa Loop feels suitably off the beaten track, but with a range of comfortable digs along the way, cyclists can recharge before tackling Ecuador's tremendous inclines.

For those unfamiliar with the topography of South America, let me assure you of this: the Ecuadorian Andes are a deeply crumpled land. A slim band squeezed between the expanse of the Pacific Coast and the vast sprawl of the Amazon, it abounds with microclimates, determined more by geography and altitude than by any season. Within these folds, one steep-sided valley dovetails into the next. Cradled between two volcanic ranges, they form the Avenue of the Volcanoes, as coined by Alexander von Humboldt, the Prussian naturalist who journeyed through the continent in the 19th century.

Big mountains, big views... and, above all, big climbs: adventurous cycling, without doubt. But family friendly? Yes, and somewhat surprisingly, very much so.

We shared our Ecuadorian adventures with three brothers I'd first met while cycling through the country three years prior. Mountain guides by trade, they lived off-grid on an organic family farm outside Quito. In the interim, we'd kept in touch – and we'd all had children. When the chance came to visit Ecuador once again, this time I travelled with my partner and our young son, Sage, so we might experience this beautiful and unfeasibly rugged country together.

In any shape or form, this ride would have been epic enough. Apart from the quiet dirt tracks, small mountain settlements, and fluffy roadside llamas, its backdrop was nothing short of spectacular: high altitude Ecuadorian *páramo*, the alpine tundra for which the country is known, and the emerald-tinted, 2-mile wide Quilotoa crater lake, a definitive highlight along the Avenue of the Volcanoes.

But factor in no less than eight bicycles and five accompanying trailers, charged with a payload of children ranging in age from six months to three years, and such a journey takes on an even more memorable character. Despite the afternoon downpours and the occasional synchronized meltdowns, our pint-sized expedition proved to be an incredible life experience for everyone.

Together, we blazed a trail of family mayhem through the countryside. We rubbed shoulders with poncho-clad horse riders, picnicked among fields of quinoa, visited an indigenous market, and lingered in village playgrounds.

We kept distances short, and tried to harmonize riding times with napping schedules. When our three toddlers needed a break,

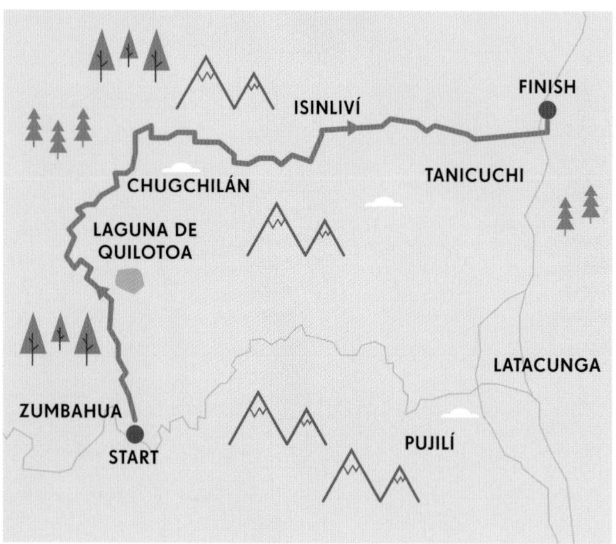

"Reaching the summit was rewarded with a feast of local produce, cheese and ripe avocados that had filled our panniers"

we stopped and played football, helped them climb trees, or just explored the land. And what a land it was. A fertile patchwork of vertiginous fields clung to steep-sided slopes, surrounded by both soaring peaks and crumbling canyon cliffs. Pigs scuffled around by the road, men sauntered by with machetes on their hips, and women crammed their colorful shawls with fresh corn, their felt hats peeking out through the foliage.

The route itself looped southeast through Ecuador's Central Sierras. After stopping to applaud the natural watery wonder of Quilotoa, and scout briefly along the knife-edge of its crater, it took us through the small settlement of Chugchilán, where we detoured into the dewy delights of the Illiniza Cloud Forest. There, fingers of mist curled through the trees, enveloping the land, filling every nook and cranny with silence. When the sun occasionally permeated through, it was subtle, painting the mountains in gigantic, camouflaged swatches.

Up and down we rode, rarely a flat moment for respite. Climbs had our derailleurs clattering frantically through the gears, spinning our legs in the lowest cadences we could find, the ballast of our toddler cargo weighing us down. In immediate riposte, descents demanded we pull on brake levers like reins on a horse, lest our trailers shunt us forwards. Added to this, the terrain was often bumpy, sometimes even cobbled. Yet when I looked back to check on Sage, more often than not he was sound asleep, oblivious to our efforts.

Travelling over the winter holidays, we celebrated Christmas in Isinliví, a picturesque settlement perched in one of the region's verdant valleys. As we came to appreciate, South Americans know how to party, whatever the time of year. The main square was awash with revellers, countryside cowboys and a roving brass band that relentlessly circled its stony streets. To Sage's delight, it even boasted an antiquated funfair, featuring a carousel that spun with dizzying speed.

Isinliví was also our last staging post before we tackled the longest climb of the trip, a Herculean undertaking that involved 3300ft in altitude gain, on an unpaved road at that. Inevitably, this final undertaking had us all off the bikes and pushing, our Lilliputian team of toddlers enthusiastically lending a helping hand too. When the summit finally came, it was rewarded with a feast of local produce, cheese and deliciously ripe avocados that had filled our panniers. Then, with a last gaze out towards the highland *páramo*, we dived into the whirligig descent that lay ahead, the flags of our trailers snapping in the wind.

Despite the diminutive daily distances, I won't lay claim that family bikepacking is easy; without doubt, it poses its own set of mental and logistical challenges, quite apart from any physical toils. But I couldn't more highly recommend trying it out, wherever you may be in the world, for however many days you may have. Gather the troops and brew up a plan. Choose a route that everyone will enjoy. Take the time to luxuriate in being off the bike as much as you are on it. I can guarantee that such undiluted family time will warm the heart and feed the soul. **CG**

MARKETS

Ecuador's markets are not to be missed: vibrant colours, towering displays of food and a real sense of community. Fresh fruit juices and delicious snacks abound – grilled plantain is safe to eat, and a surefire toddler favorite. Usurping the main square each Saturday, there's Zumbahua's market – at the beginning of the Quilotoa Loop. Or, as a separate trip, don't miss Otavalo, the best place to stock up on beautifully knitted jumpers and ponchos for children.

Clockwise from left: cosy cargo; public transport; climbing gravel roads, one step at a time

TOOLKIT

Start // Zumbahua
End // Lasso, on the Pan-American Hwy
Distance // 68 miles (110km)
Getting there // Both Zumbahua and Lasso can be easily accessed by bus from Quito.
Where to stay // Hostal Llullu Llama in Isinliví. For eco-minded luxury, the Black Sheep Inn, near Chugchilán.
What to take // Pack light and make use of traveller-friendly accommodation en route.
Climate // Put aside several days in Quito to acclimatize before heading into Ecuador's high country.
Hot tip // Ecuador's inclines can be long and unreasonably steep (but ultimately rewarding!). Trucks regularly ply Ecuador's mountain roads. For a few dollars, flag down a driver, and enjoy a lift to the top of the next mountain pass.

Opposite: riding through downtown Salida, Colorado

MORE LIKE THIS
FAMILY BIKEPACKING RIDES

SALIDA, COLORADO

The Great Divide Mountain Bike Route (GDMBR) is famed for its Herculean race, in which self-supported riders tear across the Rockies. But broken up in bite-size portions, it also has all the ingredients for a series of wonderful family bikepacking adventures. Indeed, things don't get much better than the high grasslands and aspen groves above Salida, Colorado, especially during the technicolored splendor of fall. There, a dirt road loop can be formed using Aspen Ridge and the backbone of the GDMBR. Salida's polished, historic redbrick downtown – distantly echoing an insalubrious past as a Wild West railroad settlement – also features a park in which to picnic, a playground, a climbing wall and a river to soak in. Kids' trailers are almost as common as the dual suspension mountain bikes that roam the streets.
Start/End // Salida, Colorado
Distance // 52 miles (84km)
Info // www.bikepacking.com/routes/family-bikepacking-salida

BEARS EARS, UTAH

Just west of mountain bike hotspot Moab, newly designated Bears Ears National Monument has been in the news for political reasons recently. Never mind the politics, it's a fascinating area to explore by bike, rich in Native American history. Ancestral Pueblans inhabited the Abajos mountains 1000 years ago and left many reminders of their communities here, including ruins and rock art. Doubletrack dirt roads thread through pinyon and juniper forest, offer easy riding for young or beginner bikers. But what makes this area particularly suited to family-friendly bikepacking trips is that local outfitters, such as Western Spirit in Moab, can organize supported introductions to bikepacking by helping carry gear from one camping spot to the next and helping set up tents, leaving you free to cycle 10 to 15 miles per day on a typical five-day trip. For those who have never camped independently, it's an accessible experience.
Start/End // near Moab, Utah
Distance //approx 75 miles (120km) over five days

CONGUILLÍO NATIONAL PARK, CHILE

The Conguillío National Park lies at the northern tip of the Chilean Lake District, and envelopes the 10253ft Llaima Volcano. It's a lunar landscape where islands of fertile earth lie stranded between lava flows frozen in time – or at least until the next eruption. Quiet mountain roads make for great, if challenging, family bikepacking, combining an exploration of the park with a ride to Lonquimay, through the neighboring Reserva China Muerta. Dotted through the area, standing nobly in tranquil groves, are the enchanting *Araucaria araucana* or 'Monkey Puzzle' trees, so named as it was thought that climbing them would flummox even a monkey. These bizarre, bandy, Seussian-like creations reach up to 130ft high, their tentacle-like branches surely protecting them from any primate intrusion while also fascinating children.
Start // Melipueco
End // Lonquimay
Distance // 50 miles (80km)

A.T.HENRY
1886
Ruby BLUES
DOVETONS
SALIDA
MOUNTAIN
SPORTS
SH 291

BAJA CALIFORNIA'S CAPE LOOP

As the finale to the long-distance Baja Divide bikepacking route, the Cape Loop makes a wonderful journey in itself. Complete with idyllic camping and wild beaches, it has all the makings of a manageable yet adventurous family ride, too.

Family bike holidays are always a delicate balancing act. Get it right and you'll strike parental gold: an abundance of laughter, a sense of discovery, good sleep and, in our case, a happy five-year-old. Picking the right destination, however, is key. After much around-the-table deliberation, we set our sights on the Cape Loop because it offered an escape from winter, mile upon mile of empty beaches, and the promise of a daily menu of fresh fish tacos...

As a family we've completed a number of biking adventures together; we spent a few weeks in Chile when our son, Sage, was 18 months old, Ecuador a year later, and Bolivia after that. For the most part, our trips have involved towing Sage behind us in a trailer. Distances were best covered when he napped and we paused regularly so he might expend some of his toddler energy. Our bike ride around the most southerly portion of the Baja California peninsula would, however, be different. For the first time, Sage would provide a part of the propulsion, riding a tag-along bicycle, which my partner and I would pull behind us.

As with all bike trips, it didn't take long before we developed our modus operandi: start the day early to beat the heat; set our watches for a mid-morning slather of sunscreen; push on for an hour before finding a beach at lunchtime; splash around in the water, enjoy a picnic lunch of avocados and tortilla chips, then take a nap; ride again in the afternoon; swing by a village for a few rounds of fish tacos; scout out a good camping spot for the evening and unpack the football; set up the tent, make a fire with driftwood, and settle in for the night.

After all, bike trips don't have to be only about cycling: fire building, beachcombing and tent time were undoubted highlights

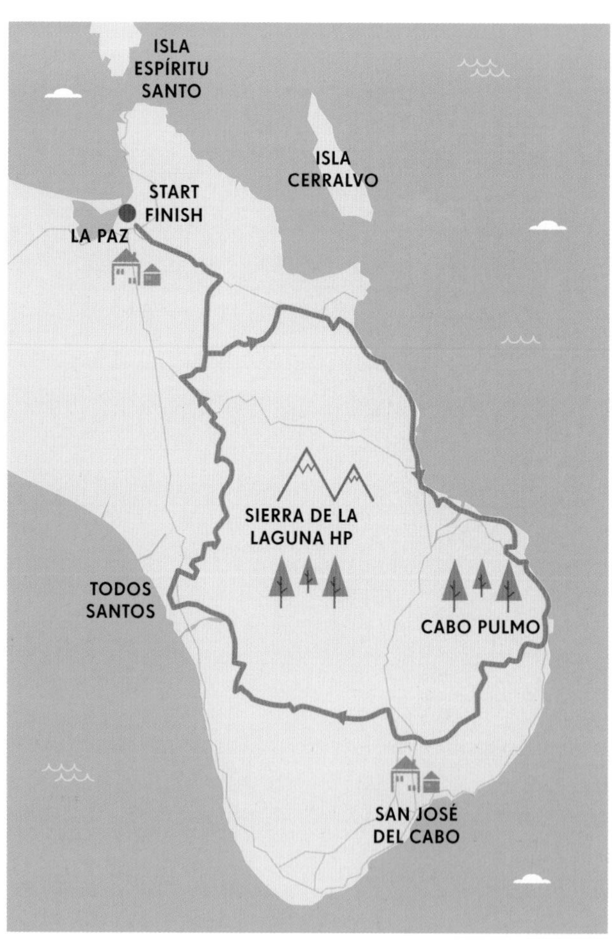

of our time in Mexico. 'You've got to admit, this is shell central!' Sage announced delightedly at one of our lunchtime stops, his eyes feasting upon the sheer variety before him; some tiny and intricate, others weathered by years in the sea, all seen with the fresh eyes of a five-year-old. Sage also took charge of setting up the tent, as well as prepping the mattresses and laying out the sleeping bags. Using only the tent's inner mesh without the need for the fly meant spectacular vistas of Baja's starscapes every night, framed by the tent's poles. It was like peering through the window of a rocket ship floating across a star-filled Milky Way. Worried about screen time for your kid? This is the best alternative to a TV show, ever.

Allow me to remind you, however, that touring as a family can be a Slow Moving Experience. From the gentle pace of the riding itself to the time spent packing up our campsite or stopping for afternoon siestas, it's not about covering miles. For the Baja Divide, we set our sights on a target of 20 miles a day but were happy to cover far less, with more hours spent off the bikes than on them. In fact, much of our journey revolved around a search for shade. The Cape Loop crosses the Sierra de la Laguna, a rugged range that divides the warmer climes of the Sea of Cortez from the windier, cooler Pacific coast. There, respite from the heat can be especially hard to come by. Hollow-hipped cows know the best shady spots but wouldn't give us an inch. We discovered that roaming donkeys are also astute to where best to while away the hottest hours of the day. Thankfully they were more open to co-sharing, so we could sit out of the midday sun.

Five-year-olds can also be wonderfully verbose; by this age, Sage was connecting thoughts and sharing personal opinions. Leaving the kitesurfing idyll of La Ventana, I took a turn pulling the tag-along up a steep and rocky pass that separated us from the next string of beaches, the wildest and most scenic part of the loop. 'Here we go, Sage, pedal, pedal, pedal!' I called out, dropping

ACCESSORIZE YOUR ADVENTURE

A family-style, beach-themed adventure benefits from a little extra gear, on top of the usual packlist. A football or a Frisbee make a welcome change from cycling. Similarly, we packed goggles to study the plethora of colorful fish; Playa Los Arbolitos was a favorite spot. We tied a mesh bag to our trailer to dry off damp beach clothes when we were riding. Also handy is a lightweight blanket for picnics and naps. As on any family bike tour, reflective tops are recommended for the occasional stints on main roads.

Clockwise from above: heading to Todos Santos; at windy La Ventana; look forward to delicious tacos at the end of your day's ride; keeping young riders amused. Previous page: pitching camp beside the sea at La Ventana

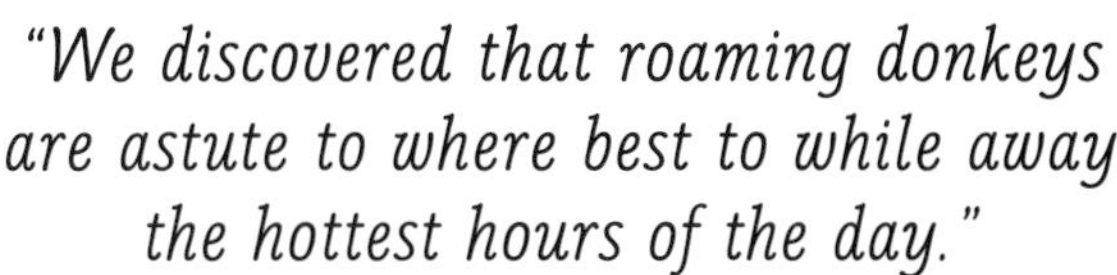

"We discovered that roaming donkeys are astute to where best to while away the hottest hours of the day."

down through the gears as the grade sharpened. 'We're doing it,' he chimed in. 'And look at that view, it's so beautiful!' I know that Sage has always enjoyed our past bike tours, perhaps because, more than the travel experience itself, we're all together as a family, away from distractions. But to hear his own reaction and a developing appreciation for the scenery around him was new.

Later, as we rode down a sandy two-track between a corridor of enormous cardón cacti and the azure waters of the Gulf of California, I expressed my thoughts. 'Sage, I want you to know how happy I am that we're sharing this experience.' I felt the need to expand. 'I hope that you enjoy the trip as much as I do, even if some bits are hard. Which is a bit like life. Hopefully we enjoy most of it. Some of it will be hard. But everything is an experience.' He replied: 'Yes, I agree. I think that exactly.' What can I say? Five-year-olds...

Sure, we could have booked ourselves a more conventional beach break. In many ways, I bet Sage would have enjoyed himself too. But this trip meant so much more. It offered a satisfying sense of movement and change. By keeping distances manageable, the riding was almost always fun, even if it was challenging. Most of all, I've no doubt that we'll look back upon out time in Baja as not just a holiday, but a real adventure. **CG**

TOOLKIT

Start/End // La Paz

Distance // 283 miles (455km). The ride is manageable in a week but allow two or more if kids are involved. Beach time is sacred!

Getting there // Both La Paz and San José del Cabo (Los Cabos) are convenient airports with budget-priced flights in and out of the US.

When to ride // Due to excessive heat in the summer and the hurricane season in the fall, November to March is the best time.

What to ride // Surfaces are often rocky and sometimes sandy. Although you can get by with less, 3in tires are recommended, as is a tubeless setup.

What else to see // Break up your riding with a visit to see turtles hatching in Todos Santos and a whale shark tour in La Paz; make sure the company you book through observes best practices.

More info // www.bajadivide.com

Opposite: Pedersen Lagoon, near Seward, Alaska, the starting point of the Kenai 250

MORE LIKE THIS
BEACH AND COAST RIDES

OMETEPE, NICARAGUA

Further south, squeezed between the Pacific Coast and the Atlantic, lies Lake Nicaragua and the Island of Ometepe. Reaching it is a journey in itself – Isla Ometepe's twin volcanoes rise out of the water like a scene from *Jurassic Park*. Once there, it's possible to make a figure-of-eight loop around Volcán Concepción and Volcán Maderas, keeping to dirt roads for much of the way. Like Baja California, the ride around Ometepe suits adventurous families, though surfaces can get rough and rowdy at times. If you want to pack light, there are a number of cheap guesthouses on the islands, as well as idyllic campsites; beautiful Finca Magdalena (www.fincamagdalena.com) combines the best of both worlds. Nicaragua's typical fare of eggs, beans and *tostones* – deliciously crispy plantains – is a surefire way of fuelling a cyclist's appetite. The country's dry season runs between November and April, and the island is best reached from San Jorge port, near the town of Rivas.
Start/End // Moyogalpa
Distance // 85 miles (135km)

EL FIN DEL MUNDO, PATAGONIA

At the very bottom of the Americas, aka El Fin del Mundo, cyclists can ride between southern Patagonia's two major settlements: Punta Arenas in Chile and Ushuaia in Argentina. There's a paved road connecting the two cities, or a meandering alternative, which keeps to dirt and gravel roads that skirt the watery edges of South America's southerly tip. Wildlife abounds along this route, including guanacos, condors, penguins, dolphins and whales. The best time to set out is during Patagonia's summer, from the beginning of November to March. Tierra del Fuego is a remarkable place to experience on a bike, just as long as its notoriously blustery winds are on your side. Given the prevailing northwest winds, which can reach over 60mph (100km/h), riders are highly advised to cycle from north to south. The route crosses a rarely used military area a day's ride from Ushuaia, which you'll need to detour around in the event of local activity.
Start // Punta Arenas, Chile
End // Ushuaia, Argentina
Distance // 390 miles (630km)

KENAI 250, ALASKA

The Kenai 250 laces together wild singletrack and quiet paved roads over its 254-mile (409km) length. Local riders have been known to tackle this epic peninsula medley in just a day and a half, but you'll certainly enjoy it more if you put aside a week, given that the route includes the very best of the Last Frontier's backcountry singletrack. The loop is best ridden in July, when the days are longest (almost 24 hours of daylight) and the weather likely to be driest. It's also important to familiarize yourself with camping protocol – bears and moose are residents of the peninsula. There are regular flights to Anchorage, from where you can catch a bus to Seward. The latest gpx track for the route can be downloaded from the official race website, www.kenai250.wordpress.com.
Start/End // Hope, Alaska
Distance // 254 miles (409km)

OAXACA CITY TO PLAYA ZIPOLITE

Pedal from the charming Mexican city of Oaxaca to a hippie paradise by the Pacific Ocean, via the rugged and mystic Sierra Madre del Sur Mountains.

Not many couples celebrate Valentine's Day by going on a five-day bike-pack over steep mountains to get to their beach vacation, but maybe they should. After all, what says 'romance' like a leg-burning elevation gain of 21,000ft over 170 miles, ending in a nudist beach?

The Oaxaca to Zipolite route follows dirt roads from the colorful, culinary, colonial city of Oaxaca, past mezcal farms, through remote indigenous villages in the Sierra Madre del Sur Mountains, to sea level, ending at Playa Zipolite, Mexico's first and only legal nudist beach. With some serious cycling effort, my partner and I intended making this vacation's good times even sweeter.

Our romantic trip began in Oaxaca City, in southeastern Mexico. Oaxaca City is home to one million and visited by more for its colonial-era architecture, cultural charm, exquisite *mole* cuisine, lively festivals, and the ancient pyramids of Monte Alban. Oaxaca's appeal makes for an inspiring location to start a bike tour and a tough place to leave. We meandered through markets, sipped hot chocolate in the *Zócalo* and explored the vaulted ceilings of the many cathedrals, monasteries, and convents lining Oaxaca's narrow cobbled streets. With our bellies full of *chapulines* (fried grasshoppers seasoned with chilli), *mole* (spiced sauce), and fresh *piña* (pineapples), we reluctantly set out into Oaxaca's Valle Centrales.

The route flows quickly out of the city and into the countryside where crops of agave are grown to make mezcal, a distilled alcoholic beverage similar to tequila and for which the region is famous. We stop at a roadside cafe for a home-cooked meal of chicken and *mole*. As we finish, our host brings two shot glasses of mezcal. It's smoky and strong, and makes the next few navigation

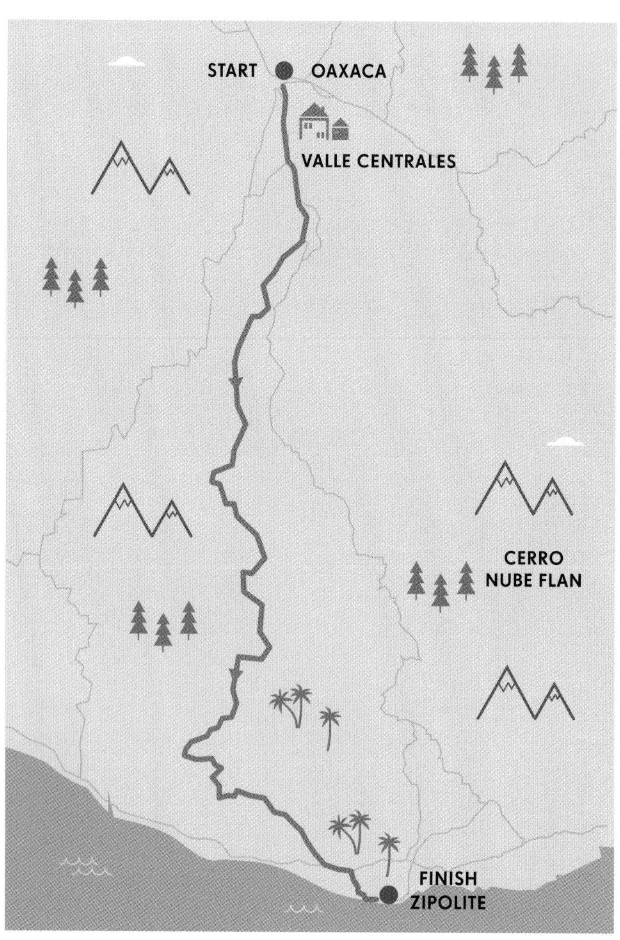

decisions that bit trickier. But soon our heads clear as we make our way along flat dirt roads lined with succulents and cacti to the foothills of the Sierra Madre del Sur Mountains, stopping to chat to farmers driving oxen to the fields and laden donkeys carrying supplies to the next village.

With the elevation gain the mountains grow steeper, the sun stronger, and we begin to notice the pesky itchy bites we are getting from the all-but-invisible no-see-um gnats. Despite the heat we put on long pants, high socks, and long-sleeved shirts and like magic, we stopped getting bitten and burnt.

Up in the Sierra Madre del Sur Mountains ranges we roll at between 5500ft to 6500ft. Even within this limited elevation change the biome changes as well, with pine-oak forests at the higher elevations and tropical dry forests at the lower. Sprinkled throughout are small, isolated villages perched high above the clouds and nestled deep within the forest, the only sign of their existence the cheerful music reverberating through the surrounding mountains. These communities are convenient places to stock up on supplies and to meet the indigenous Zapotec and Mixtec people, who are direct descendants of the Mesoamerican civilizations. Each group has its own language, customs, religious beliefs and traditional dress, with artisans specializing in crafts such as *Alebrije* (brightly painted, wooden mythic figures), woven rugs, or *barro negro* pottery (black clay) to sell at markets.

One particularly hot day we stopped at a roadside store to refill our water bottles. As we rested in the shade, a woman emerged

TRIP ADVISER

A two-day easterly detour from San Pedro de Coatlán (at about mile 75 along the route) is a high mountain town called San Jose del Pacifico known for the hallucinogenic mushroom *Psilocybe Mexicana* that grows in the region (its consumption purely for recreational use is illegal). Regardless of its reputation, San Jose del Pacifico is worth a trip, not least for the indigenous steam baths (known as *temazcal*) set in the mountains high above the clouds.

Clockwise from above: the beautiful beach at Zipolite; and the rocky shore; even the dead ride their bikes in Oaxaca. Previous page: pausing for breath on a dirt track

from her home with two bowls of a cool, corn-based liquid soup. It was a welcome gesture, and typical of the indigenous people whom we encountered – best of all it hit the spot, a nourishing and refreshing feed station, Oaxaca style. (If you're in the area and want to try the soup, ask for *Atole*.)

As the route begins its 6500 ft descent to sea level we become stifled by the heat and make frequent stops to sip coconut juice and to eat fresh mango, pineapple and melon.

The route turns to pavement and short, steep coastal hills tug us closer to the Oaxaca coast and its remote beach and fishing communities. Our destination is Playa Zipolite, a 1-mile stretch of golden sand between rocky sea cliffs, lapped by inviting turquoise Pacific waters.

In the 1970s, the isolated nature of the Oaxaca coast attracted hippies from all over the world, particularly to Playa Zipolite. As a result, the community exudes a free-love paradise vibe with a relaxed attitude toward most things, including the human body in all its glory. The beach in Zipolite was unofficially nudist for over 30 years and has been legally so since 2016. Want to rid yourself of those cycling tan lines? You won't find a more picturesque place to strip off: over a mile wide, with golden sand (though be aware, there are strong undertows).

It may only have three paved roads, yet the village has a variety of good restaurants, cafes, and lodging ranging from rustic to luxurious. If you manage to tear yourself from the relaxing shade of a open-sided, palm-thatched *palapa*, there are plenty of opportunities to surf, do yoga, get a massage, or snorkel.

As for us, we roll into the hip streets of Zipolite, sun-baked, tired and dusty, and make straight for the beach. We drop our bikes in the sand, pull off our dirty clothes, and leap into the Pacific's chilly embrace. Let the vacation begin. **SS**

"The Playa Zipolite community exudes a free-love paradise vibe with a relaxed attitude toward most things, including the human body in all its glory."

TOOLKIT

Start // Oaxaca City
End // Zipolite
Distance //170 miles (274km)
Getting there // Oaxaca City Airport
Getting away // There are airports at Huatulco (60 minutes' drive) or Puerto Escondido (90 minutes)
Where to stay // Oaxaca City – Quinta Real Oaxaca, a convent converted to luxury hotel. Zipolite – Lo Cosmico, basic palm thatched huts directly on the north end of the playa (other, luxurious accommodations are available).
Best time of year to ride // November through February.
What to take // GPS device, camping equipment, cookware, clothing layers, a battery charger, your climbing legs and an open mind!
More info // www.bikepacking.com

Opposite top: the Lost Coast of California; bottom, Costa Rica's Nicoya Peninsula

MORE LIKE THIS
COASTAL GETAWAYS

NICOYA PENINSULA BEACH ADVENTURE, COSTA RICA

There aren't many routes that reward a hard day in the saddle with a dip in a crystal clear ocean and a beach to yourself. The Nicoya Peninsula of Costa Rica delivers this and more, and is just a hop from the international airport in Liberia. You'll spin along sandy tracks on desolate beaches, climb steep coastal dirt roads, and ford a few rivers. The route passes many small towns, and a couple of touristy ones, with a range of lodging. But if you pack to camp wild, most nights the route will deliver you to your own private shoreline site. Bring your goggles: the turquoise waters teem with Pacific sealife, and you may even get a chance to spot some sea turtles nesting on one of the beaches. Ride during the dry season from December to April but be sure to bring a handkerchief to cover your mouth, as it does get dusty.

Start // Liberia
End // Paquera
Distance // 182 miles (293km)
Info // www.ridewithgps.com/routes/5717460

THE LOST COAST RIDGE TRAIL, CALIFORNIA

In the most populous state in America, what a treat to find such a remote challenge. The Lost Coast is the most undeveloped portion of the California coastline, defined by the rugged and steep slopes of the King Range that prevented road builders from establishing major routes through the region. Be aware, though, of the severity of the terrain and the prevailing weather: the King Range National Conservation Area is one of the wettest places in the US. The route begins among the ancient, giant trees of Humboldt Redwoods State Park and winds its way south through the subtropical forests of the King Range along a combination of paved, dirt and jeep roads, delivering you to the idyllic Usal Beach – once you arrive, look for elk in the surrounding hills.

Start // Burlington, California
End // Leggett, California
Distance // 75 miles (121km)
Info // www.ridewithgps.com/routes/12307187

THE KING RIDGE DIRTY ROAD RIDE, CALIFORNIA

This epic paved and gravel adventure is famous for including several celebrated roads, such as King Ridge Rd and Hwy 101. King Ridge Rd is the crown jewel, climbing to a rolling ridge through green or dry pastures (depending on the season), with sweeping views to the Pacific Ocean in the distance. More delights are to come: gravel roads lined with eucalyptus and redwood, the scenic coastal sections along Hwy 101, quad-burning climbs and formidable descents. Doable as a single-day adventure ride on road bikes with wide tires, or more casually over several days. Just be sure to bring your climbing gears! Note that the route is remote, with little to no cell signal, and requires a degree of self-sufficiency.

Start/End // Jenner, California
Distance // 63 miles (101km)
Info // www.ridewithgps.com/routes/17254724

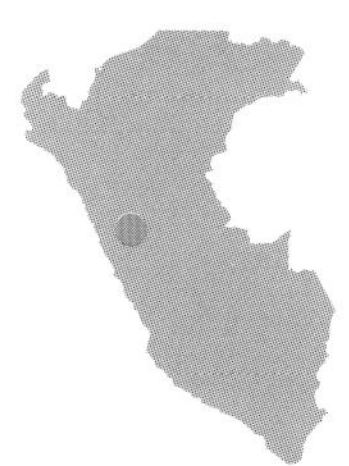

THE PERU DIVIDE

The Peru Divide hurdles one high mountain pass after another, replete with a succession of glaciated peaks along the way. Far removed from the usual Gringo Trail, it reveals a side to the country that juxtaposes both natural beauty and man's desire to plunder and control.

There are many ways to cross a country. Unfold a map and a knot of colored arteries and veins, coursing across mountains, jungle and coastline, are revealed. Knit together the very faintest of these paths and, chances are, the promise of adventure will beckon.

The rich network of mining roads that crisscross the Peruvian Andes, in this case between the towns of Huaraz and Huancavelica, is a good example of such a latent promise. Take the time and trouble to link them up, and you'll unearth a high-altitude roller coaster of a ride that straddles Peru's Divide: the mountainous boundary that forms the watershed between the Pacific to the west and the jungly sprawl of the Amazon and the Atlantic to the east.

Mines aside, it's a ride that's shared with little more than herds of wiry llamas and fluffy alpacas, and the occasional intrepid and dilapidated bus, bouncing by with a serenade of its horn. Settlements are few and far between, often little more than the most minuscule of *pueblecitos*, a collection of stone houses, a well-kept plaza and a small church. Here, the women wear fresh garlands of flowers in their sombreros, procured from the warmer lowlands, or broad-rimmed black hats along with bright skirts and dark leggings, offset with the quintessential, technicolored bundle of produce. Ticlios, Mangas, Acobambilla, Viñas... a string of welcoming, remote and high-elevation villages linked by the merest scraps of road and footpaths, painstakingly chiseled into the sheerest and most stark of mountainsides.

Indeed, the noise, or rather the lack of it, is the reason why locals call such remote highlands 'El Silencio,' treating them with a definite air of apprehension, and even fear. For, despite the poetic

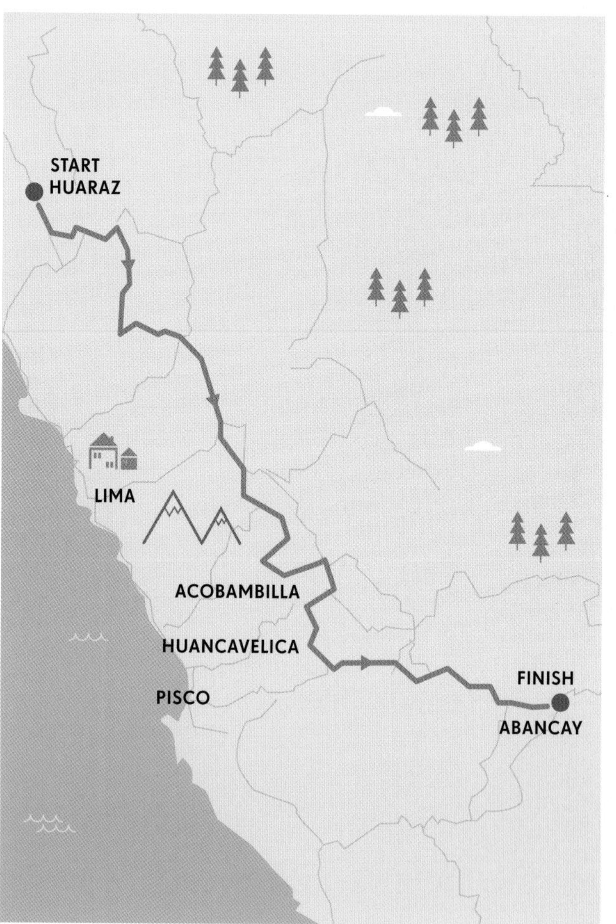

allusions we attach to such a name, Peruvians are a cacophony-loving people. Noise is reassuring, and that's something in short supply in these parts.

Over the course of 600 miles, my riding companions and I pedaled our way over an almighty medley of high-altitude passes, up among the condors, tackling climbs that sometimes unfurled for over 6500ft in elevation. Even though it was the dry season, mountain storms reserved all right to darken the sky with menace and pelted us with heavy rain; chasing us tirelessly 'like a pack of hungry, grey wolves,' as one of our team put it.

We bounced along unmaintained roads from one settlement to the next, gathering basic supplies where we could, savoring every packet of stale biscuits we could find. When we occasionally chanced upon larger settlements, promising bowls of hot soup, grizzled meat and all, or mounds of rice and fried eggs – the Peruvian mountain staple – then our lives felt complete. 'Entre gringitos,' said one restaurant owner with a smile. Come in, little gringos – despite our need to stoop through doorways, or the way our lanky frames towered over all the local mine workers around. Like a favorite aunt, she invited us to platters of food and cups of steaming tea, on the house, and bid a warm and heartfelt 'feliz viaje,' when the time came for us to head back out into the sierras. Parked up as they were against weathered walls, our bikes – and the way they coped with such hardy terrain – were objects of marvel. The tires drew particular attention; even grandmothers approached to give them a gentle squeeze, as they would a neighbor's baby. Kids danced around us: coolness by association.

As for the riding, it was among the most challenging I've experienced in all of my travels through the continent. At times, the high walls of the Andes felt impregnable and endless. Altitudes reached over 16,000ft. Road surfaces were almost exclusively unpaved and generally strewn with jumbles of rocks, just for good measure. After one long day, when dirt had turned to quagmire, our Gore-Tex was long soaked through and a storm raged around us, we bedded down gratefully in a corrugated shack we'd chanced upon – only to have its owners, two shepherd girls, gingerly return some time later, calling to us from a distance to find out what these strange, bicycle-riding gringos wanted. We brokered a deal to stay the night and they headed back to their family home, returning early the next morning with a pink Chinese mobile phone to film us. Yes, this was 21st-century touring.

But it's hard to ignore the reality that now frames much of the Cordillera Central. Riding through the Peruvian Andes is akin to a journey through the ugly guts of a land, from which resources are sought and goodness is stripped. The stark and

ANIMAL COMPANIONS

A highlight of this ride, and indeed, many similar journeys across the Peruvian Andes, are the welcoming committees of llamas and alpacas, native to South America. On occasions, the wilder, more wiry camelid vicuñas will make an appearance. In preparation for the cold night temperatures, there's no better way to keep warm than by buying a hat and socks, often made from a blend of sheep and llama wool, from the market in Huaraz.

Left to right: Punta Pumacocha, at 16500ft (4990m), is the most challenging pass on the Peru Divide; local attire in the hamlet of Rapaz; be sure to pack light. Previous page: mining roads in the Central Cordillera are largely free of motorized traffic

"The unrelenting sense of remoteness captured my imagination, as did the dirt roads that unfurled into the distance."

buckled landscape, so pocked with mines, juxtaposed such heart-wrenching natural beauty with the blight of humanity's insatiable hunger. Of the mines we passed, a few were working at fever pitch, overloaded trucks shuttling backwards and forwards. Most mines were long since abandoned; only husks of buildings, boarded-up tunnels and railway sleepers remained. The land had been exploited and it was time to move on.

Yet despite it all, the journey proved to be everything that I hope and strive for in my travels. Without the mines, these very roads would never exist, the irony of which did not escape me. The unrelenting sense of remoteness captured my imagination, as did the traces of dirt road that rolled and curled and twisted into the distance. Far removed from the chaos and freneticism of the Pan American Highway, these unpaved roads are the real lifeblood of the country. Trust them and they will take you on a truly remarkable journey, revealing the most remote of *pueblecitos*, and the warmest of Peruanos. **CG**

TOOLKIT

Start // Huaraz
End // Abancay
Distance // Roughly 620 miles (1000km). The complete route takes a month to complete. Huaraz to Huancavelica is a highlight and takes two weeks, plus time to acclimatize.
Getting there // Lima's international airport is the best access point. Cruz del Sur is a reliable bus company that runs from Lima to Huaraz and from Abancay back to Lima. There is a small fee for a bike, based on weight.
When to ride // May to September. Avoid the rainy season.
What to ride // Any mountain bike-style tourer will work, the key component being to pack as light as possible. Carry food for two to three days at a time and pack a filter for water along the way; be aware of runoff from mines.
More info // www.andesbybike.com

Opposite: circling Ausungate is a highlight of the Tres Cordilleras; expect to hike-a-bike too!

MORE LIKE THIS ANDEAN PASSES

RUTA DE LAS TRES CORDILLERAS

For more Andean delights, consider the Ruta de las Tres Cordilleras. As the name suggests, it revolves around three mountain ranges – the Cordillera Real, the Cordillera Apolobamba and the Cordillera Vilcanota, connecting the mountain settlements of Sorata in Bolivia to Pitumarca in Peru.
In doing so, it provides a beautiful and remote high-elevation traverse between the two countries, as well as an assortment of Andean passes, backcountry singletrack, and a few demanding hike-a-bikes. You'll need two to three weeks to cover it; the mini loop around Ausangate is a highlight, while nearby Cuzco makes a great base for acclimatization and cultural sights like Machu Picchu.
Start // Sorata, Bolivia
End // Pitumarca, Peru
Distance // 493 miles (793km)

CONES AND CANYONS, PERU

A little further south, yet more epic Andean passes await. The Cones and Canyons route takes two weeks to cover. This high-elevation route connects Arequipa, one of the country's most appealing cities, with the Peruvian high *pampa*. En route, it winds its way past one of the world's deepest and longest canyons, El Cañón de Cotahuasi, before hurdling a medley of 16,000ft passes, set to a backdrop of white-capped volcanoes. Like the Huascaran Circuit (right), it can also be linked with the Peru Divide, making for one epic bike tour. All riding in the Peruvian and Bolivian Andes requires several days to acclimatize and to serve as a buffer for the vagaries of mountain weather, so bear this in mind when planning your days in the saddle. Common to this region, both rides are best tackled between May and September for the best chance of reliable weather.
Start // Arequipa
End // Albancay
Distance // 488 miles (785km)
Info // www.bikepacking.com

HUASCARAN CIRCUIT, PERU

When it comes to breathtaking rides, it's hard to imagine a loop that packs in as much jaw-dropping scenery as the compact Huascaran Circuit, set in the heart of Peru's fabled Cordillera Blanca. If you have the time, treat it as warm-up ride to further explorations; nearby Huaraz is the start point of the Peru Divide. The loop is also endearingly known as the Triple Heart Bypass, on account of its three 13,100ft plus passes that crisscross the Blanca, providing the perfect opportunity to shock your legs into shape. Expect a number of supremely photogenic whirligig mountain climbs, but hold on to your teeth during its rough, unpaved descents. The website www.blancahuayhuash.com has up-to-date details for an associated guidebook about riding and hiking in this region. As with the Peru Divide, there are regular overnight buses between Lima and Huaraz, the hub of the region.
Start/End // Carhuaz
Distance // 142 miles (230km)

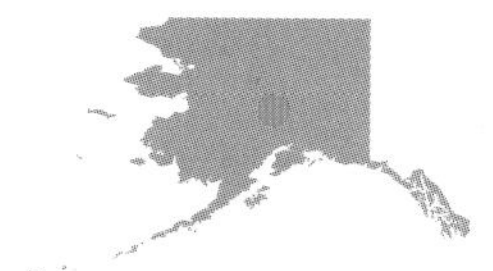

DENALI PARK ROAD

Lael Wilcox has ridden every single road in Alaska – and this 92-mile route, lit by the midnight sun, in the shadow of North America's highest peak, accompanied by the state's 'big five' beasts, is the wilderness itinerary to beat them all.

Last year, I set out to ride all of the major roads in Alaska in a single summer. Alaska is a vast land, over twice the size of Texas, but with only 12 numbered highways and 4500 miles of road, including dirt spurs.

I am fourth-generation Alaskan born and raised. My grandfather was born in Fairbanks and moved to Anchorage as a boy. He tells stories of wooden sidewalks and traplines in downtown Anchorage, and the blueberry fields that used to populate midtown. There were so many tales about places that I'd only heard of and never seen – Cordova and McCarthy, Eagle and Deadhorse. I wanted to see it all from the seat of my bicycle – every inch of road, where it leads and why. Over thirteen long rides, with work and life sprinkled in between, that's what I managed to do.

But which ride encapsulated the spirit of my journey through Alaska? The Denali Park Rd: over 92 rugged miles from the entrance to Denali National Park to the former gold-mining town of Kantishna, in the shadow of Denali itself, the highest mountain in North America at over 20,000ft. Pavement ends at mile 15 – thereafter, it's a scenic dirt road that runs through wilderness inhabited by Alaska's 'big five' (bears, wolves, caribou, moose and Dall sheep), alongside braided rivers and rolling tundra, climbing past the tree line to gain 11,000ft over four mountain passes.

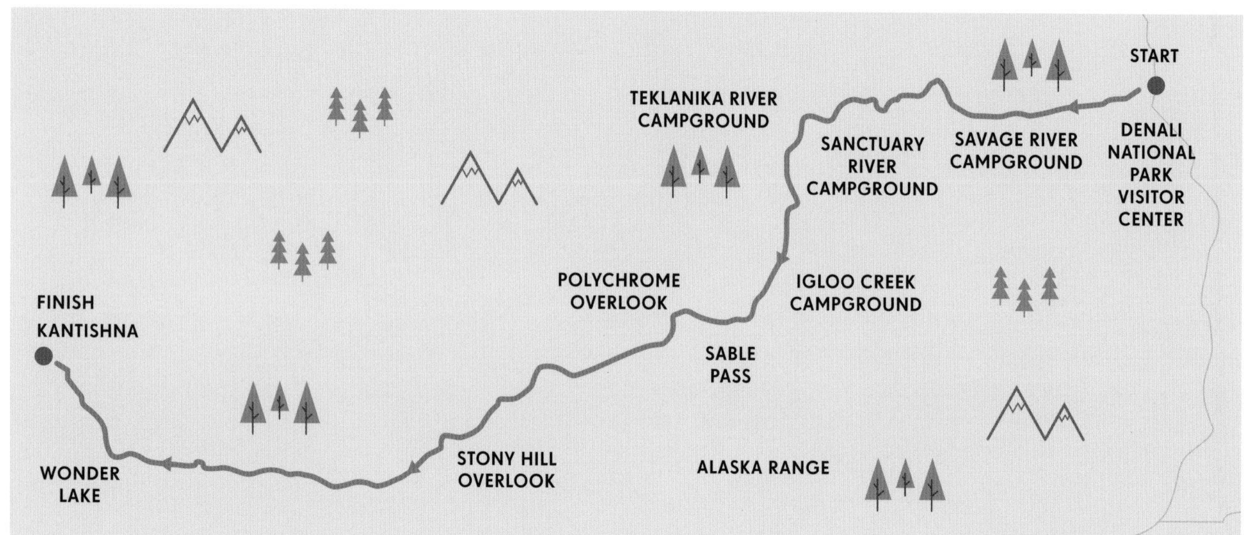

I begin my Alaskan bike journey a week after the summer solstice. The plan is to meet my friend Rugile at the park entrance, then catch a bus to Kantishna, from where we'll cycle back (joined part of the way by another friend). But the bus to Kantishna is fully booked, so Rugile and I (and our bikes – all buses are equipped with a two-bike rack) take the bus to Wonder Lake (at mile 85). It's a sightseeing service, stopping frequently over 5½ hours, but it's a clear day so Denali is in full view and we spot a herd of caribou and, at a distance, a momma grizzly bear with her two cubs.

We get out of the bus in the late afternoon and wade into Wonder Lake to cool off. But even though the days are long, we don't hang around, spinning on past Kantishna to pick up Tessa (who works as a chef at Denali Backcountry Lodge) and tag the end of the road. Only then does the ride proper begin.

It feels like the day will never end and it almost doesn't. At summer solstice this far north, the sun sets at midnight and rises again at 4am, but it's never dark, not really. After 20 miles, we take a break at a high point to eat some blueberry coffee cake that Tessa brought along. Around 9pm she turns back to Kantishna and we continue east, into a headwind. The buses are gone and the only people we see are a road maintenance crew at work. In general, the road's in terrific condition, suitable for gravel or mountain bikes. Pedaling on, we ride in our own separate worlds. At one point, I stop next to a herd of caribou to wait for Rugile.

The light fades to twilight and then remains constant. We climb and descend, rolling alongside tundra. Down the road, on a flat stretch, we spot four bull moose standing in a line. It's a powerful image, and though Rugile has her camera, she scolds herself for not having the right lens. But we don't mind – we saw it in the flesh and it's a breathtaking moment nonetheless.

CAMPING

Apart from the 92-mile ribbon of road through the park, there are very few trails and no designated routes across the park's six million acres of wilderness – and backcountry camping (at least a quarter mile off the road) is permitted, so if you truly want to get away from it all, Denali National Park is the place. Same day backcountry permits are issued at the Visitor Access Center at the entrance of the park (bear-resistant containers available). The process is free of charge and takes an hour. There are six official campgrounds in the park, too.

Clockwise from top: pedaling towards Denali, the highest peak in North America; caribou migrate through these lands; camping at Wonder Lake; buses carry bikes here. Previous page: the wilderness and mountains of Denali National Park

The wind gets stronger riding along the Toklat River and over a long bridge – we're relieved to climb out of the valley and up towards Polychrome Pass. By now, it's past midnight, and though we consider riding through the night, why should we? To arrive exhausted at a parking lot by morning? We're tired. We push the bikes through the tundra, away from the sight of the road and set up the tent. The ground is springy, like a trampoline. We blow up our sleeping pads, lay out our sleeping bags and then we're asleep on the comfiest mattress Mother Nature can provide. (Free backcountry camping permits are easy to attain.)

The next morning is bright. The tourist buses are back. We descend from Polychrome and fill our water bottles from a stream. I shake up instant coffee in one of them and we eat cookies for breakfast and wave at the tourists passing by on the buses. The second half of the ride is fast, hitting a high point at Sable Pass at 4000ft then rolling up and down to 1500ft. We descend back into the trees and down to Sanctuary River. We see one other biker, without gear – I catch him on the last climb and on the uninterrupted 9-mile descent to the visitor center, he flies past me.

Before lunch, we're out of the park, and the entire ride feels like a dream. Rugile heads back to Anchorage for work and I continue north – to Nenana, then Fairbanks, Coldfoot and Deadhorse. I ride north past the Arctic Circle where the summer sun never dims. I feel like I can do anything and I want to. I want to ride through the night and fill my bottles from cold streams and watch the muskox graze by the pipeline. I want to see every mile from the seat of my bicycle. And I do. **LW**

TOOLKIT

Start // Entrance to Denali National Park, mile 240 George Parks Hwy

End // Kantishna

Distance // 92 miles (148km) one way

Getting there // Anchorage (240 miles/386km south) and Fairbanks (123 miles/198km north) both have international airports, with trains or shuttles to Denali National Park.

When to ride // Mid-May to mid-September, when tourist buses with bike racks run from the Visitor Access Center at the park entrance.

What to take // Camping equipment; bear-resistant containers; insect repellent; stock up on food in Cantwell (26 miles/42km south) or just north of the park in an area locally known as 'glitter gulch'; drinking water from the Eielson Visitor Center at mile 66 along the park road. Plenty of surface water is available along the road (bring water filter or treatment tablets).

Bike rentals // Available from Denali Adventure

Tours // www.denaliadventure.com

More info // Further information can be found at www.nps.gov.

Opposite: a clue to the name of your starting point on the Taylor Hwy

MORE LIKE THIS
ALASKAN ADVENTURES

THE RICHARDSON HIGHWAY

The original incarnation of Alaska's first road began construction in the late 19th century as a pack-animal trail from the port of Valdez to the Alaskan interior at Eagle. By 1910 it had been upgraded to a road suitable for motorized vehicles in the 1920s. Today, the Richardson Hwy terminates at Fairbanks, about 366 miles (590km) from Valdez. Much of it is now a major four-lane highway but that doesn't mean that the scenery is any less spectacular than it was a century ago. And, heading north, once you pass the turning for Anchorage or Tok, the tourist traffic drops off a lot and you can enjoy the views as the road cuts through tundra valleys, dark forests and the Chugach mountain range, with rivers rushing beside you.
Start // Valdez
End // Fairbanks
Distance // 366 miles (590km)

THE TAYLOR HIGHWAY

Situated on the Yukon River, Eagle is one of the oldest communities in Alaska. Incorporated in 1901, the settlement was a supply point for gold rush miners and boasted a population of 1500. Presently, only a couple of hundred people reside in Eagle year-round. But it's a thriving metropolis compared to your start point, Chicken, population 10. That's another old gold mining town, little more than a quirky truck stop with a rowdy saloon and cabins. The road between the two is the northerly half of the Taylor Hwy, mostly gravel winding up and down, and topping out at 3652ft at American Summit with spectacular views of the surrounding mountains and the Yukon River. The road to Eagle is seldom visited because it is a dead end and difficult to access. The journey is well worth it – telling stories of Alaska's forgotten cultural history and its rough, natural beauty.
Start // Chicken
End // Eagle
Distance // 90 miles (145km)

THE DENALI HIGHWAY

The Denali Hwy is a low traffic, scenic road connecting the two small communities of Paxson and Cantwell on the Richardson and Parks Hwys. So much for the facts – for the rider, it offers much spectacular riding above the tree line, with never-ending views of the Alaska range, passing by glacially fed rivers and lakes. If you're in Alaska on a bike, it's not a route to be missed. The first 22 miles (35km) to Tangle Lakes are paved and the remaining 103 (166km) are good-quality gravel. It's a remote itinerary, so backcountry route supplies are limited. There are three lodges along the way at Tangle River Inn (mile 22), Maclaren River Lodge (mile 42) and Alpine Creek Lodge (68), and unlike the Denali Park Rd, no permits are required for camping along the road.
Start // Paxson
End // Cantwell
Distance // 135 miles (217km)

THE SKY ISLANDS ODYSSEY

In the vast borderlands of the Wild West there are still untouched mountain idylls where you and your trusty mount can camp out under the stars.

When winter rolls in with its grey, cool days, we all look for some relief to get through it. Me, I know just the place for a dose of the outdoors and vitamin D: Southern Arizona. A one-hour drive south of Tucson delivers me to the small, eclectic town of Patagonia and the beginning of my Sky Islands Odyssey.

The Sky Islands is an eco-region within the Sonoran Desert, named for a series of isolated, forested mountain ranges surrounded by radically contrasting lowland desert and grasslands. The Odyssey circumnavigates one of the Sky Islands, the Santa Rita Mountains, and over its 230-mile course offers views of many others, each with its own distinctive topography. Together, these habitat 'islands' host some of the highest levels of biodiversity in the world, ensuring ever-changing scenery, terrain, and critter sightings: it's not uncommon to see hundreds of bird and reptile species, as well as pronghorn antelope, javelinas, and jackrabbits – even jaguars, occasionally.

The land management agencies along the Sky Islands Odyssey are almost as diverse as the ecosystems they protect, which lie within a range of state, federal, and private lands (permits required – see Toolkit). They offer educational information about the region, quiet gated roads open to cyclists, preserved wild

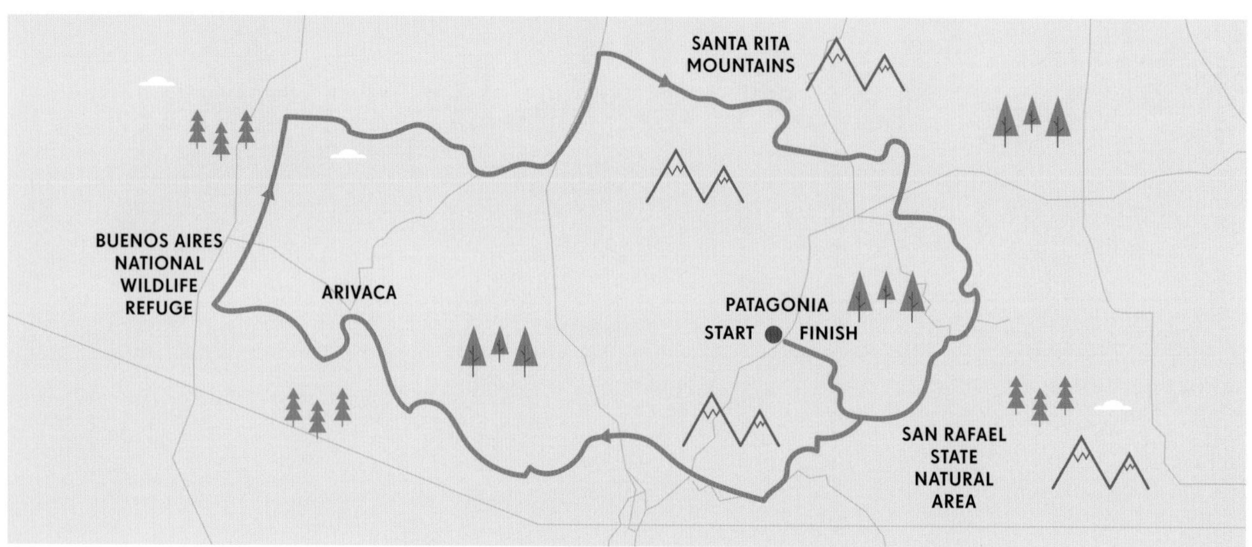

spaces, and ideal places to camp and spot wildlife.

The Odyssey is a loop and I head off clockwise, south from Patagonia to the wide-open spaces of the San Rafael Valley. Here I climb from grasslands into the rocky pine-oak forests of the rugged Patagonia Mountains, to the route's highest point on Mt Washington at 5800ft, where I take in the view of the Santa Cruz River Valley in front of me, all the way north to Tucson, and to the south, Mexico.

From Mt Washington I enjoy the zigzag, sandy descent along granite cliffs covered in lichen to the valley I had gazed at from above. This odyssey is not entirely a wilderness – there's a brief stretch through suburbia and some tempting fast-food outlets, but no, I have my mind set on a cool dip at Peña Blanca Lake 10 miles up the road, and soon enough asphalt gives way to dirt again and an otherworldly landscape rich with succulents.

After camping near the lake, I make my way to the small town of Arivaca by 11am, to catch the farmers market, to stock up on water, supplies and some fresh hot tamales for the road. Then it's back into the borderland hill country to make my way to the Buenos Aires National Wildlife Refuge – and a sight of Baboquivari Peak. This land remains home to the Tohono O'odham tribe who regard Baboquivari as the 'navel of the world,' the most sacred place at the center of their cosmology. Today, its unmistakable, rectangular peak against the desert sky serves as a monumental landmark, visible throughout the west side of the loop.

Just as eye-catching is the wildlife thriving in these overwhelming landscapes. At the Buenos Aires National Wildlife Refuge Headquarters, I grab a checklist of the myriad bird species common in the area and set off for the Refuge's conserved wetlands and grasslands. Before long, my ride has become a two-wheeled safari. In tunnels of tall grass savannas and yucca trees I spy birds of prey perched on old growth oak trees, camouflaged pronghorn antelope napping in the grass, and jackrabbits rapidly hopping in all directions.

Eventually the grasslands give way to lowland desert, which feels harsh and hot. Some ice cream from a highway store does the trick, cooling my insides ahead of the wilds of the Santa Cruz River Valley. I skirt another stretch of populated land along the Juan Bautista De Anza Trail, which doesn't just meander through cacti, sandy arroyos and olive groves but commemorates the expedition route taken by Spanish colonizers from Sonora, Mexico, to eventually establish the city of San Francisco, California, between 1774 and 1776. Fortunately, I'm not riding that far.

After climbing the pass of Box Canyon, I am grateful to leave the desert behind and to be welcomed by the shady forests of the

BORDER PATROL

This region is an illegal border-crossing corridor at the center of the US immigration crisis. The Border Patrol are a noticeable presence in certain areas of the route. Encounters with migrants are extremely unlikely, since they stay off established roads and on more discreet trails. While this aspect of the route may deter some, for others it offers a humanizing perspective of a very current issue in the US.

Left to right: descending a dirt track; Arizona natives: a mammillaria pringlei cactus and Yarrow's spiny lizard. Previous page: the grasslands and flowers of Arizona's Sky Islands

> *"This land is home to the Tohono O'odham tribe who regard Baboquivari as the 'navel of the world,' the center of their cosmology."*

Canelo Hills. Here, on the east side of the Santa Rita Mountains, is my spot for the night, with views to envy. As the sun sets, another island in the sky, the Whetstone Mountains, is laid out before me. Then, thanks to the dry climate and absence of insects, I bed down under the stars, watching Orion's procession across the heavens through the night.

In the morning I make my way to the old gold mining town of Kentucky Camp, for a look at historic mining life in a small museum curated within the walls of the town's old adobe buildings. Then it's into Elgin Wine Country and a stop at the Village of Elgin Winery for a celebratory self-toast. I'm almost there! I conclude my ride along the route though the private ranches that offer permitted passage to cyclists through their conserved grasslands – it's yet another opportunity to see an abundance of wildlife and a land untouched.

As I roll into Patagonia, Odyssey complete, I feel refreshed and energized. Winter, do your worst! **SS**

TOOLKIT

Start/End // Patagonia, Arizona
Distance // 230 miles (379 km)
Getting there // Tucson International Airport, a one-hour drive from Patagonia.
What to take // GPS device, plenty of water storage and filter, camping equipment, cookware, clothes for the drastic change in temperatures, a battery charger, and some binoculars, tires no less than 40mm wide (tubeless ideally).
Where to stay // Kentucky Camp, Appleton-Whittell Research Ranch and camping on public lands.
When to ride // November through April.
Permits // Call ahead for permits to pass through the Appleton-Whittell Research Ranch (+1-520-455-5522) and Babacomari Ranch (+1-520-455-5507).
More info // www.ridewithgps.com/routes/26902258

Opposite: the Sonoran desert, through which the Camino del Diablo passes

MORE LIKE THIS
BREAK FOR THE BORDER

MONUMENTAL LOOP, NEW MEXICO

The Monumental figure-of-eight loop explores the four geologic and biodiverse regions encompassed within the Organ Mountains Desert Peak National Monument around Las Cruces, New Mexico, just north of the US–Mexico border. This 315-mile (507km) route is challenging but the payoffs include great camping, peerless star-gazing opportunities – and a chance to stop at Sparky's Diner in Hatch (the green chili capital of the world) for a world-famous green-chili burger. Against the jagged peaks of the Organ Mountains, the loop winds its way through woodland pines and flat grassland plains, to a volcanic landscape of cinder cones, lava flows, and craters (3in tires recommended). Plan your food and water carefully and brush up on your navigation skills. Beware, too, the thorny desert flora of ocotillo and barrel cactus – however you set up your tires, bring spares. This route is best ridden between October and April (bring at least a 30°F/0°C sleeping bag).

Start/End // Las Cruces, New Mexico
Distance // 315 miles (507km)
Info // www.ridewithgps.com/routes/26945575

CAMINO DEL DIABLO, ARIZONA

El Camino del Diablo (aka The Devil's Highway) is an ancient travel route covering 130 miles (209km) through some of the most remote sections of the Sonoran Desert along Arizona's Mexico border. Its historic name, Camino del Muerto (road of the dead), reflects the harsh and unforgiving desert conditions you'll encounter: the route consists of mostly sandy roads and tracks, which require the fattest of tires (3–4in). This route may be desolate but it is beautifully varied, traversing mountain ranges, basins, and expanses of lava flow. Wild camp throughout the route, filtering water from the few wells and pools – but be prepared to carry all of your food. Navigation along the Camino del Diablo is simple: it is listed on the National Register of Historic Places and signed throughout.

Start // Ajo, Arizona
End // Yuma, Arizona
Distance // 130 miles (209km)
Info // www.ridewithgps.com/routes/6580710

BIG BEND BIKEPACKING ROUTE, TEXAS

In the remote border region of West Texas lies Big Bend Ranch State Park where miles of old jeep roads, singletrack, and ideal backcountry camping await in the Chihuahuan Desert. Expect striking geologic features (especially along the Crystal Trail) and vast starry nights. Treat yourself to a free shower and a soda at the halfway mark at the Sauceda Ranger Station. Ride in the spring or fall but pack for cold nights. Any mountain bike will do but 3in, tubeless tires are preferable. There is no food resupply and water is scarce, so before heading out, ask a ranger at The Barton Warnock Park Station which water tanks are active along the route. You will also be required to buy a daily park use and camping permit. Ride over, head to the Terlingua Trading Post for a post-ride local beer.

Start/End // The Barton Warnock Park Station, Lajitas
Distance // 90 miles (145km)
Info // www.ridewithgps.com/routes/6847612

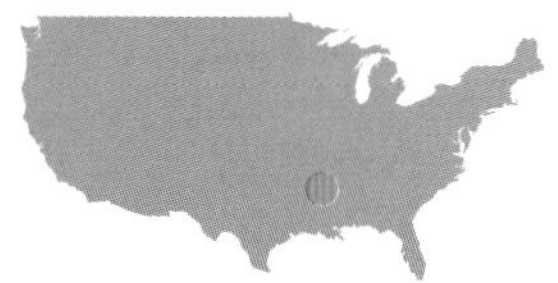

BLAST BENTONVILLE'S TRAILS

Are you a trail rider who dreams of a town with endless miles of varied cycling – from family fun to hard-core technical – on the doorstep? Then beat a path to Arkansas.

I never believed I'd say this. But somewhere between pointing-and-flowing down the slabby rock gardens on Rock Solid, and achieving actual hang time over the smooth tabletop jumps on Fire Line, a thought occurred to me: 'When we leave, I'm going to miss the trails in Arkansas.'

I acknowledge the obnoxious assumption in that statement – that anyone should be surprised that there are ripping, fun trails in Arkansas. As a cycling journalist who has ridden all over the place, I should know better. There's truly fantastic riding all over the US. Still: historically, Arkansas was just not a place known for killer mountain biking.

The key word is 'historically.' Today, Northwest Arkansas is squarely on the mountain bike destination map, thanks to the town of Bentonville, and to a surprising benefactor: the Walton family. Yes, of Walmart fame.

Bentonville is home to Walmart's corporate headquarters, and to attract a young, educated, professional workforce, Walmart and the Walton Family Foundation – in partnership with various nonprofits and public entities – have made huge investments in the Northwest Arkansas region. And the trails are a significant part of that effort. Tom and Steuart Walton – grandsons of Walmart founder Sam Walton – are cycling fanatics, and have spearheaded the efforts to build nearly 400 miles of new cycling infrastructure over the past 10 years, including a 36-mile paved path that goes from Bentonville to the neighboring city of Fayetteville; and three distinct singletrack trail networks that are riding distance from town: Coler, Slaughter Pen, and Blowing Springs. Just 10 miles away in the town of Bella Vista, there's also a 20-mile network called the Back 40. In the past decade,

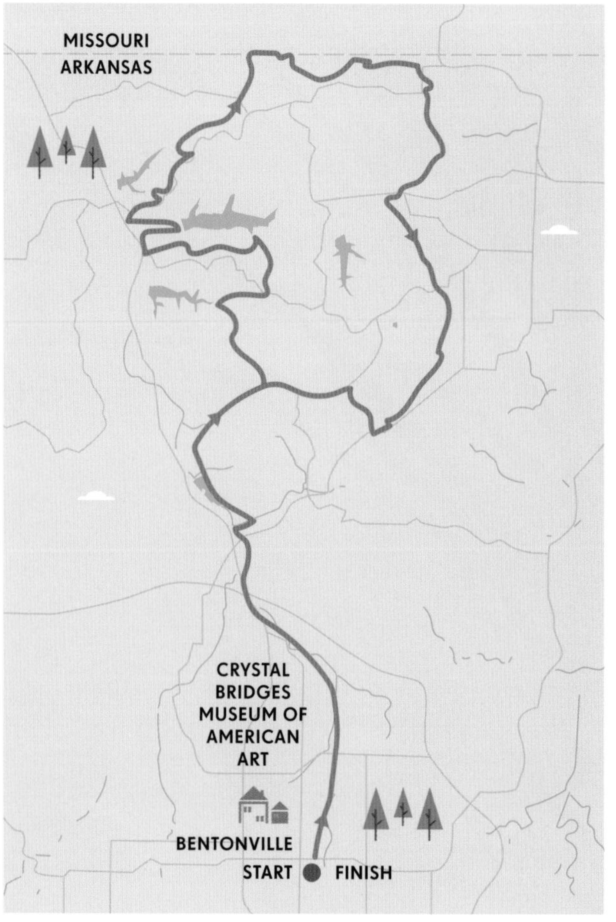

the Walton Family Foundation has invested $74 million in trail construction alone.

And we get to ride what they paid for. I came to Bentonville with a team from *Bicycling* magazine, to test mountain bikes. When you're testing bikes, you want a variety of terrain – from cross-country and flow trails, to features and tricky technical segments – and you want easily accessible, and repeatable, loops. Bentonville delivered.

Access to the Slaughter Pen trail network is from the center of town. We rode The All-American Trail, a flat, winding ribbon with optional play lines for children, and children at heart: wooden skinnies, ladder bridges, man-made rock gardens, even a short downhill berm section. (At the beginning of the trail network are two side-by-side jump lines, adorably named Choo Choo and Boo Boo. *D'aww.*)

Slaughter Pen itself is a playground of natural-feeling singletrack (over 20 miles) winding through oak trees, ferns, and vines. Everything was clearly marked: signs even denoted technical rock features and drops. On the sides of the trails, features of all sizes beckoned, from 1ft drops suitable for teaching total beginners, to bridges-to-nowhere that were taller than me. My friend Taylor did her first real drop; I practiced my skinnie-riding skills through a series in the grass. Most impressive, we marveled that these features were just pedal strokes from the main road – on our home singletrack, similar drops and jumps usually get torn down, for concerns about liability. Instead, in Bentonville the public is encouraged to enjoy them, and build their skills. We saw kids out with their friends after school, and families out riding together.

The next day, we pedaled about 20 minutes to the 16-mile Coler trail network, along quiet residential and farm roads. Coler is like a collection of every trail you might want to ride, woven into one trail network, with a strong freeride influence. Fire Line was a sweet flow trail with smaller, progressive tabletop jumps. On Rock Solid, armored-up rock gardens challenged our technical skills. Drop the Hammer featured a massive road gap and large drops (spotted the trail naming convention here?).

It was late March, cheerfully sunny, and already, temperatures were in the low 80s. After four or five hours on the trails our first day, fully wrung out from the heat and exertion, we pedaled straight from the Coler trails to the Spark Café, an original, '50s-style ice cream parlor/soda fountain inside the Walmart Museum in the town square. Apparently, Sam Walton loved ice cream, and it turns out he and I share a favorite flavor: butter pecan. Outside the site of the first Walmart, our large group of dirt-streaked, sweaty mountain bikers sprawled out across two tables. The scene was idyllic, so perhaps that was why it felt somewhat jarring to see a car with a Confederate flag drive by, a reminder that we were in

LOCAL FLAVORS

High South Cuisine – seasonally available, locally sourced, and Southern influenced – was born in Bentonville. At the Tusk & Trotter, the menu offers dishes like the 'High South Banh Mi,' a fusion-style sandwich with smoked pork loin, pork jowls, and Vietnamese pickled vegetables. The Preacher's Son serves an upscale dining experience inside a converted church. But it's not all highbrow: our default refueling stop between rides became a taco truck called Yeyo's.

Left to right: find trails for beginners and advanced riders at Bentonville; the town is home to the Walton family; trails are well signposted. Previous page: hitting the big jumps at Bentonville

"After hours on the trails, wrung out from the heat, we pedaled to the Spark Café, an original, '50s-style ice cream parlor"

the South. (The statue in Bentonville's town square, I later learned, is also dedicated to Confederate soldiers.)

On the one rainy afternoon during the week, most of the group took advantage of free admission to the Crystal Bridges Museum of American Art, which holds works from Jean-Michel Basquiat to Andy Warhol, with a permanent art collection extending back to the Colonial era. The museum is yet another creation of the Walton Family Foundation. My friends were unanimously impressed. The one regret I have from the trip is not joining them that afternoon.

We left Bentonville on a Friday, and I did so reluctantly. I'd seen something in that week that I wouldn't soon forget: what's possible for trail building when real money and influence is poured into it. Beyond that, I simply found myself daydreaming of that swoopy, feature-rich singletrack, long after I'd returned home. Bentonville will be a hard situation to replicate until we lure some more big-time corporate shot callers (and dollars) to our sport. But in the meantime, the town is welcoming and waiting to change what you think you thought of Arkansas. **GL**

TOOLKIT

Start/End // Bentonville, Arkansas

Distance // Various

Getting there // Fly into Northwest Arkansas Regional Airport, 25 minutes from Bentonville. Or it's two hours' drive from Tulsa, three or four from Little Rock or Kansas City.

Where to stay // The boutique 21c Museum Hotel is on the town square, and is bike-friendly. By late 2019 you'll be able to camp at the Coler trail network.

When to ride // You can ride year-round in Northwest Arkansas, but July and August are hot; April to early June is ideal.

Bike shop // Phat Tire rents Trek and Santa Cruz mountain bikes, and has local beers on tap for your post-ride refreshment.

Info // www.visitbentonville.com; www.bikebentonville.com

Opposite: railing a turn in Brevard, North Carolina

MORE LIKE THIS
MOUNTAIN BIKING TOWNS

BREVARD, NORTH CAROLINA

Forty-five minutes from Asheville, this small mountain town sits next to 200 miles (322km) of singletrack within the Pisgah National Forest and DuPont State Forest. From flowy, family-friendly trails in DuPont to rugged, all-day backcountry adventures in Pisgah, and endless gravel roads for adventurous drop-bar bike riders, the 'Land of Waterfalls' has something for everyone. Get a map and local trail information at The Hub and Pisgah Tavern, a local bike shop and bar (it's a Santa Cruz dealer, and offers top-of-the-line demos) that literally sits at the gateway to the national forest – then swing by on your way back for a post-ride brew on their patio. But don't get too sauced: you'll want to save some room for a visit to the Oskar Blues and Sierra Nevada taprooms.
Start/End // Various
Distance // Various
Info // www.brevardnc.org/

EAST BURKE, VERMONT

Kingdom Trails is a special place. At one point, East Burke was a tiny town with a nearly defunct ski resort. John Worth, the owner of the local ski shop, started selling mountain bikes in the summer as a second revenue source – then he figured he better build some trails for people to ride, too. Today, Kingdom Trails offers over 100 miles (160km) of singletrack built on private property: the trail center charges $15 per rider for a day pass, which helps fund trail maintenance, maps, a visitors center, and a parking lot with coin-operated showers. Today, East Burke attracts 80,000 visitors a year to ride the twisty, rooty New England trails, and while most of the network is family friendly, steeper terrain on Burke Mountain satisfies hard-core riders too.
Start/End // Various
Distance // Various
Info // www.burkevermont.com

CRESTED BUTTE, COLORADO

You could spend months exploring all the trails in Colorado, but the state's spiritual home of mountain biking is unquestionably the funky little ski town of Crested Butte (population 1500). It's the jumping-off place to legendary rides like the 401 Trail and Doctor Park, and is now even home to Evolution Bike Park, which offers 30 miles (48km) of lift-accessed downhill and cross-country trails. Altogether, Crested Butte and neighboring Gunnison claim a staggering 750 miles (1200km) of singletrack between them. For dirtbag mountain bikers, backcountry campsites abound outside town, with breathtaking views (wait, is that just the altitude?) of the dramatic Elk Mountains. Or stay in the Crested Butte Hostel, which offers dorm and private rooms in a clean, homey, lodge for as little as $50 a night. Come in July for the spectacular natural display that has also earned Crested Butte the title 'Wildflower Capital of Colorado.'
Start/End // Various
Distance // Various
Info // www.colorado.com

SOCAL DESERT RAMBLE

Far removed from the veneer of Orange County and its shopping malls, Southern California's sprawling's deserts come replete with desert blooms, starry nights, anthropomorphic Joshua Trees, and a touch of the bizarre...

Cycling across Southern California – or SoCal, in local parlance – is an established ride within the bike-touring world. Throughout the year, two-wheeled travelers make the coast pilgrimage from San Diego to Los Angeles, linking a number of dedicated bike paths that lie in between. But as good as the bike infrastructure is, it's impossible to ignore the heavy traffic and sheer population density along the Pacific. Sure, there are beautiful camping spots overlooking idyllic beaches and coves, but there's also a dizzying amount of people and their cars.

Heading inland to connect the two cities, however, unveils a completely different world: it's desert solitaire with a twist of the bizarre. Yes, such a journey triples your distance. But its distracted wanderings are infinitely more remote and appealing. Besides, if you want the quintessential Californian beach action, there's plenty of Baywatching to be had in San Diego or Los Angeles' Santa Monica Beach.

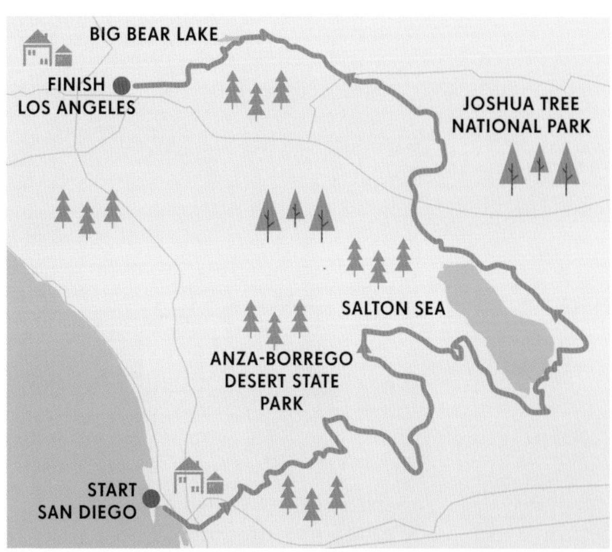

The Television Will Not Be Revolutionized by Flip Cassidy

For this ride, I follow the road less traveled, up and over the San Ysidro Mountains for an introduction to the remarkable Anza-Borrego State Park that lies just on the other side. There, a number of desert washes and backroads promise the most peaceful sleep imaginable... and provide a gateway to the unexpected.

I time the ride so that my first clue to the Sonoran Desert's dual personality comes with the astonishing sight of it in full bloom, from bursts of technicolor cacti to carpets of wildflowers draped across ochre scrubland. But I make sure I dodge the tentacle-like ocotillos as I pick my way through more than 100 ironwork sculptures that dot the landscape – life-size prehistoric mammals and dinosaurs reenacting scenes from the land they once roamed, twinned with a fantastical 330ft-long serpent diving through the sand, only to reappear on the other side of a paved road outside of Borrego Springs.

Pushing on down the sandy Salado Wash, I am deposited onto the fringes of the equally improbable Salton Sea. Here, fans of historical oddities will take particular delight in exploring what was once coined the Californian Riviera, even if this failed tourist experiment is now more voyeuristic than romantic. In the early 20th century, water from the Colorado River was redirected into the valley through a series of engineered canals, to establish a farming economy in the heart of the desert. But a breach inundated the basin for two years, creating the 'Salton Sink' in the process. In the late 1950s, this body of water was rebranded to Salton Sea and developed as a resort getaway for Los Angeles highfliers: the likes of Frank Sinatra frequented its shores and Sonny Bono water-skied on its waters. But within a couple of decades, high salinity levels and agricultural runoff turned the Sea into a toxic soup, bringing about the demise of the resort culture, remnants of which still stand incongruously within its desert backdrop.

Just when I thought things couldn't get any more peculiar, a grid of levy roads – running past date plantations promising delicious milkshakes to quench my thirst – funnel me into counter-culture country. I enter Slab City, inhabited by the Slabbers and Snowbirds who've settled down in cheap, off-grid living; the latter so named on account of their clockwork migration north come the warmer months. Slab City is quite the scene, complete with recycled dwellings and outdoor art installations.

The intrigue doesn't stop there. Climbing back up into the higher echelons of the neighboring Mojave desert to Joshua Tree National Park, it's impossible not to marvel at the Dr Seussian splendor of the gangly, anthropomorphic yuccas. Each is different from the next, be it the contortion of double-jointed arms, height, or just a sense of being. The area is a playground for climbers, too, who cling like colorful little ants to gargantuan limestone rocks that

LIFE ON THE EDGE

Slab City appears in an early scene of *Into the Wild*, Jon Krakauer's book about Christopher McCandless. This pocket of land takes its name from leftover concrete slabs used in now abandoned barracks. These days, it's often described as a counter-cultural hangout, complete with off-grid dwellings, be they repurposed water towers or former school buses. Aside from a knot of residents escaping 'the man,' there's a bandstand and a library, plus art installations, such as the TV Wall.

Left to right: Flip Cassidy's art installation The Television Will Not Be Revolutionized; named by Mormon settlers, the Joshua tree; welcome to Slab City. Previous page: big skies and dirt roads on the Socal Ramble

"My first clue to the Sonoran Desert's dual personality comes with the sight of it in full bloom, with carpets of wild flowers"

soar skyward. Truly, this is a magical place, especially mid week, when the roads are quietest.

Then, one of the most scenic forest roads of the trip wends its up in elevation to Big Bear Lake, via Pioneer Town. This quirky, photogenic settlement was once a Hollywood Wild West film set. Now, it's a regular venue for bands, both local and international, hosted at Pappi and Harriet's jam-packed Palace. I keep an eye on the weather as the higher reaches of this road will likely be impassable after a heavy storm. Even though the skies are clear, as they usually are, I decide to find accommodation here, given that it doubles as a ski resort. Next day, there's little more to do than enjoy the ensuing loss in elevation to the desert floor once more, before catching the train from San Bernardino into the heart of Los Angeles, suddenly catapulted into a noisy, concrete metropolis, far removed from the desert-solitaire experience that preceded it. Still, it captures perfectly the remarkable dichotomy between nature and 'civilization' in Southern California, and how closely they can rub up against each other. **CG**

TOOLKIT

Start // San Diego
End // Los Angeles
Distance // 497 miles (800km)
Getting there // San Diego is easily reached by Amtrak from Los Angeles. There is a frequent and bike-friendly Metrolink service between San Bernadino and Union Station, LA, to complete the loop by public transportation.
When to ride // Between fall and early spring. Given the short winter hours, start early and bring a book for bedtime. Note that the route reaches over 6560ft (2000m) in elevation at Big Bear Lake, so check the forecast for winter storms.
What to ride // It's a very straightforward ride, technically speaking, though the arroyos can be sandy. The wider the tire, the better. It should take about 10 days.
More info // www.bikepacking.com

Opposite: views to savor on Utah's White Rim Trail

MORE LIKE THIS DESERT SOLITAIRE

STAGECOACH 400, CALIFORNIA

Little brother to the SoCal Ramble, the Stagecoach 400 makes a loop out of the fairy-tale-like town of Idyllwild, striking out to San Diego and back through Anza Borrego. Designed as a race that's held each April, the latest yearly gpx track is available for a small donation from the organizers, suiting those who want to enjoy it at a more leisurely pace. This route takes a solid five days to complete; expect sandy arroyos and rough and tumble singletrack, as well as a network of bike paths through San Diego. The Stagecoach packs in a little of everything that Southern California has to offer: forested mountains, empty desert and ocean stretches, along with San Diego and its city life. Idyllwild is tricky to get to by public transport, so you can also start in San Diego, which is well served by Amtrak trains.

Start/End // Idyllwild
Distance // 385 miles (620km)

CAJA DEL RIO, NEW MEXICO

For an overnight fix of the high desert – plus petroglyphs at La Cieneguilla – head for the Caja del Rio region just 15 miles (24km) west of Santa Fe. You can pedal out of Santa Fe via a rail trail and bike paths before the ascent proper to this peaceful plateau begins or take a train to the Santa Fe County/NM 599 station. The route is hard to follow so download an up-to-date GPX file from www.bikepacking.com. You'll need to scramble off the trail to find the petroglyphs, which date from the 13th to 17th centuries – spot all the bird figures! Rejoining the route, prepare for the technically challenging Soda Springs descent – which may not be rideable for some – to the Rio Grande, then a climb back up to the plateau to camp on the public land. After savoring the sunrise, it's a 15-mile (24km) ride back to Santa Fe, refreshed and ready for the week.

Start/End // Cannonville (or any point along the circuit)
Distance // 61 miles (98km)
Info // www.bikepacking.com/routes/caja-del-rio

WHITE RIM TRAIL, UTAH

This ranks as one of the most beautiful mountain bike rides in the Southwest. It may not be as technical as anything in nearby mountain biking mecca Moab, but it packs in one view after another. Local ironmen choose to grind out the route in a day, but it's far more enjoyable splitting it into two or three. After all, there's nothing like camping under a star-filled Utah desert sky, so why not make the most of it? Plan this trip in advance, as campsites need to be booked up to a year ahead. A backcountry permit is also required, which can be reserved online, or at the Island in the Sky Visitor Center. Spring and autumn are the best times to ride the White Rim as it's searingly hot in the summer and icy cold at night come winter. Given how beautiful the route is, the shoulder seasons offer the best chance of enjoying the emptiness to yourself.

Start/End // Shafer Canyon lookout
Distance // 97 miles (156km)

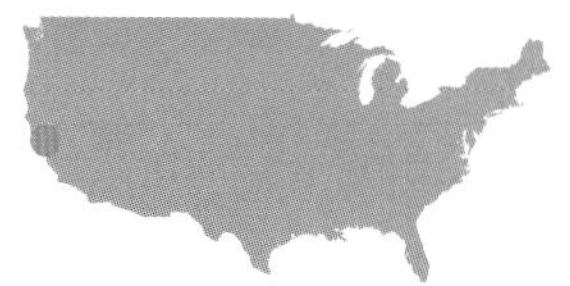

SAUSALITO TO POINT REYES LOOP

European galleons, shipwrecks and indigenous peoples: explore a region rich in Californian history on this day ride to Point Reyes in Marin County.

It was a foggy, blustery June evening in 1929 when Captain Enstrom misjudged a course correction and ran the 200ft schooner *Hartwood* aground just off Point Reyes peninsula. Its passengers, including Enstrom's wife and six-year-old son, took to the lifeboats, but the captain and six seamen stayed aboard with the ship's cargo of lumber. Rescuers from the Drakes Bay Lifeboat Station raced to the scene and plucked the passengers from their skiffs just as the tumultuous surf forced them toward rocks. It was another successful rescue from the 45 wrecks along this short stretch of treacherous coast that the station attended in the first nine years of its operation. Captain Enstrom was suspended, the timber cargo was salvaged and sold, and six months later the *Hartwood* broke up, adding to the driftwood that washes up on these wild shores.

Almost a century later to the day, the weather is bright and breezy when I set off on my ride up to Point Reyes Station and back. Marin County and its wealth of recreational cycling is, of course, no secret to San Franciscans. That great wedge of hills and coast on the north side of the Golden Gate Bridge – much of it protected by Point Reyes National Seashore, Mt Tamalpais State Park and Muir Woods National Monument – has long attracted weekending city-dwellers. But for an out-of-towner like me it was uncharted territory, much as it was to English explorer (and privateer, slave trader, mariner) Sir Francis Drake way back in 1579, when he landed on the Point Reyes coast to repair his treasure-laden ship during his circumnavigation of the globe.

To explore this corner of Marin County, I craft a 60-mile route from the seafront hot spot of Sausalito, north via minor roads through Larkspur, Fairfax and Nicasio to Point Reyes Station,

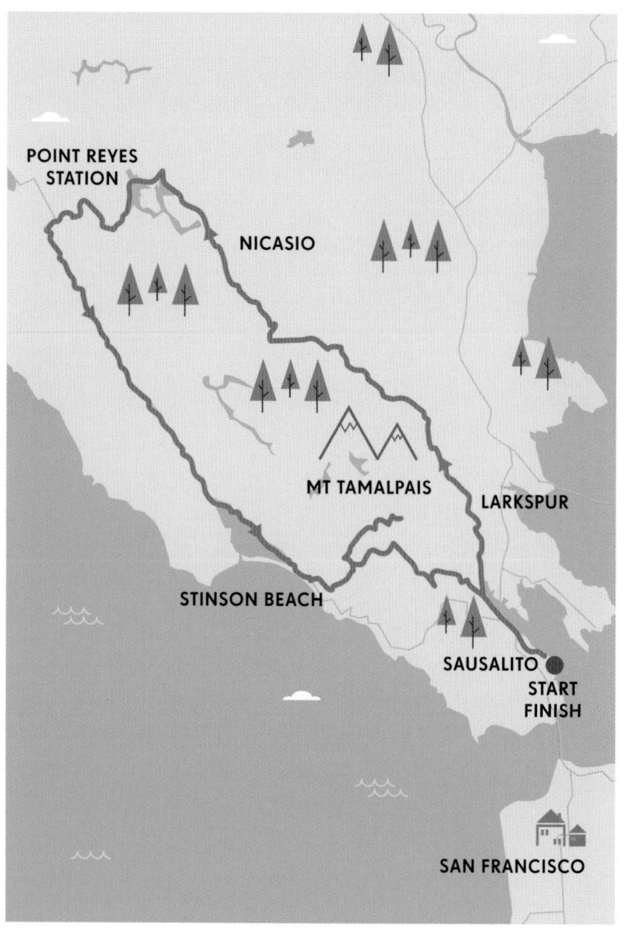

and then back south on famed Hwy 1 to Stinson Beach and then the leg-stretching main event of a climb over Mt Tamalpais and a descent to Sausalito. The reason for starting in Sausalito is because I've rented a Bianchi road bike from the much-loved Bicycle Odyssey shop in the town, but it is equally easy to set out from San Rafael or San Francisco (where there are alternative rental options if you've not brought your own wheels).

From Bicycle Odyssey's front door I turn north and follow a bike path along the shoreline, which then segues into a road that twists through the towns of Alto, Corte Madera and Larkspur. At San Anselmo I bear left, on Sir Francis Drake Blvd, toward Fairfax. If evidence was needed of Marin County's passion for cycling, you'll find it in Fairfax at the Marin Museum of Bicycling – and also in the mosaics on the town's funky street furniture. Some of the early American pioneers of mountain biking (see sidebar) would take their basic balloon-tired bikes up Mt Tamalpais in the 1970s and speed down its dirt roads. They're all members of Fairfax's international Mountain Bike Hall of Fame, which has been inviting inductees since 1988. The town is also home to one of America's most successful High School teams, the Drake Pirates Mountain Bike Team, eight-time California State Champions since 2009.

Much as I would like to stop, I speed onward and town turns to forest. I'm looking out for a right turn, Nicasio Valley Rd, which takes me off the main highway and into slightly hillier country, before circling Nicasio Reservoir at about the 25-mile mark. Rounding the bulk of Black Mountain I reach Point Reyes Station, the halfway way point and where I turn back south for home. But not before stopping to refuel: 90 years ago Point Reyes Station was

MT TAMALPAIS

Was mountain biking invented in Marin County? No, people have been riding up and down unsurfaced mountain tracks ever since the bicycle was invented. But did Fairfax locals like Gary Fisher, Joe Breeze and Charlie Kelly commercialize the mountain bike's modern form? Yes. The improvised bikes on which they skidded down Mt Tam's Repack Road are direct antecedents of the $5000 machines in your local shop. And Marin County deserves its place in cycling legend.

Clockwise from above: the Golden Gate bridge leads to Marin County and Sausalito; a sweet treat at Bovine Bakery; climbing through the rolling meadows from Stinson Beach to the summit. Previous page: on the way to Mt Tamalpais

a rough-and-ready outpost, but today it's packed with delicious diversions. I grab a blueberry muffin from Bovine Bakery on the main road and stand outside to eat it. Just around the corner on 4th St is Cowgirl Creamery, the original outlet for what is now a NorCal cheese empire. Sue Conley and Peggy Smith, founders of Cowgirl Creamery, made their first artisanal cheeses in a restored hay barn in Point Reyes. Their Red Hawk cheese is still made here, its unique flavor down to the wild bacteria in Point Reyes' air – if you want to taste the place, this is how to take a bite of the salty marine climate of Tomales Bay.

Revitalized, I hop back on the Bianchi and pedal south on Hwy 1, now with the Pacific on my right. Until Stinson Beach, the ride has been relatively easygoing, but taking the left turn onto the Panoramic Hwy leads me to what is a rite of passage for local cyclists – an ascent of Mt Tamalpais, which tops out at about 2500ft above sea level. The detour to the top of Mt Tamalpais and back down adds about 20 miles to this 55-mile loop, but the name has resonated with me since I was a teenage mountain biker.

It's a wonderful climb – a steep, narrow road with lots of fellow riders ahead and behind me. The road glides over grassy meadows and Stinson Beach disappears into the distance beneath me. As I keep a steady if not speedy pace, I imagine what the views over San Francisco will be like from the top. There's an observatory up there – they've got to be pretty special, right? I round the final few corners and arrive at the East Peak Visitor Center and realize that the Bay Area climate has foiled me, as it did Captain Enstrom: I'm in thick cloud, unable to see further than 100ft, let alone to the city. The descent back to Sausalito is a blustery experience but six hours after setting off, I pitch up safely at the shop with the memory of Mt Tam a little more vivid. **RB**

"Fairfax is also home to one of America's most successful High School teams, the Drake Pirates Mountain Bike Team."

TOOLKIT

Start/End // Sausalito, California
Distance // 55 miles (88km) without Mt Tam detour, 75 miles (120km) with.
Get there // Daily ferries to Sausalito from Pier 41 in San Francisco take about an hour. Driving from downtown San Francisco can take about 30 minutes. Or cycle.
Bike rental // Bicycle Odyssey (www.bicycleodyssey.com) at 1417 Bridgeway, Sausalito, offers road bike rentals (often Italian brands) and also does repairs.
Where to stay // San Francisco has accommodation options for every pocket, as do Sausalito and San Rafael.
When to ride // The route is accessible all year round but weather will be variable whatever the season. June, July and August often bring foggy conditions.
What to take // An inner tube, pump and puncture kit; water and food but Point Reyes has great snacking options.

Opposite: the searing challenge of climbing White Mountain

MORE LIKE THIS
CALIFORNIAN CLIMBS

MT SHASTA

If your appetite for Californian climbs has been whetted by Mt Tam, head further north and tick off one of the most demanding ascents in the state. The 14,179ft peak can be seen for miles around, which is just as well as it's a huge and active volcano ('a very high threat' according to the US Geological Survey in 2018). But, unless your timing is terrible, cycling up the road (which tops out at over 7000ft) poses few dangers: it's a long but gradual ascent, averaging less than 6% gradient over 14 miles with over 4000ft of elevation gained. That makes it tough but totally achievable. Other plus points are that there's a low speed limit (35 mph) on the road, the surface of which is of very good quality. Once you get above the trees, there are incredible views over the county and towards the snowcapped summit.
Start/End // Mt Shasta City
Distance // 30 miles (48km) round trip

GIBRALTAR RD

Northern California doesn't get all the gems. Gibraltar Rd, ascending out of Santa Barbara, is one of the very toughest climbs in the state for several reasons. It might be relatively short at about six miles in length (if you start from the El Cielito Rd intersection) but it's steep, with an average gradient of 8% and some stiff double-digit stretches as you gain about 2600ft on the ride north to the East Camino Cielo intersection. It's easy to add some extra miles into the canyons if you feel the need but local pros, such as Alexis Ryan, use the climb for interval training. And in 2018 the Tour of California made Gibraltar Rd the summit finish of stage two, which was won by Colombian superstar Egan Bernal (who also holds the Strava King of the Mountain title with a time of 27 minutes).
Start/End // Santa Barbara
Distance // 6 miles (9.5km)

WHITE MOUNTAIN

There is a climb that looms over all others in California in terms of difficulty and distance: White Mountain in Inyo National Forest. It's not the highest mountain in the state – that would be Mt Whitney, a fellow fourteener (a peak of more than 14,000ft) a short distance to the south. But it is the highest summit to which you can pedal a bicycle. Don't underestimate the dangers of doing this: you will need a lot of water and you will need to work out how to carry it. The altitude means that storms are a real risk. Oh, and the road is dirt so you will need a gravel or mountain bike. Next, figure out where to start from: the summit is at 14,252ft. The Grandview Campground is at 8500ft and the Ancient Bristlecone Pine Forest visitor center is at 10,500ft; starting from the latter gives an arduous round trip of 48 miles and almost 9000ft of climbing.
Start/End // Ancient Bristlecone Pine Forest visitor center
Distance // 48 miles (77km) round trip

TOUR OF THE UNKNOWN COAST

Giant trees, giant gradients and a windswept beach are some of the highlights of this 100-mile tour through remote northwest California.

'See this?' The extravagantly tattooed man beckons me over, as I walk my bike over a footbridge across the Eel River in Humboldt County. His pit bull dog sniffs my bike's tires. It's 8am on a Sunday morning and we're the only people about.

'I watched them wade across from the shore,' he says, pointing to a pair of black-tailed deer stepping delicately through the clear shallow river below. Light sparkles off the water around them.

'Beautiful,' he adds. 'Only in Dell Rio.'

I'm riding the route of the Tour of the Unknown Coast, an annual Gran Fondo ('big ride') that takes place in late spring and starts and ends in Ferndale, about 30 minutes north of Dell Rio. This is deep in the northwest of California, just over 100 miles south of the border with Oregon, and the air here seems to hum with a natural energy from the dark, coniferous forests of giant trees and the vast Pacific ocean beyond – if one believes in that sort of thing, which is quite likely if you're a northern Californian. Or it's the local pot plantations.

The ride has been enchanting cyclists since 1977, when a group of Humboldt County riders scoped out the route for a training ride and loved it so much that they put it on as a tour open to all the following year. Few rides in the world combine elemental ocean scenery and forests of giant redwoods. But don't ignore the numbers: the ride is 100 miles with almost 10,000ft of ascent – not for nothing is it billed as 'California's toughest century.'

But that's all to come. After Dell Rio, the next section of road is more awesome than arduous. After a 5-mile pedal along Hwy 101 – quiet at this hour – I turn left to coast along the Avenue of the Giants, the famous road that passes through groves of redwood trees (pro tip: bring a bike light and wear hi-vis clothing – little light filters past these behemoths).

On exiting the Avenue of the Giants, the route leads under Hwy 101 and into Humboldt Redwoods State Park where the

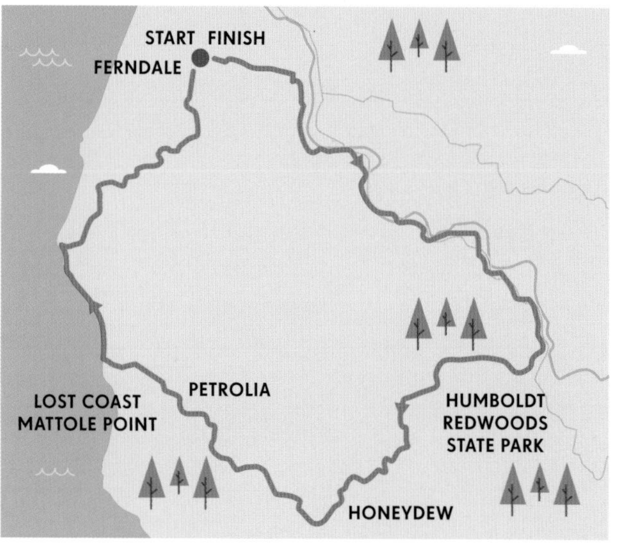

© Michael Overstreet | Shutterstock

arboreal attractions are even more impressive. Among the massive redwoods here are the Rockefeller Tree, the Bull Creek Giant and more than 150 other redwoods taller than 345ft. Weaving in between impossibly large trunks can't fail to bring to mind the *Stars Wars* speeder scene.

After 30 miles I've not done any climbing – that all changes when I reach a 7-mile ascent after Bull Creek Flats. The road switchbacks up through the forest and I find a comfortable groove until about halfway up, when I turn a corner to see a large black bear amble across the road 50ft ahead of me. I stop. It's a very large bear. 'Hey!' I shout, the internationally recognized greeting. The bear stops to regard me, then continues on its way into the forest. I don't see any cubs following so I sprint past, in so far as twiddling uphill in a small gear can ever be called sprinting. Rounding the next corner, three deer are grazing on the verge. They too ignore me. 'Only on the lost coast,' I think.

Gradually, the forest thins until I reach the most southerly point of this diamond-shaped route. Homeward bound now. But there's a reason this ride is called California's toughest century: most of the climbing is back-loaded into the final 20 miles. First I must pass through the village of Petrolia, today hosting a farmers market. I pause in the fragrant shade of some eucalyptus trees for a snack. Now 30 miles from the finish in Ferndale, I refuel as a hummingbird whirs about my head. Mattole Rd descends down to a grey-sand beach dotted with driftwood, and beyond the ocean breaks onto black rocks offshore. If you ride in spring, look out for migrating whales beyond the breakers.

The sand-blown road follows the shore for a while – savor this stretch because it's the calm before the storm. At the end of the

THE REDWOODS

For anybody seeking awe and peace, Humboldt Redwoods State Park is home to many of the world's tallest trees, grouped in about 160 groves around this undulating forest. One of the largest is Stratosphere Giant – at 372ft high it's about twice as tall as the Statue of Liberty. Before you reach it, there's a tree named Tranquility. The Rockefeller redwood is named after John D Rockefeller, who donated $2m to the Save the Redwoods League in the 1920s. Stash your bike and hike to some of the groves off the road.

Clockwise from top: Mattole beach; Ferndale's Victorian shop fronts; a club ride along Mattole Rd, near Petrolia. Previous page; pedaling along the Avenue of the Giants

"If you survive the 'Endless Hills' you've earned a victory lap of Ferndale, the 'best-preserved Victorian town' in the US."

beach the road jacks upward abruptly: this is 'the Wall,' a one-mile climb with a 20% gradient that breaks legs and hearts. From here on to Ferndale, this stretch of road is known as 'the Wildcat' or 'the Endless Hills,' as it is either going up or down. Each descent is bittersweet because you know you'll need to pedal back up again. The road here, as in other parts of this ride, is exceptionally rough and pocked with potholes, often in the shady areas beneath trees. It's here that the little suspension unit in the stem of my borrowed Specialized Roubaix – developed for the cobbles of northern France – earns its keep. Take care on all the descents of this route because a broken spoke or rim could end your ride in a very remote location.

Survive the 'Endless Hills' and eventually the road dips sharply to the centre of Ferndale, where you've earned a victory lap of the 'best-preserved Victorian town' in the US. After showering, I head to the Farmhouse on Main restaurant and reward myself with a locally sourced rib eye and a glass of Sonoma cabernet sauvignon.

I'm not sure whether this is California's toughest century but I do know that on a warm, still, summer Sunday I didn't see a single other cyclist on this spectacular route, so it may well be America's most under-appreciated century. **RB**

TOOLKIT

Start // End Ferndale, CA
Distance // 100 miles (160km)
Getting there // The closest major airports are in Sacramento and San Francisco, both about 270 miles (435km) south or southeast.
Where to stay // There are several quaint inns and B&Bs in Ferndale and a selection of private accommodations available online for a range of budgets. Alternatively, there's a RV park at the Humboldt County Fairgrounds.
Where to eat // Enjoy local produce at the Farmhouse on Main. The pizzas at Ferndale Pizza Co. are also good. Eel River Brewing supplies the local beer.
What to take // Carry enough food and water for 100 miles as there are few places to stop on the remote route. Also, be sure to bring a couple of spare tubes, a pump and puncture repair kit as the roads are rough.
More info // Visit www.tuccycle.org for details. Outside of the official organized ride, you could always ride the route in reverse and get the climbing done first.

Opposite: the Tour of California rolls into Big Bear Lake

MORE LIKE THIS
AMERICAN CENTURIES

RED ROCKS CHALLENGE, COLORADO

Clip in for what is likely America's toughest century ride (that's an imperial century not the metric variety). Colorado's Red Rocks ride has been around for many years and is now a charity challenge raising money for research into ALS (motor neurone disease). What's the challenge? Answer: 130 miles (209km) and 13,000ft (3962m) of ascent straight out of Morrison, on the outskirts of Denver, and into the foothills of the Front Range. It's not nicknamed 'the Beast' for nothing. You'll feel it on the first monster climb up Bear Creek to Evergreen and the elevation gain keeps coming, with the high point being at about 9000ft, which is why arriving early and acclimatizing to the Centennial State is a wise strategy. Riding the charity event (usually scheduled for September annually) brings the advantage of food and mechanical support, but the route is widely available and can tackled at other times. Start training today.
Start/End // Morrison, Colorado
Distance // 130 miles (209km)
Info // www.deathridetour.com

TOUR DE BIG BEAR, CALIFORNIA

Sandwiched between Los Angeles and Joshua Tree National Park, Big Bear Lake lies at an altitude of 6500ft (1981m), which means that in winter it's a ski resort and in the summer it's southern California's (self-proclaimed) cycling capital. There's some substance to the claim: Tour of California organizers first picked Big Bear Lake as a host town in 2010 and there are beautiful on- and off-road routes around the region. When the pros aren't in town, the big event of the year is the Tour de Big Bear, which celebrated its 10th anniversary in August, 2019. The century (and there's a 125-mile/200km option if you've the legs and lungs) takes in some of San Bernardino National Forest's toughest ascents, including Onyx Peak, which tops out at 8500ft (2591m). Total ascent for the century event is around 10,000ft (3048m) but the altitude will make it feel like double that. Proceeds from riders' pain have supported bike-to-school programs and local cycle paths, which softens the sting.
Start/End // Big Bear Lake
Distance // 109 miles (175km)
Info // www.bigbearcycling.com/tour-de-big-bear/tour-de-big-bear-routes

ROLLFAST GRAN FONDO, INDIANA

And now for something completely different. With a mere 1500ft (457m) of ascent, this century out of Carmel, Indiana is one of the fastest in the US. If you want to break four hours (yes, that's averaging 25mph/40km/h for 100 miles/160km) and earn the event's commemorative belt buckle, this is the route to try. Riders head out in the warm September sun in an anti-clockwise direction that usually delivers a tailwind for the last 20 miles (32km) ('usually' being the operative word). The League of American Bicyclists rated the 90,000-strong city a bronze-level bicycle-friendly community and the Gran Fondo makes sure to welcome cyclists of all abilities, with 25-/40km and 65-mile (105km) options also available. Similarly, the city has invested in its citizens' quality of life by investing in bike-friendly infrastructure meaning that it's a pleasant place to pedal around even if you're not trying to join the Sub4 club.
Start/End // Carmel
Distance // 100 miles (160km)
Info // www.rollfast.us/rollfast-cycling/rollfast-gran-fondo

htc
htc
GARMIN
htc

RIDE TO THE SUNSET IN MALIBU

Glory in southern California beach life, climb the canyons and finish with a sundowner overlooking the Pacific – is this America's most glamorous spin?

Until I went to Los Angeles to ride the canyons north of town, I'd never seen the sunset over the ocean, never seen the brilliant reds, oranges, and yellows brought to life by the Pacific's endless ripples as the sun itself nestled down into an uninterrupted horizon.

In LA, one of the world's great cities, day transitions seamlessly to night: streetlights, marquees, and ocean-side bonfires come to life, the sun's rays fade until the open water becomes indistinguishable from the inky sky, the sounds of the wind and waves blend together, and the stars appear overhead.

For cyclists, there is perhaps no better time to appreciate the setting sun than at the end of a long ride. And there may not be any better ride to put you in the mood for appreciation than a tour of the Malibu canyons.

Malibu, the community just west of Santa Monica, is home to Pepperdine University, some of the world's most famous performers, and some equally eye-catching riding. I first got a taste of Malibu's inviting, punishing, endless hills in 2016, on a spin that started in Santa Monica.

There may be more efficient ways to get to Malibu, but the most relaxing route out of town is on a bike path that puts you – quite literally – on the beach, and which stretches the length of the LA

© holbox | Shutterstock

coast, from Torrance all the way to Santa Monica. Pick the path up anywhere you like and head north. You'll roll past countless surfers riding the morning break, club kids contemplating the waves and the previous night's events with one last cigarette, runners out to sweat in the morning light, remnants from the previous night's bonfires, and all manner of cyclists cruising the shoreline of the mighty ocean. Some people race along the path, zipping to their destination. For me, the ride along the beach was a chance to ease into the day while taking in an urban melting pot that cyclists don't always get to see when hunched over the bars.

Where Santa Monica meets Malibu you'll take to the Pacific Coast Hwy, a four lane road punctuated by occasional traffic lights. Cars treat this stretch of road as a drag strip and unless you happen to be linked up with the NOW Ride – one of LA's many weekly group rides, which attracts enough riders on a Saturday morning to safely take a whole lane – it's best to stick cautiously to the shoulder, looking out for errant car doors, and oncoming vehicles making left turns.

As you head northwest, you ride past a roll call of familiar canyon roads: Tuna Canyon Rd, Las Flores, Malibu, Coral, Encinal, and Decker. Turn up anyone one of them and you'll be confronted with endless switchbacks, steep ramps, and relaxing false flats. You leave the ocean – the bustle of the beach, the rush of the highway – quickly behind.

Despite the number of people living in Malibu, the canyon roads are surprisingly quiet. You'll see other cyclists, motorcyclists and sports cars, but mostly, it will be just you and your companions.

My favorite Malibu climb is Encinal. One of the westernmost ascents in Malibu, Encinal can take a couple hours to reach if

TO LIVE AND DINE IN LA

LA is a working town; folks here wake up early and – often – turn in early. So, don't dawdle on the beach after sunset before heading out to eat. To keep your dining dollars in the cycling family, check out Jeff Mahin's artisan pizzeria, Stella Barra, in Santa Monica – Mahin is the force behind Chefs Cycle, a fundraising event that supports No Kid Hungry. He also owns Do-Rite Donuts, M Street Kitchen, Summer House Santa Monica, and other tasty venues.

Clockwise from above: the Malibu coast; surfing and cycling – both are popular here; pedaling above the Pacific Ocean in Malibu. Previous page: Santa Monica beach

you're starting from southern LA. You can fill your bottles at a gas station near the bottom and then make a right turn up pavement that was coarse and lumpy when I last rode it, and showed no signs of being repaved. But the bumps are a gift – a reason to slow down and take in the scenery of the the desert meeting the ocean. The views are pure California: endless rolling hills, dream homes, a landscape that looks nearly manicured, and an ocean that recedes from view as you grind higher and higher. Encinal isn't as steep as some of the others, giving you the chance to choose how hard you want to push yourself, and taking you gradually up, up, up.

At the top, you can savor the view one last time, before dropping downhill, away from the coast. Merge on to the Mulholland Hwy, and then turn left at Kanan Rd to get to Kristy's Roadhouse Malibu, a well-stocked general store that can refresh you and your companions with snacks and drinks – or wine and BBQ, depending on your mood.

A few quick turns takes you through the town of Cornell on Mulholland Hwy. Follow it to Las Virgenes Rd, and then take a left on Piuma for the kind of descent that will thrill roller coaster enthusiasts, and give you the chance to keep up with the motorcyclists in leather racing suits riding Kawasakis. Make a right at the bottom on to Las Flores Canyon Rd and follow it down, back to the ocean.

Soon enough, you'll be back at the Pacific Coast Hwy. Make a left and all that remains is to head southeast, back to LA. If you time your ride just right, you'll hit the beach at cocktail hour, all the better to settle in and wait for the sun to dip into the Pacific, while you relish the day's climbs and descents, views and company. **AB**

"If you time your ride just right, you'll hit the beach at cocktail hour, as the sun dips into the Pacific"

TOOLKIT

Start/End // You can start anywhere along the Los Angeles coast, but there's easy parking at Will Rogers State Park, where Malibu meets Santa Monica.
Distance // About 85 miles (137km) from Venice.
Getting there // There are lots of direct flights into LAX. Once you're on the ground, use the bus system to get around with your luggage, or call an Uber.
Where to stay // LA has many hotels to choose from, or look for an Airbnb near the beach.
When to ride // Southern California offers near-perfect weather year-round.
Bike shop // There are nearly as many bike shops in LA as there are canyons in Malibu. Take your time to find one that fits your sensibilities, or check out the Helen's Cycles chain.
More info // www.socalcycling.com

Opposite: agricultural scenery in Waitsfield, Vermont

MORE LIKE THIS
DAY-TRIPPER CLIMBS

BOULDER TO WARD LOOP, COLORADO

Boulder sits at an elevation of 5250ft (1600m) and is famous for its bike-friendly culture, not to mention a populace boasting the highest concentration of Olympic-calibre VO2 maxes. Start your ride from Pearl St and you're likely to see current and former pros taking in pre-ride espressos. Climbing to the town of Ward (elevation: 9450ft/2800m) from Boulder takes you through lush forests, beneath sheer cliffs, and alongside clear mountain streams as you ascend steep ramps high up into the Colorado Rockies. From Ward, enjoy breathtaking views of Boulder and the plains beyond. Back in Boulder, this Front Range college town offers endless dining and drinking establishments to toast your achievement.
Start/End // Pearl St, Boulder
Distance // The most popular route is 44 miles (71km)

TUCSON TO SUMMERHAVEN LOOP, ARIZONA

Starting in downtown Tucson, this 86-mile (138km) round trip packs in a 27-mile (43km) climb that begins on the eastern edge of the city and concludes in the town of Summerhaven, beneath the summit of Mt Lemmon. The road climbs more than 5900ft (1798m) to an elevation of 9150ft (2788m) through a beautiful desert landscape of juniper, pinyon pine, and sagebrush. You hardly notice the extreme elevation gain – the road is engineered so that its grades never feel like more than a gentle ramp and strong riders need never drop out of their big ring. When it comes to the descent, that same careful grading – along with perfectly arched switchbacks and banked turns – encourages even the most timid descenders, and, with due care, most will be able to fly downhill with only a few pulls on the brakes.
Start/End // Downtown Tucson
Distance // 86 miles (138km)

THE APP GAP, VERMONT

In Vermont, mountain passes are called 'Gaps,' sandwiches are called 'grinders', the liquor store is called a 'packie' and 'wicked' is a term of approval – as in, 'That descent down the App Gap was so wicked! I think I hit 60 without pedaling!' The best way to achieve that wicked experience is to take off from the ski town of Waitsfield and head east (and up) toward the Appalachian Gap. The road isn't long – the climb is less than 5 miles (8km) – but rises 1750ft (533m) with ramps approaching inclines of 20% as you labor through a lush green forest (or, take in multicolored foliage in autumn). You'll want an easy gear to make it to the top of the climb without having to dismount. Savor the view from the summit before ripping back down the hill, past the nation's only single-seat chairlift at Mad River Glen.
Start/ End // Waitsfield, Vermont
Distance // 10.5 miles (17km)

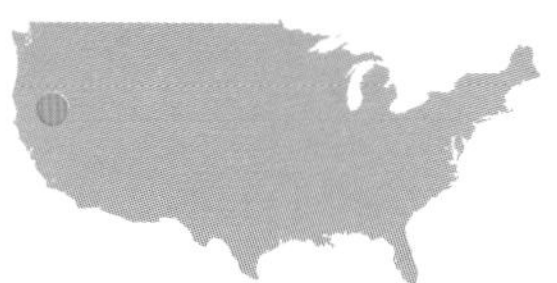

THE DOWNIEVILLE DOWNHILL

Gold Rush take two: a team of trail builders is restoring singletrack trails deep in the Lost Sierra of Northeast California and mountain bikers are reaping the rewards.

The shuttle driver, TJ, unclips my rented mountain bike from the van's roof rack and hands it down to me. We're at 7100ft in a section of the Sierra Nevada known as the Lost Sierra, a couple of hours' drive northwest of Lake Tahoe and this is the start of the most storied mountain bike trail in the US: the Downieville Downhill. Ahead lies more than 5000ft of descent over 15 miles of rocky, dusty, rooty singletrack nirvana. The route is actually several trails threaded together and I roll over to the trailhead of the first section, the newly inaugurated Gold Rim Trail, formerly part of the Pacific Crest Trail.

Pedaling up a gentle switchbacked climb and through a grove of red fir trees, a vista of mountains, lakes and forest opens before me. I pause overlooking tree-fringed Deer Lake to watch a lone kayaker leave a V-shaped wake far below, the only other human in my sight. Naturalist John Muir rhapsodized over landscapes like this in 'My First Summer in the Sierra': 'I tremble with excitement in the dawn of these glorious mountain sublimities, but I can only gaze and wonder...'. I wonder what the great protector of the Sierra Nevada would make of today's adventure-seekers in his beloved Sierra.

For mountain bikers, the town of Downieville – population 300 – is the gateway to an expanding network of off-road trails. In 1849 a Scottish major and prospector, William Downie, struck gold where the North Fork of the Yuba River meets the Downie River. Within a year the town that sprang up at the confluence of the rivers had 15 hotels and soon a population of 5000. Of course, when the gold dwindled within 20 years (or at least most of it...), so did the town. But the miners left behind a priceless legacy: narrow trails navigating the peaks and valleys of the Lost Sierra. Greg Williams is a co-founder of the Sierra Buttes Trail Stewardship. His family pitched up in Downieville with the gold rush: 'My great-, great-, great-grandfather ran pack mules and helped construct the trails in

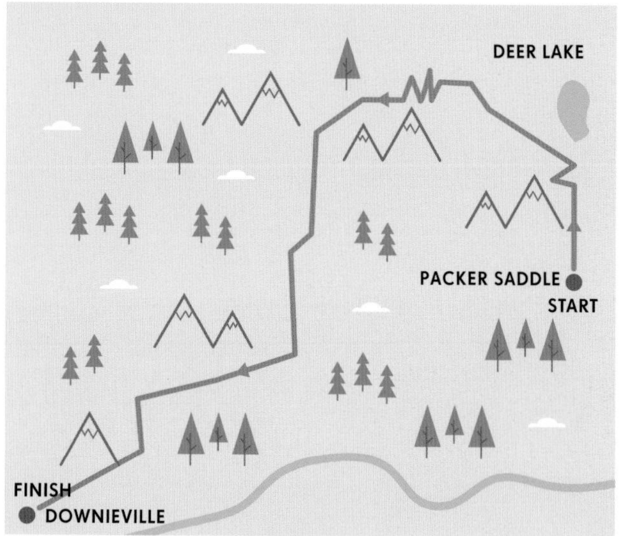

© John Watson | ww.theradavist.com

Downieville,' he tells me. In the 1980s he began riding these trails on his mountain bike and by the early 1990s he was providing guided trips into the Sierra. A bike shop in Downieville followed and then he started shuttling riders to the top of the trails. In 1995, Greg founded the first Downieville Classic race, with 277 mountain bikers battling it out. By the time of the event's 25th anniversary in 2020, the number of entrants was capped at 1150 over two days of racing, some taking on both the cross-country course (which includes a climb from Sierra City christened the Trail of Tears) and the downhill.

The cross-country route includes the Gold Rim Trail, then follows much of the route of the downhill. The newly completed extension is perfect judged, with enough rock features to keep it challenging at speed. Halfway down the Gold Rim descent I meet a party of Forest Service trail builders, chainsaws buzzing, mattocks swinging.

'How do you like that new section of trail?' one asks. 'Nice and flowing? We figured the switchbacks were getting a bit eroded.'

They pause while I pass.

'Have a good ride!'

With more riders visiting Downieville, Greg decided to put the proceeds of his bike shop into a nonprofit organization dedicated to creating and maintaining multiuse trails in the Lost Sierra. The Sierra Buttes Trail Stewardship was formed in 2003 and now employs more than 40 local people seasonally; the trails they build and repair are used by 200,000 visitors each year – hikers, mountain bikers, motorcyclists and equestrians. 'Mountain bikers have brought an economy to Downieville, along with a sense of pride for the folks being able to raise their families there because they have a job,' says Greg.

THE SBTS

The Sierra Buttes Trail Stewardship is a global benchmark for local trail advocacy and maintenance. The key, says founder Greg Williams, has been to represent all trail users. This gives the nonprofit greater influence with landowners. The result is that the SBTS is responsible for a trail network that helps people to lead healthy lifestyles and supports a local economy. Donations, memberships and entry fees from three annual bike races that SBTS hosts keep the good work rolling. See www.sierratrails.org.

Clockwise from above: post-race shenanigans at the Downieville Classic include a river jump; racers navigate rocks and roots; riding the Gold Rim trail above Deer Lake. Previous page: musical accompaniment on race day

The trail twists between pine trees, moss covering the leeward side of their trunks. Then, after a section of 4WD track through meadows filled with spring wildflowers – the phlox is in bloom, orchids and daisies are just appearing – the route joins Pauley Creek trail and the descent quickly becomes narrow and vertiginous. The downhill racers follow an alternative trail, Butcher Ranch, but having ridden this the previous day, I know they're of similar difficulty – except on race day when you'll have riders breathing down your neck in steep, rocky chutes. The Downieville Classic is a great leveller. Better descenders catch quicker climbers and as often as not the race winner will be decided by a sprint down the main street.

But for every white-knuckled stretch, there are moments of respite: where runoff crosses the trail, butterflies rest and sip water, fluttering upwards in a Marquezian cloud as I pass.

After Pauley Creek, a short climb leads to the start of the fastest section of the route: Third Divide trail. Dust motes float in the golden light. Blue jays hop from tree to tree. My eyes are focused on none of these things. Scientists say that signals from the brain controlling muscle movement travel at 120m per second. At this moment that's only just cutting it because – exceeding 30mph on the singletrack – all my attention is focused on what's happening next. Roots send me airborne, rocky sections are dispatched almost subconsciously, trusting the bike to find the route of least resistance. And all the while the trees flash past on either side of my handlebars and the momentum pushes me deep into banked corners and over water bars. Time seems to slow down but it's only a matter of minutes until the joyride ends at the Lavezzola Rd.

After a second fix of the Third Divide trail I head back to Yuba Expeditions shop, dusty and elated. 'Would you like a beer from the keg?' asks Alex from behind the shop counter. Hell, yes. **RB**

"The trails that radiate from this hamlet were forged by gold prospectors, leading pack horses ever higher into the Sierra."

TOOLKIT

Start // Packer Saddle, California

End // Downieville, California

Distance // 15 miles (24km); 5333ft (1625m) descent

Get there // It's a four-hour drive from San Francisco (or half that from Reno), there are no public transport options.

Bike rental // Yuba Expeditions (www.yubaexpeditions.com) has Santa Cruz mountain bikes for $125/day and also runs shuttles to the top of the Downieville Downhill, Mt Hough and Mills Peak from $25 per person.

Where to stay // The Carriage House Inn (www.downievillecarriagehouse.com) is conveniently close to Yuba Expeditions and offers balconies overlooking the river.

When to ride // The higher elevations of Lost Sierra trails tend to open in June, though there may still be snow; lower reaches may be rideable year-round.

What to take // Eye protection for the dust; water.

Opposite: tandem cyclists take on the Mt Hough descent during the annual Grinduro event

MORE LIKE THIS
LOST SIERRA RIDES

MILLS PEAK

Break in your legs and lungs with the two-hour climb to the top of Mills Peak and the one-hour descent. The trail starts just outside the rustic little town of Graeagle, blessed not only with good-for-the-soul High Sierra lake scenery but also restaurants, a gas station and a golf course. Mills Peak, maintained by the Sierra Buttes Trail Stewardship is one of the easier trails in the region but, it climbs through a classic Sierra Nevada landscape of pine trees and rocks that was sufficiently rugged to break off the arm of SBTS' trusty trail dozer during the construction period, which finished in 2018. You can take a shuttle to the top but the gentle ascent is a pleasant pedal. It's an 8-mile (13km) descent, dropping 3033 vertical feet – there are some rocky sections but nothing steep or exposed. Yuba Expeditions runs shuttles on Fridays and Saturdays.
Start/End // Mills Peak trailhead, south side of Graeagle
Distance // 16 miles (26km) round-trip
Info // www.yubaexpeditions.com

MT HOUGH

Continue northwest past Graeagle and you'll reach the town of Quincy, the base for any trip up Mt Hough. The trail down this mountain is perhaps the most groomed and flowing of those in the Lakes Basin, especially on its lower reaches. The route from the summit starts at an elevation of around 7000ft and drops 3800 vertical ft in 12 miles (19km). The catch? It's a long haul up to the top on gravel logging roads if shuttles aren't running (though a new Sierra Buttes Trail Stewardship bike shop in Quincy might increase the frequency of shuttles). The region hosts the annual SBTS-owned Grinduro gravel race each September, which features timed sections up and down the mountain. At the time of writing shuttles with Yuba Expeditions could be booked for Fridays and Saturdays.
Start/End // Quincy
Distance // 24 miles (38km) round-trip
Info // www.yubaexpeditions.com

MT ELWELL

On the opposite side of Gold Lake from Mill's Peak, Elwell is an altogether chunkier proposition. It's not a trail to be tackled unless you're a skilled and confident rider, comfortable with technical rock gardens, drops and steep turns coming at you from the outset. The trail mellows out lower down and sections can be walked if necessary. It will help if you're also able to make basic bike fixes (broken derailleurs, punctures and the like). But go with a group (for reassurance) and expand your boundaries. The reward will be classic Sierra scenery with Feather River to the north and the Lakes Basin to the south. Most riders climb up from the south and descend to the north, all the way from the granite peak, through old-growth forest to Graeagle. Guided rides are available from Yuba Expeditions in Downieville.
Start/End // Graeagle
Distance // 17 miles (27km) round-trip
Info // www.yubaexpeditions.com

910

THE PACIFIC COAST

With the shimmering Pacific horizon to your right and an endless ribbon of blacktop ahead, this ride traces the dramatic western edge of North America.

For cyclists who live to ride, this is a once-in-a-lifetime trip, the kind of experience that's a culmination of years of daydreaming and months of planning. I'd wanted to ride an extended stretch of the Pacific Coast Hwy for years, but the challenge is no joke: the jagged western edge of the continent has plenty of long, tough climbs and lonely stretches of blacktop that demand tenacity and self-sufficiency. But the rewards make it one of my favourite rides. Sunsets inflame the horizon, dizzying cliffs drop into the crashing surf, and redwood giants tower above. Over the years, I've ridden plenty of beautiful miles on Hwy 1, but none more exciting than the stretch between Seattle and San Francisco – an epic 980 miles with incredible sights, great camping and plenty of diversions.

Scores of cyclists make the southbound trip on the Pacific Coast Hwy every year – mostly in the summer. I took the trip solo, but the camaraderie of the riders who gather around nightly fires at the hiker-biker campsites balanced a month of solitary days in the saddle. I met John and Margaret, a pair of sweetly sardonic teachers sporting classic '80s touring rigs, gadget-obsessed twin sisters from Victoria BC on their way to Los Angeles, and a handful of grizzled vagabonds attempting solo trips to Mexico and beyond. And everyone had a story – about troubleshooting a mechanical nightmare in the rain, or a truck-driving redneck with an axe to grind, or climbs that seemed never-ending.

Although I was determined to camp – there are established campgrounds every 50 to 60 miles along the route with sites designated for cyclists – there are also plenty of opportunities for so-called 'credit-card' touring, for riders who travel light and prefer a soft bed.

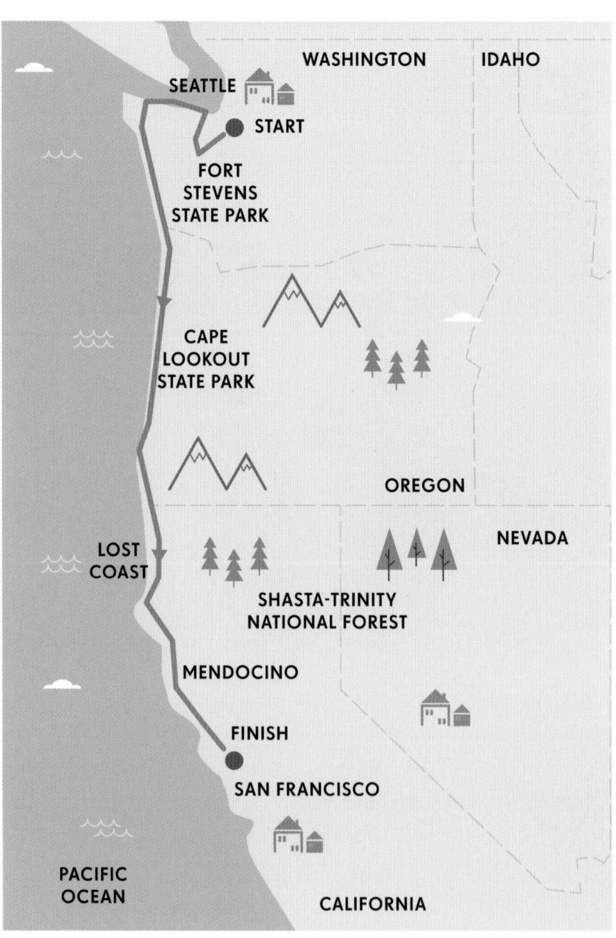

The complete trip between Seattle and San Francisco can be done in 15 days (for a powerhouse cyclist with very little gear), but I took twice as long with a fully loaded touring bike. Although I met plenty of riders ticking away miles on a tight schedule, I knew quickly that this wasn't my style. The flexibility of my itinerary enabled some of the trip's rewarding memories: pints of world-class beer at the Six Rivers Brewery, naps under swaying redwood trees, and cliff-top whale-watching. In other words, little pieces of heaven.

Before leaving Seattle, I spent an extra day or two fuelling up on the city's excellent food scene. Exploring the narrow alleys and bustling stalls of Pike Place Market, I got some fancy campfire supplies for the days ahead, and dug into the city's best: steaming bowls of ramen and fresh-that-day crab.

My detours began as soon as the trip did, tacking on several days to cruise around the Olympic Peninsula. With misty rides on near-empty roads, the trip began with a surreal tranquility. It didn't take long to get what I came for: brackish ocean breeze and mind-blowing vistas, as I cruised along spine-tingling cliffs, shoveling down snacks at quirky little roadside bodegas.

It took a long three days to get around the whole thing, but it was worth every minute: views of the Strait of Juan de Fuca, quiet farms, remote beaches and ancient forests. The camping was a superlative highlight.

Some of the best Pacific Coast lies in the coastal campgrounds of Oregon, which make up the bulk of the trip. I loved Fort Stevens State Park, a 4200-acre park that has incredible biodiversity – displaying everything from gusty dunes to freshwater wetlands – and a number of historic military sites dating from the WWII fortification of the coast. Many of the coastal Oregon parks further south made me consider lingering a bit longer than planned, like Cape Lookout State Park, where the beachside

CONTINUING ON...

Although the ride from Seattle to San Francisco is a favorite section of the Pacific Coast, because of the quality of the scenery, the relatively quiet roads and the superlative options for camping, a cyclist with enough time and energy can keep pedaling for weeks along the Pacific. The stretch from San Francisco to Los Angeles is also a scenic stunner, though narrow shoulders and heavier traffic make it more of a challenge.

Clockwise from top: fog rolls in off the Pacific along the North California coast; the Avenue of the Giants; campfires at dusk on Cannon Beach, Oregon; Pike Place Market, Seattle. Previous page: Cape Sebastian State Park in Oregon

hiker-biker sites are blissfully remote from the RV sites.

Although the camping in Oregon was the best on the trip, I discovered the most staggering vistas south of the California border. The ride here is a constant parade of awe-inspiring natural beauty, particularly when you get to the smoothly paved Avenue of the Giants, a byway surrounded on all sides by towering old-growth redwood trees. (If you're into mid-century kitsch, there are even several that you can ride through, near Leggett.)

Cycling along the edge of the so-called Lost Coast, I paused for a breather and saw the white flumes of whales, in their migration to Mexico. As I pedaled further south, I slowed for the seaside holiday towns lining the coast of Northern California. In one of them, Mendocino, there's a tidy grid of cute shops and four-star restaurants next to gorgeous headlands. I also paused for fresh seafood in Point Arena – which has an amazing bakery and a historic theatre.

By the time San Francisco drew close, I was in great shape for the most challenging section of the ride, Sonoma County. Thankfully, this also has the best views, with rock formations in the waters that rival the dramatic power of the famed Big Sur coastline south of San Francisco. Here, Hwy 1 offers paved rollers along the cliffs – three days in the rhythm of 20 minutes of lung-burning climbing followed by five minutes of glorious descending.

Reaching the coastal farms that supply San Francisco's famed foodie culture, I knew the end was near, and stopped into Point Reyes Station for fresh oysters and locally made triple cream cheese at the Cowgirl Creamery. By the time I crossed the Golden Gate – 28 days and 980 miles after my departure – this epic trip proved that the most magical part about going somewhere was the process of getting there. **NC**

"The ride is a constant parade of awe-inspiring natural beauty, particularly when you get to the Avenue of the Giants"

TOOLKIT

Start // Seattle
End // San Francisco
Distance // 980 miles (1577km)
Duration // Just over two weeks, though it's much more enjoyable with three weeks or more.
Getting there // If you fly in and out of Seattle, you can return with your bike via Amtrak at a modest additional fee, or ship your bike for a flat fee through REI (www.rei.com).
Where to stay // Hiker-biker campsites at the Oregon State Park System are exceptional value and they never turn away cyclists – even if the park is sold out.
What to read // *Bicycling the Pacific Coast* by Vicky Spring & Tom Kirkendall.
When to ride // You can do this trip any time of year, but summer and autumn are best.

Opposite: the marina at Key West, the full stop of the Florida Keys Overseas Hertiage Trail; below, the Flume Trail beside Lake Tahoe

MORE LIKE THIS
WATERSIDE RIDES

FLORIDA KEYS OVERSEAS HERITAGE TRAIL

Although still in development, the Florida Keys Overseas Heritage Trail (FKOHT) is shaping up to be as popular with locals as visitors. The completed trail will run for 106 miles (170km) from Key Largo to Key West and the 'Overseas' part of the name is appropriate because it will cross 37 bridges – many formerly part of Henry Flagler's turn-of-the-century Florida East Coast Railway – as it follows the chain of islands that dangle from the tip of the mainland. At the time of writing, about 90 miles was ready, on a mixture of road and trail. Running alongside Hwy 1 for some of the time, the FKOHT is very much life in the slow lane, allowing you to notice Floridian details the drivers pass by, such as manta rays in the water, the Flagler-era work camp on Pigeon Key, and the No Name Pub on Big Pine Key. Tip: ride south with the wind at your back. You may prefer to rent a vehicle or take the Greyhound to travel in the other direction.
Start // Key Largo
End // Key West
Distance // 106 miles (170km)
Info // www.www.floridastateparks.org

LAKE TAHOE, CALIFORNIA

At times it can seem that Lake Tahoe is the go-to weekending destination for most of California and Nevada. As such, you can expect one of its most famous mountain bike trails, the Flume Trail, to be popular from Memorial Day onwards. On the other hand, if you pick your time carefully, you can enjoy some of the best views of Lake Tahoe and also great singletrack on this 14-mile (22.5km) section of the full 168-mile (270km) Tahoe Rim Trail (largely off-limits to mountain bikers). Although busy, it's a bucket-list ride for good reason. It's typically tackled as a one-way ride that starts with a shuttle to the trailhead at Spooner Lake and, after an initial climb to Marlette Saddle at 8157ft (2486m), descends all the way to Tunnel Creek Cafe. Take your time to savor the lake views and also be aware that this trail attracts plenty of beginner bikers.
Start // Spooner Lake
End // Tunnel Creek Cafe
Distance // 14 miles (22km)
Info // www.flumetrailtahoe.com

DOWN EAST SUNRISE TRAIL, MAINE

This 87-mile (140km) section of the East Coast Greenway is all off-road – being part of the former Calais Branch rail line and now New England's longest rail trail – and is an accessible introduction to the east coast's scenic conservation areas. You might spot beaver or moose as you pedal past marshes and through forest with the Gulf of Maine a constant companion on one side, depending on whether you're heading north or south. Your other companions may be ATV drivers, horse-riders or hikers since this is a multiuse trail (obeying the rules helps all the users get along). Typically, the Down East Sunrise Trail is divided into three stages: from the western terminus of Washington Junction to Cherryfield; from Cherryfield to Machias for the central section; and from Machias to Ayers Junction for the eastern trail.
Start/End // Washington Junction / Ayers Junction
Distance // 87 miles (140km)
Info // www.sunrisetrail.org

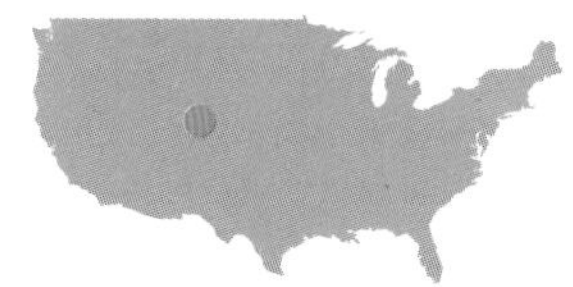

THE COLORADO TRAIL

Running the length of the USA's most fabled mountain state, the Colorado Trail has it all: high passes, historic settlements, microbreweries, and some of the best singletrack in the country.

If there's a US state that's earned itself near-mythical status among mountain bikers, it's Colorado. And for good reason. The Coloradan swathe of the Rocky Mountains is laced with a dense network of superb singletrack, expertly maintained by a devoted group of trail builders. Climbing well above the tree line, these trails wend their way across high pastures and through dense, forested glens. The descents they promise unravel for mile upon mile, in number and scale that's hard to find anywhere else in the world.

Taking it all in, in one sublime hit, the Colorado Trail is top of the list of bikepacking routes. Yes, there's a race of the same name, in which hardened, bleary-eyed mountain bikers pit themselves against each other. Day and night, they pedal their way through the very heart of the Rockies, winching their way up hour-long climbs, hurtling down technical trails and lugging their bikes across rugged, sometimes impossible-to-ride passes. The record finishing time stands at just three days and 20 hours, which is almost impossible to imagine given the overall length of the route and its wildly mixed terrain.

But I wanted to focus on something completely different. A ride on which there was no shame in taking some time off to rest tired legs, nor in dallying at the craft breweries that line the route. Nor stopping early when the perfect camping site was discovered, or if there was the opportunity to enjoy some fly-fishing along the way. By allowing two indulgent weeks to ride the CT, instead of racing the clock, this classic bikepacking route took on a different character altogether.

Given so much variety and such a high calibre of trails, experiencing the Colorado Trail was also a fine way of spending

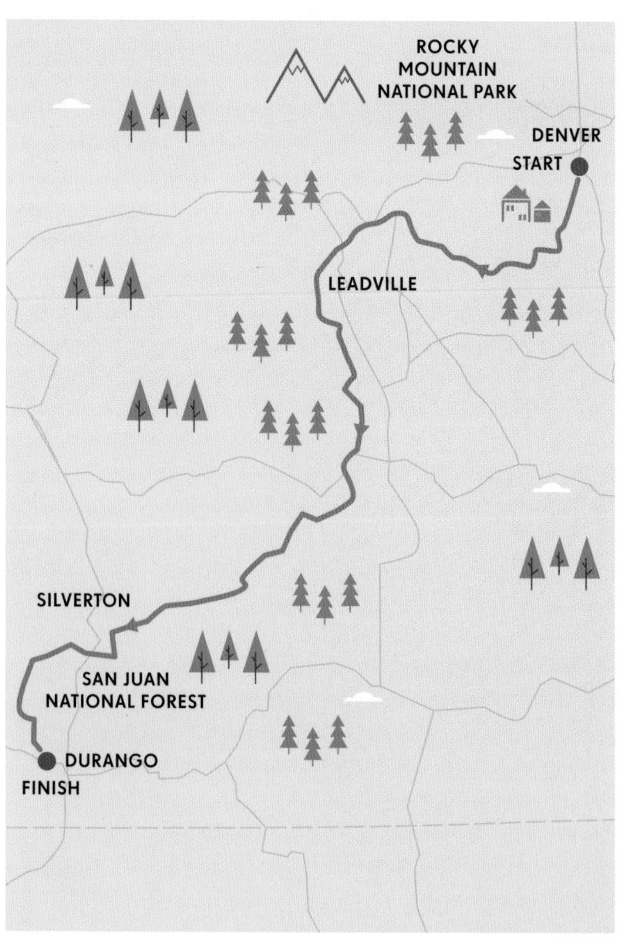

time with like-minded friends. In fact, my own group was drawn from around the globe, united by a mutual love of pushing ourselves hard in the saddle, tempered by a willingness to kick back and relax. Michael, of German descent, hails from Ecuador, where he and his brothers live on a permaculture farm. If you've familiarized yourself with the Trans Ecuador Mountain Bike Route (see p82), you'll know the kind of terrain he calls his backyard. Paul had made the journey from Minnesota; given winter's snowy embrace of his homeland, he was no stranger to either good bourbon or digging deep when required. Zach lives in nearby New Mexico and in a former life was a professional mountain bike racer. As a firefighter by day, he helped ensure the fires we lit each evening followed proper protocol, especially important within Colorado's National Forests.

In terms of understanding the big picture, the CT runs southwest across the state, connecting the outskirts of big, sprawling Denver to petite, picture-perfect Durango, via mostly singletrack and dirt roads. Stints of paved roads exist as part of bike-specific detours to avoid the six Wilderness Areas crossed by the route; these protected lands are open to hikers but not cyclists. Given its substantial 72,500ft of vertical gain, the CT is a monster of a ride and as such requires a certain degree of stamina, skill and willpower to complete. A sufficiently streamlined payload is strongly advised too, to ensure its frequent hike-a-bikes are manageable. This is no rack-and-pannier bike tour.

But as dazzling as it was, the Colorado Trail isn't just about white-knuckle singletrack and arduous portages. Crossing the Mountain State also provided a daily lesson in Southwest frontier history, even if its towns have largely been reinvented to cater to the desires of Colorado's well-heeled outdoor enthusiasts.

Situated almost halfway through the ride, the old mining settlement of Leadville is a perfect example of this historical and modern-day outdoorsy interplay. Lying at the headwaters of the Arkansas River, it boasts the largest number of fourteeners – peaks that stand over 14,000ft – within eyeshot of town. Aside from being a magnet for the country's best climbers, the Leadville 100 draws international endurance foot racers and mountain bikers alike.

And yet the town is also steeped in historical intrigue, should you dig a little deeper. Its Main St is a throwback to the rowdy times of the Wild West, back when Leadville was home to such characters as the infamous outlaw Doc Holliday, who moved there shortly after the gunfight at the OK Corral, and the 'Unsinkable Molly Brown,' famous for surviving the sinking of the 1912 RMS *Titanic*. Meyer Guggenheim, the Swiss patriarch of the

WEIGHT LIST

Hike-a-bikes are part of the Colorado Trail experience. How much of the route is rideable will vary between riders, depending on skill set, gear carried, the weather and acclimatization. For the most part, hike-a-bikes are relatively short, though there are several longer stretches to contend with. This said, it's easy to let the mind dwell on what's not rideable. For the vast majority of the time, the CT's singletrack is flowy, fast, rambunctious and fun!

Left to right: singletrack heaven; pitching camp on the Colorado Trail; a four-legged trail companion. Previous page: breathing thin alpine air on the Colorado Trail

famously wealthy Guggenheim family, earned his first fortune thanks to Leadville's mining riches. And the town's impressive Tabor Opera House, named after Horace Tabor – the quick-shooting, hard-drinking Irishman who whipped Leadville into shape during its early, lawless years – hosted a lecture by Oscar Wilde in the late 19th century.

But I digress. Beyond Leadville, the Colorado Trail became more remote and the miles that went by were especially hard fought; flowy singletrack gave way to rough moto trails and hike-a-bikes became longer and often protracted. The route passed the railroad town of Silverton, until it breached the tree line one last time, opening spectacularly into the high tundra of the San Juan Mountains. This sub-range of the Rockies was an undoubted highlight of the entire ride, thanks to the sense of pure mountain-biking bliss to be found there. Streams, brooks, mountain peaks and high pastures were in abundance, all of which lured us into lingering picnics or calling an early end to the day, if only to enjoy the view from a prime camp spot and delay those inevitable last few miles of a great adventure. And enjoy it we did. Because once we dropped out of the San Juans and hit the outskirts of Durango, we left behind one of the most challenging, well-rounded, singletrack-infused bikepacking routes on the planet. **CG**

TOOLKIT

Start // Denver, Colorado
End // Durango, Colorado
Distance // 539 miles (867km). Factor high elevation passes into route planning, especially if arriving from lowlands.
When to ride // July to September are the most reliable months. (Early summer promises wildflowers but beware snowy passes. Late September brings autumn colors and more settled weather). This is a high mountain ride, so monitor the forecast. Storms will dictate how you break up your days; make sure you're below the tree line if they roll in.
What to take // Front or even full suspension will help you enjoy the trails to their utmost. The Trail is signposted but a GPS is important, especially for bail-out options. The Colorado Trail Databook is also worth carrying, as it lists re-supply points, water access, campsites and passes.
More info // www.coloradotrail.org

Opposite: taking on the Oregon Timber Trail

MORE LIKE THIS SINGLETRACK EXTRAVAGANZAS

OREGON TIMBER TRAIL

The newly formed Oregon Timber Trail is a long-distance bikepacking route that crosses the entire state, lacing together as much singletrack as possible along the way. Give yourself 25 days to cover it and, like the Colorado Trail, bear in mind this is a tough ride with its fair share of hike-a-bikes, so pack light. There's a similar amount of cumulative climbing, although the altitude is lower, so it's easier on the lungs. The OTT is best ridden between mid-July and mid-October, on a mountain bike with front suspension. From a navigational standpoint, you'll want to be comfortable using a GPS, as it isn't signposted. This is a work in progress, so check www.oregontimbertrail.org for updates, new route alignments and the latest gpx file.
Start // Lily Lake, California
End // Hood River, Oregon
Distance // 668 miles (1075km)

ARIZONA TRAIL

Completed in 2011, the Arizona Trail is another classic singletrack extravaganza, crossing the entire length of Arizona. There are those who race it in just over six days, tearing along its challenging trails both day and night. Mere mortals will likely enjoy it more in two or even three weeks. The route includes a crossing of the Grand Canyon, during which bikes have to be carried (tires aren't permitted to touch the ground), making it a true 'bikepack', in every sense of the word. Expect all manner of vegetation, from ponderosa forests and the red rock of Sedona to corridors of saguaro cacti further south. With these come techy slabs, loose rock and sand. Spring and autumn are the only seasons the trail is passable from one end to the other. Summer is dangerously hot and the mountains will be snowbound in winter. Visit www.aztrail.org for the latest gpx file and notes on the route.
Start // Montezuma Pass, near Mexican border
End // Buckskin Mountain, Utah border
Distance // 739 miles (1189km)

TAHOE TWIRL, CALIFORNIA/NEVADA

Shorter in length but boasting equally good singletrack, Lake Tahoe's Rim Trail offers more classic bikepacking opportunities. There are variations, depending on how close to the official Rim Trail you want to keep (and, by association, how much you want to ride versus carry and push your bike). Consider bikepacking.com's Tahoe Twirl for a balance between the two: long, flowing ribbons of singletrack are interspersed with mellow bike paths and dips in the lake's azure waters. The route begins in Nevada but spends much of its time in California, given how Lake Tahoe straddles the two states. Give yourself four to five days to enjoy the route without rushing unduly. Like the Colorado Trail, it's worth taking altitude into account if you're coming from the lowlands; the highest point of the ride reaches just under 9600ft (3000m). Because of this, it's best ridden between early summer and autumn, depending on the snowfall that year.
Start/End // Reno, Nevada
Distance // 187 miles (301km)

FOX

COLORADO BREWERY TOUR

Year-round sunshine, world-class cycling, and hundreds of breweries – quench your thirst after a long day on the bike with some of America's best craft beer.

I get off the bike, legs full of lead and heart thundering, face tingling from the wind and mouth full of cotton. If this was a typical ride, I'd grab my water bottle and find the nearest cheeseburger. But taking in the scenic regions of Colorado's north by bike is anything but typical. On this ride, I'll savor the marriage of the region's two perfectly complementary pastimes at every stop: mind-blowing cycling and mouthwatering beer. A blissful 20-mile descent from the mountains and an icy pint of citrusy, grassy, dry-hopped double IPA? This is my kind of recovery regimen.

Colorado has long been a hot spot for road cycling and mountain biking, and boasts more microbreweries per capita than anywhere else in the US. For a beer-loving cyclist, it's a no-brainer.

I started in the state's capital, Denver, which has transformed from a frontier cow town into an urban capital of the American west. The city itself might be destination enough for casual cyclists – an excellent bike network includes long, leisurely routes along

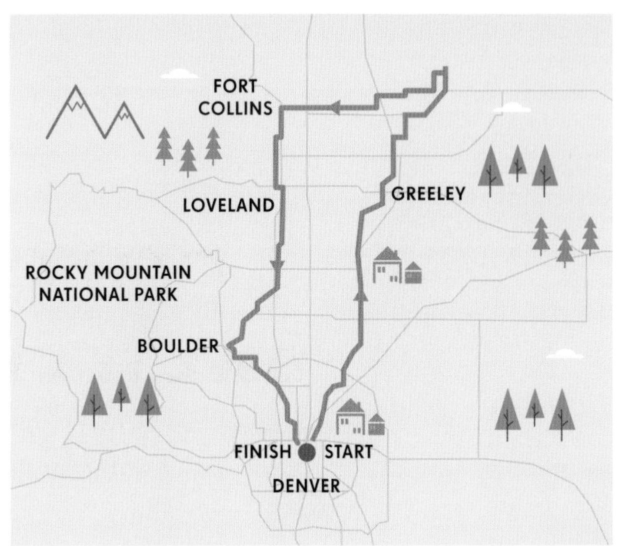

the Platte River Parkway, the Cherry Creek Bike Path, and trails to neighboring suburbs. You can even use the excellent B Cycle program, which has bikes stationed throughout the city. But one look at the peaks of the 'fourteeners' (local speak for a mountain of 14,000ft or more) looming on the horizon, and I knew that a serious two-wheel adventure was ahead.

Denver was the perfect embarkation point for my beer-themed trip. I was a month early for the endless tasting at autumn's Great American Beer Festival – but consoled myself with a fun, boozy overview of the city's breweries from the Denver Microbrew Tour. A few of my favorites included the Great Divide Brewing Company, where the spectrum of seasonal beers are all beautifully balanced (be careful, many of them are over 7%), an outpost of the excellent Breckenridge Brewery, and the weekly rotation of taps at the Denver Beer Co.

Fully hydrated and rested up, I hit the road. My next major stop would be Fort Collins, a college town that perfectly merges Colorado's beer and bike cultures. Although a serious cyclist could do the trip in a long day, I took the 100-mile route into two days with an overnight in Greeley. With the pancake-flat roads and a tailwind, I blasted out of Greeley for a cruise through the unending green expanse of the Pawnee National Grassland, a sea of swaying hip-high grasses that were once prime buffalo hunting land. There's something hypnotic about the rhythmic sway of the prairie.

"Riding west brought me to Fort Collins, the essence of the trip, its bike-packed streets dotted with great breweries"

Navigating a few extra miles brought me to the Pawnee Buttes, two 300ft formations that leap dramatically out of the flatlands. Aside from free-roaming cattle, these back roads are mostly free from traffic, and toward the end of the day I caught the flash of a white-tailed antelope bounding through the fields.

Riding west brought me to Fort Collins, which straddles Colorado's topographical divide, at the point where the Rockies begin their rise. This town is the essence of the trip: the bicycle-packed streets of Fort Collins are dotted with great breweries. And the city is mad about cycling: the Fort Collins Bike Library offers free bikes to anyone who passes through.

This first stop in Fort Collins is the New Belgium Brewery. This employee-owned operation has brought its passion for bicycles, beer and sustainability to an international audience in recent years. The guides give me a playful walk through the facility that ends in a carnival-like tasting room before I head back to town for a stop at the Odell Brewing Company, a remarkable small brewery with the best IPA of the trip. If the sun was up, I would have hit the beer garden at Equinox Brewing, but the jagged horizon suggests

that a good night's rest is in order.

Anyone could close this loop by riding straight south on the relatively flat roads that skirt the edge of the Rockies. I've got a pint of stout or two to work off, so I'm up for the challenge of climbing Rist Canyon to Stove Prairie Rd. This route (loved by locals and a recent stage for the USA Pro Challenge) is tough, but the scenery is incredible. Ahead, mountains roll into view in shades of purple and blue. Behind, plains reach out in a checkerboard of green. All day, I'm surrounded by pines, massive boulders and rushing creeks. Heading south on Stove Prairie Rd, I lose all that elevation through the sweeping curves that lead to Loveland. Of course, there are plenty of places to fuel up in this small town as well, starting with the family-owned Loveland Aleworks, where the creative selection of taps is frequently rotating. This stop includes a pucker-inducing explosion of summer flavor with the Strawberry Sour.

The next day, I take the 35 miles between Loveland and Boulder in a few hours, allowing plenty of time for exploring the Boulder Creek Bike Path to end the penultimate day. Snuggled up against the Flatirons, this bohemian college town is in love with the outdoors. After chatting with local characters on the Pearl St promenade, I grab a beer at Avery Brewing, and take a self-guided tour from the catwalk. The evening ends with some noodling guitar warriors at the Draft House, which brings in local bands every weekend. Another half-day in the saddle brought me back to Denver for a well-earned rest for my legs and my liver. **NC**

THE COLORADO TRAIL

With some 535 miles of twisting singletrack, jaw-dropping views, and rollercoaster elevation, the Colorado Trail is one of the world's great long-distance mountain bike journeys. Riding the entire trail – from Denver to Durango – takes about 20 days, and requires resupply in mountain towns along the way. For the more casual rider, there are numerous day rides that will give you a taste of this epic adventure. For complete information: www.coloradotrail.org.

Left to right: autumn colors at Boulder Creek; not a state for indecisive drinkers; Colorado is singletrack heaven for mountain bikers. Previous page: Denver's skyline

TOOLKIT

Start/End // Denver
Distance // About 350 miles (563km) in five or six days.
Getting there // Denver International Airport is an easy connection to many cities in the US and has several daily routes to Europe, Japan, Canada and Latin America.
Bike rental // A number of Denver shops will rent bicycles suitable for multi-day trips, including The Bicycle Doctor (www.bicycledr.com), and Bicycle Village (www.bicyclevillage.com). The big REI (www.rei.com) in Denver also rents bikes and camping equipment, and can arrange bike shipping.
Where to drink // The Beer Drinker's Guide to Colorado has reviews and maps to Colorado breweries. Denver Microbrew Tour offers a great brewery overview.
More info // See www.bikedenver.org and www.denvergov.org, which has downloadable bike maps.

Opposite: quiet vineyards in the north of Napa Valley

MORE LIKE THIS
REFRESHED RIDES

CALISTOGA WINE TOUR, CALIFORNIA

A weekend amble through California's wine country is an extremely popular way to get a taste of the region north of San Francisco. Although Napa's roads can get clogged with tourists, a good alternative is to ride the relatively quieter roads surrounding Calistoga. Pedal north out of town on Hwy 29 and take Old Toll Rd up a side valley. A steep, shaded climb will pass a couple of family wineries before rejoining Hwy 29 and reaching the summit at the Robert Louis Stevenson State Park – an excellent place to rest, picnic, and take in the views. Coast downhill to Middletown and east through the lovely valley that's home to the Guenoc and Langtry Vineyards. Then climb Butts Canyon and descend into the flowering meadows of Pope Valley. From here, connect to the celebrated (car-free) Silverado Trail, through the adorable downtown of St Helena, and head back to the start.
Start/End // Calistoga
Distance // 62 miles (100km)

VALLEY BEER TOUR, MASSACHUSETTS & VERMONT

The region of Western Massachusetts and southern Vermont gets called the Napa Valley of Beer for good reason – the clutch of creative craft breweries and excellent brewpubs makes it a beer-lover's dream. Start this trip in Springfield, a half-day train ride from New York City. Here, you can enjoy old world beer-making traditions at The Student Prince, one of the best German restaurants in Western Mass. After a stein and a schnitzel, make your way along back roads to North Hampton, a college town with a number of great brewpubs, including the 40 taps of local and far-flung beers at Dirty Truth and the rowdy outdoor beer garden at the Northampton Brewery. This ride ends just across the Vermont state line at the The Whetstone Station Restaurant and Brewery, where riders can enjoy a view of the Connecticut River and refined small plates.
Start // Springfield, Massachusetts
End // Whetstone Station Restaurant & Brewery, Vermont
Distance // 66 miles (106km)

KENTUCKY BOURBON TOUR

A ride filled with rich history, heady spirits, and Southern American charm, this trip takes in six of the best distilleries along the scenic, rolling, rural roads of Central Kentucky. The terrain is moderately challenging (particularly with a couple of samples under your belt), so this is recommended for more experienced cyclists. Start in Lexington at the Jim Beam distillery, where you can get a detailed map of the region and turn-by-turn instructions. Along the route, you'll sample America's oldest spirit at the Heaven Hill Distillery, Maker's Mark, Four Roses, Wild Turkey, and Woodford Reserve. In addition to the delicious bourbons, you'll find undulating hills of bluegrass and picture-perfect horse farms.
Start/End // Lexington
Distance // 30 miles (48km)
Info // www.kybourbontrail.com

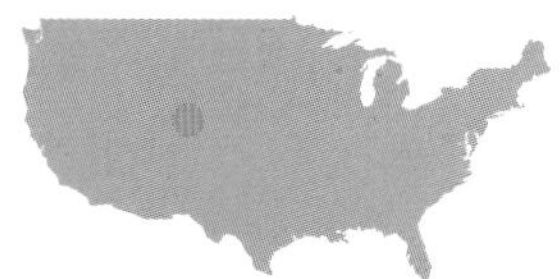

THE ALPINE LOOP

Ride through the ghost towns of Colorado gold country, up and over the 12,000ft passes of the San Juan Mountains. This one's a lung-buster!

When a group of friends from Texas, Oregon, and Connecticut planned a trip to visit me in Colorado I couldn't help but scheme the most impressive bike tour in the area: an epic journey over the high mountain passes and alpine tundra of the San Juan Mountains, following the Alpine Loop. The route makes a champion out of anyone who accomplishes the two lung-busting climbs above 12,000 ft.

The Alpine Loop is designated a Scenic and Historic Byway and circumnavigates 80 miles through ghost towns and abandoned mines along mostly well-maintained gravel and 4WD roads. But as well as the remains of these bygone communities, there's plenty else to catch the eye in this high alpine environment: it is not uncommon to see elk, bighorn sheep, black bear, moose, mule deer, pika, marmot, and red-tailed hawks in the high valleys, basins, tundras. But pick your moment. Generally, the mountain passes at this altitude are clear of snow only from July through September, and while the early summer brings a riot of colour from the blooming wildflowers, it is also the most popular time for the SUV crowds. September tends to be the quietest month, plus you'll catch the aspen trees in all their fall glory.

While the loop is relatively short, allow yourself two or three days to complete it: the two major ascents on this route can each take an entire day. Plan the timing of your ascents, know your limits, and avoid camping above the tree line. At the high elevations, sudden storms can bring rain or snow at any time of year (afternoon storms from July through August are common) so be sure to bring some extra clothing in case of sudden drops of temperature. In order to keep our bikes light up the arduous climbs and nimble descending tricky terrain, we opted for minimal bikepacking bags, strapped tightly to our mountain

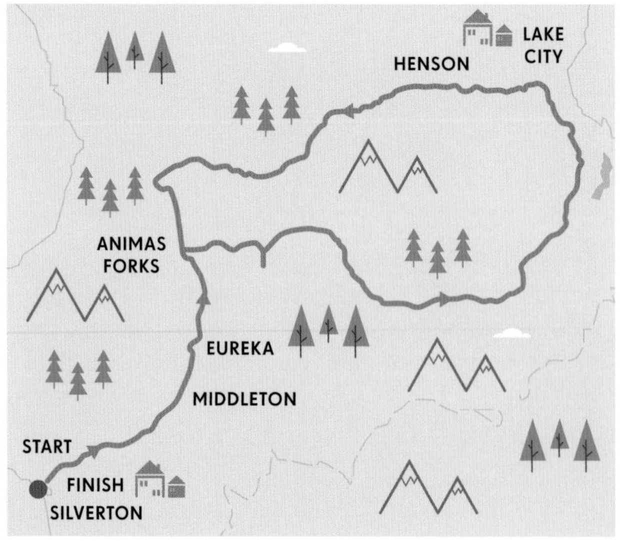

bikes, so space for clothing was at a premium.

We begin our ride in the historic mining town of Silverton, Colorado, nestled between 13,000ft peaks. In the late 19th century it was one of the richest gold- and silver-mining communities in the world (minerals to the then value of $12m were extracted from the nearby Ute Ulay Mine). Mining brought new life to the San Juan Mountains, and in its heyday the town of Silverton had 5000 residents. When the price of silver dropped overnight in 1896, the miners departed, a mass exodus from the region that left behind ghost towns that remain to this day. Silverton is now a small town of 650, a base for mountain adventures, and a destination for tourists arriving by steam train along the historic Durango and Silverton Narrow Gage Railroad.

We can't draw on steam power for the climbs that lie ahead, sadly, and we're already high – Silverton is at 9400ft. We head north out of town, climb gradually along a quiet dirt road parallel to the main road, along the Animas River. In Eureka the grade kicks up, and we settle into our individual climbing paces. After lunch in the cooling mist of a nearby waterfall, we arrive in the historic mining camp of Animas Forks. In the 1880s this town of 450 people was bustling enough to sustain its own newspaper The *Animas Forks Pioneer* – today, the prospectors are gone but the remains of their mines and many old buildings are still here for us to explore.

From Animas Forks the road steepens and becomes harder going. We may have enjoyed the views earlier but now all we can focus on is the road in front of us, while carefully balancing our

DINNER WITH MR PACKER

During the winter of 1874, Alfred Packer, along with a group of five other prospectors, attempted to cross this region of the San Juan Mountains. The snow and the subzero conditions slowed the group, and, their supplies diminished, they began to starve. When Packer showed up to his destination alone and well fed, a dark story began to unfold. Eventually, Packer was tried and found guilty of murder and cannibalism at the courthouse in Lake City. He remains part of Colorado's folklore.

Clockwise from above: big smiles per mile; wildflowers and bighorn rams in Colorado; taking a break on the Alpine Loop. Previous page: surfing the switchbacks

bikes for traction over the steep loose rocks and trying to ignore the ever-thinning air: suffer mode. If your back wheel slips, well, that's a chance to take in the otherworldly alpine tundra: it's wildflower season, so between the islands of remaining snowpack are dashes of red, purple, white and yellow. We reach Cinnamon Pass and cheer for the backmarkers making the last effort.

While we revel in the accomplishment of climbing to 12,600ft by bicycle, we don't linger. It's cold and windy. Instead, we're rewarded in the descent along the technical 4WD mountain road which offers new views and valleys to explore. We drop into American Basin, an alpine valley famous for its wildflowers – orange and yellow paintbrush, scarlet king's crown, pink elephant's head, purple aster, white alpine sorrel, and the state flower, the purple colorado columbine in midsummer – and they do not disappoint. We happily set camp in this sea of color, in a pre-established spot along a creek, with a firepit already lined with rocks – we go to sleep lulled by the sound of mountain water trickling by.

From American Basin the Alpine Loop drops down to Lake City, a small town at an elevation of 8671ft, well equipped for resupply and recovery. We need it, because we've another big stretch in the saddle up to Engineer Pass (12,800ft), and it just gets steeper and more rugged – by way of consolation, we pass yet more vestiges of Colorado's mining history and enjoy magnificent views of the 14,000ft peaks characteristic of the San Juan Mountains. What remains? A 3000ft technical descent back into Silverton, where we find a little gold dust of our own: a celebratory drink at an old-time saloon. **SS**

"We drop into American Basin, an alpine valley famous for wildflowers – including the state flower, purple columbine"

TOOLKIT

Start/End // Silverton, Colorado
Distance // 80 miles (129km)
Getting there // The closest airport is the Durango-La Plata County Airport. Rent a car for the 1½ drive to Silverton.
Where to stay // The Raven's Rest Hostel in Lake City. There are also many pre-established camp spots along this route between 9000ft and 10,000ft. The only official campground is at Lake San Cristobal.
What to take // GPS device, water filter, camping equipment, cookware, clothes for the drastic change in temperatures, repair kit, spare tubes, a battery charger, your climbing legs, and a camera!
More info // www.bikepacking.com

Opposite: Oregon's Elkhorn Crest Trail

MORE LIKE THIS
ELEVATED ALPINE-STYLE LOOPS

THE ELKHORN CREST TRAIL, OREGON

The Elkhorn Crest Trail is the highest trail in northeast Oregon and runs along the Elkhorn Mountain ridgeline in the Blue Mountains. This technical mountain-bike ride traverses subalpine forests and grasslands on dirt roads, jeep tracks, and singletrack and offers constant panoramic views of Baker Valley and the Wallowa Mountains to the east, and the Blue Mountains to the west. Don't get too distracted by the views, though – certain trail sections hug exposed cliffs and will require your full attention. Break the ride up over two days by camping at one of the many high mountain lakes, enjoy views of the nearby rocky peaks, and maybe even catch a glimpse of a herd of elk or resident mountain goats.
Start/End // Haines, Oregon
Distance // 52 miles (84km)
Info // www.ridewithgps.com/routes/17987857

LA GIRA DE SUR YUNGAS, BOLIVIA

Relish relentless climbs to high elevations? The La Gira De Sur Yungas loop outside La Paz, Bolivia is for you. The route negotiates the eastern slopes of the Andes in a striking transition zone between the Bolivian Altiplano and the Amazon, called the Yungas. Along primarily dirt roads, the route undulates between arid high alpine mountains and deep humid valleys of subtropical rainforest, including the notorious Death Road and its precipitous drops. La Gira De Sur Yungas is not for the faint of heart with a leg-burning cumulative elevation gain of 40,300ft (12,283m) over 230 miles (370km). If you are looking for an accessible route that will whip you into shape for further Andean adventures, plus a taste of the colorful Bolivian culture, add La Gira to your bucket list. Along the route you will enjoy friendly hospitality, and plenty of opportunities to resupply water and good food. Best attempted during the dry season from April to October.
Start/End // La Paz, Bolivia
Distance // 230 miles (370km)
Info // www.ridewithgps.com/routes/15288056

MONARCH CREST TRAIL, COLORADO

This is one of Colorado's most epic alpine mountain-bike trails, but if a lung-busting opening climb doesn't appeal, book one of the many shuttle services to take you to the top of Monarch Pass. From there it's a test of your technical skills on singletrack, doubletrack, fire roads, smooth dirt and rocky jeep tracks. Don't let the shuttle ride fool you, though – as well as 6000ft (1828m) of descent, you've still nearly 2000ft (610m) of climbing, which is what makes this ride an all-day adventure. Come prepared with enough food, water, and clothing for all types of weather as conditions can change drastically and quickly at the higher elevations.
Start/ End // Poncha Springs, Colorado
Distance // 35 miles (56km)
Info // www.ridewithgps.com/routes/29034961

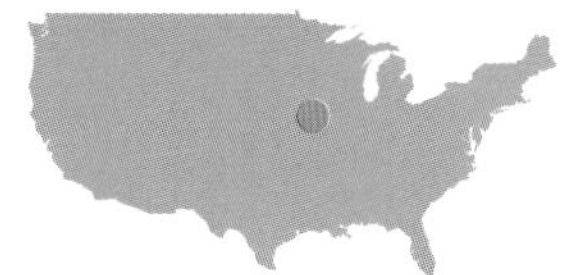

THE REGISTER'S ANNUAL GREAT BICYCLE RIDE ACROSS IOWA

Nestled in the belly of the Midwest is an organized ride so hometowny, welcoming and wonderful that you'll swear you've been there before.

This seven-day, 450-mile ride has been held every summer since 1973, when two editors from *The Des Moines Register* newspaper decided to ride across the state for a story and invited the public to join them. It has since grown from 500 participants into the oldest and largest organized ride in the world, featuring more than 10,000 riders in 2018. It's become one of the most storied rides in the country, known as a giant, week-long party. This ride crosses Iowa, starting at the western border of the state, where most riders dip a wheel in the Missouri River, and finishes up on the eastern side, with another rubber baptism in the Iowa River. Though the exact route varies from year to year, the authentic immersion in Midwest culture and hospitality is never underserved. We rode beside bicycle riders from all tribes, including grannies on their beach cruisers, tandems, a triple tandem and a guy blasting country music from huge speakers strapped to a rack. We saw someone dressed in a full Spiderman suit, a man riding in flip-flops and overalls, a pair of unicycles, and families on e-cargo bikes towing little kids and dogs.

At the first town we came to along the route on Sunday morning, the streets were so thick with people and bikes we had to dismount and walk, and somehow I got separated from the group between the grilled cheese food truck and the temporary tattoo booth. (I

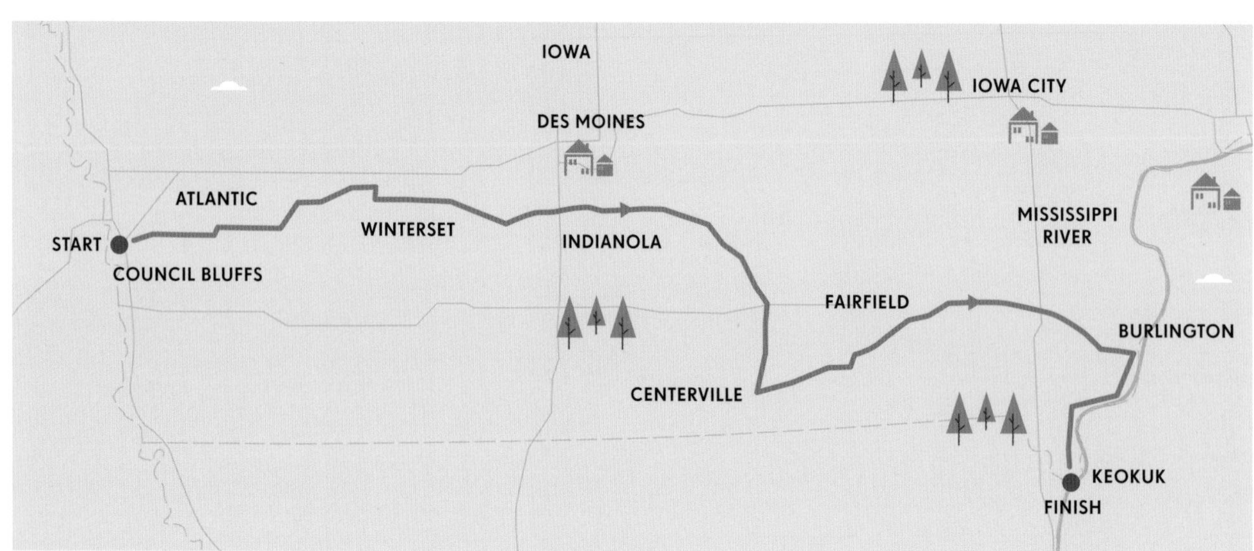

picked one out that was an ear of corn.) There was music coming from a few blocks up ahead. I realized, as we got closer, it was a stage offering karaoke. A beer-bellied man with an impressive voice was singing 'Ring of Fire.' We stopped to refill our bottles at the makeshift water fountain at the fire station. One of my friends spotted a man on a corner who was bending steel spokes into bracelets. For $5, I rode away with a shiny new bangle.

About an hour down the road, we passed a sign that read 'Free Margaritas.' We optimistically screeched to a halt, pulling into a gravel parking lot. The sign was in front of a restaurant up on a hill, overlooking a sparkling blue lake with a cement boat launch and a string of pontoon boats tied together a few meters offshore. I skittered down to the edge and clicked off my shoes, peeled off my socks and dangled my feet in the water. It was only mid-morning, but it was hot; other riders were jumping right into the cool water up to their chests. Tempting as it was, we collectively reminded each other how awful it would be to ride the next 40 miles with a soggy chamois. As we sat there on a cluster of large rocks with our bare feet in the water, a man from the pontoon chain waded over to us with a cooler in one hand.

'You guys like beer?' he asked us. We nodded gratefully, and he handed us slightly cool cans of Bud Light.

'How far you going today?' We told him we'd come 15 miles already and had about 45 to our next stopping town.

'Whoo-wee!' He offered us some protein bars from his cooler too. We sat and shot the breeze with him while people on the pontoon boats laughed and whooped.

With a long way still to go, we thanked the man and got back on our bikes.

Suffering from serious FOMO from skipping a jump in the lake, we left the house the next day with swimsuits wadded up in our jersey pockets. We promised ourselves that any sign of a lake and we would pull over and take a dip – it would feel so wonderful in the middle of a long day in the Iowa sun.

About mid-afternoon, we found what we were looking for in the form of fire hose races. The fire station had strung up a buoy on a wire about 15ft in the air, and two people with hoses were using the strong stream to push the buoy to their opponent's side. We pulled over in a convenience store car park and took turns slipping on our swimsuits in a portable toilet, then crossed the road to the park. The wet cement was warm under my bare feet, but the spray from the hoses was refreshingly chilly. Kitted-up onlookers laughed as we battled the buoy back and forth across the basketball court. While I watched two of my friends play, I realized the fireman had a lever to control how much water went into each of the hoses, and were snickering to themselves as they channelled it all into one hose and

IOWA CORN

Every day along the route, the Iowa Corn Growers Association sets up a free corn stand (donations accepted). After riding through miles and miles of cornfields, you'll want to stop to eat some. 'Butter?' the volunteer asked. I nodded, and he dipped the cob into a pot of melted butter and passed the glistening hunk of steaming starch into my hands. Holding it by the husk, I sunk my teeth into the delicious, salty gold. It was glorious.

Left to right: bicycles of all shapes, sizes and styles are seen on the RAGBRAI, including these Brompton folders; helmets are advised; an aerodynamic recumbent bike; support vehicle. Previous page: heading east on day one

my friend Vance got completely soaked by his wife Courtney. We rode the rest of the way with damp hair and giant grins.

We stopped at a family-owned slow-roasted pork-chop stand, and later at a table where women from the local church were selling homemade pie: strawberry, apple, banana cream and pecan. Families brought out their animals: in a few towns there were piglets available for photo opps, and you can even kiss one if that suits you (pigs are loud squealers – it did not suit me). I was sitting on the cool grass under an oak grove in front of a farmhouse, enjoying my pork chop, when a kitten wandered over to my feet. Even the animals were excited to greet us as we buzzed across the state.

Overnight, local families hosted us. They opened up their homes (and their fridges!) to a group of sweaty riders, eager to get to know all about us and where we came from. We spent nights on strangers' air-conditioned living room floors, our bellies full of well-earned beer and dinner.

The Midwestern route traces rolling farmland, past sparkling lakes and through acres of cornfields. The views that you don't forget, though, come at the end of the day: sitting around in a circle of camping chairs in a new friend's front yard, the ring of sunburned faces feeling like family. As the campfire died down, we slowly retreated to our campers and air mattresses, eager to sleep hard and find some more adventures tomorrow. **RM**

TOOLKIT

Start // Western border of Iowa (city determined each year)
End // Eastern border of Iowa
Distance // Roughly 435 miles (700km)
Getting there // Fly into Des Moines or Omaha (depending on which is closer to the starting city) and hop on a bus chartered by the start city to the beginning of the ride.
When to ride // Mid-July. It's hot and sunny, but pack for a few summer showers, just in case.
Where to stay // Host housing is available, as is camping, or ride-supported camping.
What to take // A support driver: if your group takes turns driving, it's feasible to bring a camper or van with everyone's gear and luggage rather than carrying it all by bike.
Tip // You don't have to commit to the whole week! Even riding a few days will give you the Midwestern experience.

Opposite: the AIDS/Lifecycle reaches Paso Robles

MORE LIKE THIS ORGANIZED MULTI-DAY ROAD RIDES

AIDS/LIFECYCLE, CALIFORNIA

The AIDS/Lifecycle is a seven-day charity ride down the coast of California. There's a fundraising minimum of $3000 per rider, many of whom choose to train and fundraise in teams for the support and camaraderie. The playful vibe of the ride is welcoming and inclusive for riders from all walks of life. It's sponsored by the Los Angeles LBGT Center and the San Francisco AIDS Foundation – all proceeds go to these organizations. Riders spend each evening at 'tent city,' set up by volunteers. There are showers and meals available for all riders at designated sites all week. This is a fully supported ride with rest stops every 14 to 20 miles (22–30km) over the daily distance of about 75 miles (120km).
Start // San Francisco
End // Los Angeles
Distance // 545 miles (877km) over seven days

JAMAICAN REGGAE RIDE

Escape to a warm, tropical island for a week and explore the western side of the island of Jamaica. Hosted by the Cycle Caribbean organization, this ride offers a fully escorted tour through fishing villages, past pristine beaches and coconut plantations. The route crosses rolling hills along the west and northern coast of Jamaica, covering 50 to 60 miles (80–95km) a day. Post-ride, you have the afternoons to explore the beaches, local farmers markets and restaurants. On the final day of the ride, participants have the option to visit Dunns River Falls and climb the 660ft (200m) gently sloping waterfall. This fully supported trip provides riders with airport transportation, lodging, food, SAG and luggage transit, official tour guides, and a police escort along the route.
Start // Negril
End // Ocho Rios
Distance // 168 miles (270km) over three days

RIDE THE ROCKIES COLORADO BICYCLE TOUR

This mountainous adventure offers some serious climbing – up to 6000ft (1800m) of elevation gain per day. Pedal through green meadows and over snowy peaks as you make your way through the Rocky Mountains of northwestern Colorado. Aid stations are available along the route in scenic locations, with free support as well as food vendors. A notable element that makes this ride especially challenging is the altitude. The ride takes place between 6000 and 12,000ft above sea level. Lower oxygen levels in the air can be managed by maintaining a slower, steady pace and staying hydrated. Ride organizers provide week-long parking and luggage shuttling, as well as free camping space and discounted hotel booking in adorable mountain towns.
Start/End // Route varies (decided in late winter each year)
Distance // About 400–450 miles (650–725km) over six days

AIDS/LifeCycle

MAINE'S EAST COAST GREENWAY

The ECG expertly guides riders through town and country, including one of the Eastern Seaboard's best off-road wilderness trails – and there are big plans for more.

The magic of long-distance cycle touring captured my imagination the summer after I turned 16. That was when my parents trusted me to make my first solo bike adventure – a month-long spin in New England. The final leg was a 150-mile pedal from Maine's southern tip to our Midcoast home near Belfast. All those years ago, I used Coastal Rte 1, already then a busy summer thoroughfare. As a practiced Maine hand, I knew to expect tough hills and town traffic, since Rte 1 paralleled the up-and-down shoreline and passed directly through maritime communities that were attracting more and more holidaymakers. But I loved the rolling landscapes, the sea-centred villages wrapped around their working wharves and the weatherworn old-timers who paused to ask, with genuine interest, where you were headed before spinning a yarn about how quickly Maine was changing.

Several decades later and a few years out of the saddle, I hatched the idea of a new biking beginning by revisiting my first epic ride in Maine and recapturing that sense of place and self-propelled

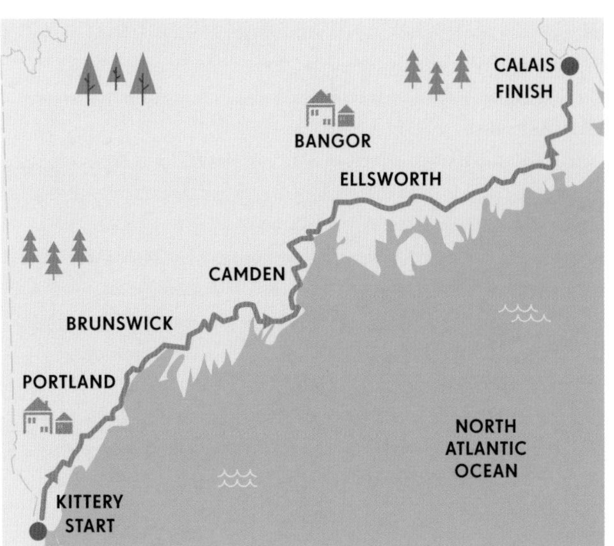

© East Coast Greenway Alliance photo

travel magic. There would, however, be one big difference: instead of battling holiday congestion along Rte 1, I'd commit to a newer, bike-friendly boulevard – the East Coast Greenway (ECG).

I was thrilled right from the start, as the terrain of southern Maine immediately set the tone for the rest of the trip: a delightful mix of the usually unbusy, well-paved back roads in small urban concentrations like Biddeford and Saco, green-lawned suburban villages full of typical clapboard houses, and lengthy rural plunges along forests and fields dotted with working farms. These fit around two shaded and gently graded rail trails of hardpacked earth leading across woodlands and wetlands, such as Maine's largest saltwater marsh at Scarborough.

To make the route even more enticing, the ECG in Maine is generously signposted; there's little need to consult maps at every turn. Leaving Kittery, the way markers are even paired with those of the Eastern Trail (ET) and US Bike Route 1 (USBR1). The ECG actually follows the ET, a 65-mile course with 22 off-road miles, all the way to South Portland. (USBR1 is another in-the-works Florida-to-Maine cycle passage, albeit one that is entirely on-road; it regularly intersects the ECG.)

A lot of this I already knew. I'd been reading about the full ECG, a 3,000-mile, multiuse trail system tracing the length of the Eastern Seaboard between Key West in Florida and Calais on the Canadian border in Maine. I was wowed by the resourceful nonprofit push of the East Coast Greenway Alliance to identify existing off-road paths – mostly municipal, county and state-owned rail trails – and stitch them together with two-wheel-tolerant, on-road routes selected for their traffic levels and speeds, shoulder widths and/or pavement quality, to complete the end-to-end connectivity.

This was on my mind as I slipped effortlessly into the city of Portland, Maine's largest. The ECG deliberately aims for major population centres, to connect people to them and vice versa. In fact, once in a metropolis, the routing adopts city cycling infrastructure, such as Portland's waterside Eastern Promenade, to cut through its busy, well-resourced and cultured core. This also helps with pacing. I planned for an average of about 60 miles a day, but with so many towns along the way, longer and shorter distances are easily possible.

Beyond Portland, I resumed riding on secondary suburban and rural roads, rising to hilltop pastures or timberland and dipping back down to cosy coastal inlets. Many of the byways were signed as local bike routes with large posted reminders to drivers that Maine law requires them to leave 3ft of space when passing cyclists. I rarely felt at risk.

In the pretty college town of Brunswick, I had to choose between the inland ECG 'spine' route or the coastal 'complementary' one. The inland incursion promised riverside rides, with traffic-free segments paralleling the Androscoggin and Kennebec rivers, not to mention the lure of cities like Lewiston, Augusta and Bangor. But

A CAR-FREE ECG?

The ECG Alliance is building new off-road segments at an average cost of $1 million per mile. More than 940 miles are on protected paths today, but the goal is to make it all car-free, even as it traverses 450 communities in 15 states (plus Washington DC) and within 5 miles of 25 million people. Incredibly, the ECG is arguably the most ambitious infrastructure project in the US.

Left to right: the Swinging Bridge across the Androscoggin River near Brunswick; a street in Portland, Maine. Previous page: the Bug Light on Portland's breakwater; the Down East Sunrise Trail

I stayed true to my youthful itinerary and took the seaside swing.

Away from the 'spine' route, however, three things happened: the challenging hills of Midcoast Maine really kicked in, while the off-road respites and ECG signage disappeared, obliging greater reliance on the ECG Alliance's (excellent) web-based mapping tool, which can be adapted for use on mobile platforms. I ended up making frequent map-check stops, embracing the need to be sure of the way as a perfect excuse for pausing between climbs.

None of this dampened my enjoyment of rolling – panting and sweating! – through gorgeous green country and noteworthy towns: Bath and its memorable architecture; art-rich Rockland, home of the Farnsworth Art Museum; touristy Camden and its windjammer-filled harbour; and historic, maritime Belfast and Searsport.

The ECG's two routes merge at Bucksport, shortly after which, in Ellsworth, the 85-mile Down East Sunrise Trail begins. At present best suited to fat tires and self-sufficient bikers, this off-road traverse of Downeast Maine's thick forests, salmon rivers and scenic national wildlife lands (keep an eye out for moose) is considered to be the most spectacular wilderness on the ECG.

In Calais, facing the Canadian border and the final yards of the ECG, it was the sense of new beginnings rather than endings that bubbled up in my mind. After about 350 miles in Maine, including more than 130 miles (at current count) of protected greenway, I was ready to do as Forrest Gump had done: turn around and head for Florida. Only 3000 miles to go! **EG**

TOOLKIT

Start // Kittery, Maine
End // Calais, Maine
Distance // 367 miles (590km) on inland 'spine' route or 332 miles (534km) on coastal 'complementary' route
Getting there // Kittery is just across the Piscataqua River from Portsmouth, New Hampshire, which is accessible by car and coach from airport, train and bus terminals in Portland, Maine, and Boston, Massachusetts.
Where to stay/eat // Along the Maine ECG, there is no shortage of markets, restaurants, campgrounds and hotels, though lodging should be booked ahead in high season.
When to ride // May through October is the best season for cycling. Summer months tend to be warmer and drier, while autumn is especially beautiful when the foliage changes color.
More info // For maps, cue sheets and other ECG details, see www.greenway.org/states/maine

Opposite: autumnal birch trees in Acadia National Park

MORE LIKE THIS
COASTAL NEW ENGLAND RIDES

CADILLAC CHALLENGE LOOP, MAINE

Mt Desert Island is home to Acadia National Park, beloved for its gorgeous and dramatic nature: high and rocky Atlantic coast headlands and seven peaks above 1000ft (305m). This alone conveys what's in store for a lengthy ride around the island, complete with a circuit of the 27-mile (43km) Park Loop Rd and climb to breath-taking summit views from the 1530ft (466m) Cadillac Mountain – this is the first place in the US to spy the sunrise (in the fall and winter). For more than 35 years, the Cadillac Challenge Century, a free organized rain-or-shine ride held on the first Sunday in October, takes this all in, surrounded by the changing colors of fall foliage. Also, ask ahead if the park will have its mid-spring Bike in Acadia month that keeps roads closed to motorized vehicles.
Start/End // Bar Harbor
Distance // 100 miles (161km)
Info // www.cadillac challengecentury.com

CAPE COD RAIL TRAIL, MASSACHUSETTS

Cape Cod is that crooked curlicue of Massachusetts reaching east into the Atlantic Ocean. Largely low-lying and fringed by pristine sandy beaches, including the protected 40-mile-long (64km) stretch of Cape Cod National Seashore, it is a very popular summer holiday destination. And, to the great satisfaction of outdoor sports folk, the Cape Cod Rail Trail slices right through the middle of it on an old, converted railroad right of way. Designed as a multiuse path, with a well-graded and smooth surface, it is a favorite of walkers, runners, skaters and cyclists eager to burn some calories without getting scorched by vehicular traffic. Bike shops set right on the trail in Yarmouth, Dennis, Brewster, Orleans and Wellfleet promise service and rentals for all would-be two-wheelers without equipment.
Start // South Yarmouth
End // Wellfleet
Distance // 25 miles (40km)
Info // www.capecodbikeguide.com/ railtrail.asp

WESTERLY TO WATCH HILL, RHODE ISLAND

Tucked into a coastal corner of New England, Rhode Island doesn't draw as much cycling attention as its larger neighbors, but it packs in plenty, especially for the smallest state in the US. One 50-mile (80km) route along rural roads well loved by the local Narragansett Bay Wheelmen club takes in the estates, estuaries and beaches of the southwest shores. Shortcuts along this loop can reduce the mileage a bit, but mean missing out on some of the most scenic and challenging parts, like the cove-line and oceanfront ride that includes views of Block Island Sound from the Watch Hill Coast Guard Station, or some lovely climbs in the hills overlooking the Pawcatuck River. For more details about this ride and others, visit the cycling club's website.
Start/End // Ashaway
Distance // 50 miles (80km)
Info // www.nbwclub.org

THE GREAT ALLEGHENY PASSAGE

Stitch together two trails that connect Pittsburgh to the nation's capital for a beautiful, if occasionally bumpy, trip through time.

Somewhere between Dam No. 5 and Williamsport, Maryland, the day began to unravel. The downed trees we'd been encountering every so often along the storm-drenched C&O Canal path began hindering our progress more frequently. Then, amid navigating the obstacle course of branches, limbs and mud puddles, my 17-year-old son's back tire went flat.

This, of course, is part of what multiday, self-supported cycling trips are all about: breaking out the new tube, channeling your inner bike mechanic and soldiering on. But, on this day, the mosquitoes along the C&O – a towpath built in the 1800s for mules to pull cargo boats down the Cumberland & Ohio Canal – proved relentless. What ensued was a sort-of 'Three Stooges' episode, with my wife showering all three of us with bug spray as the kid and I frantically tried to fix the flat.

We managed to get the job done.

Only to see the same tire deflate two miles down the road. (More on that later.)

So went the trickiest day of our trip down the C&O and then the much smoother Great Allegheny Passage Trail. Together, the paths make for a doable yet still challenging 335-mile trip that connects Pittsburgh to Washington, DC.

It's easy to see why people brave hungry mosquitoes, unexpected downpours and, at times, bumpy terrain to ride the C&O and GAP. Besides the sound of rushing rapids, smell of honeysuckle and sight of towering trees, the ride is a trip through time. Along the way, you can visit a French and Indian War fort, Colonial and Civil War sites and towns built on the infrastructural ingenuity of days gone by.

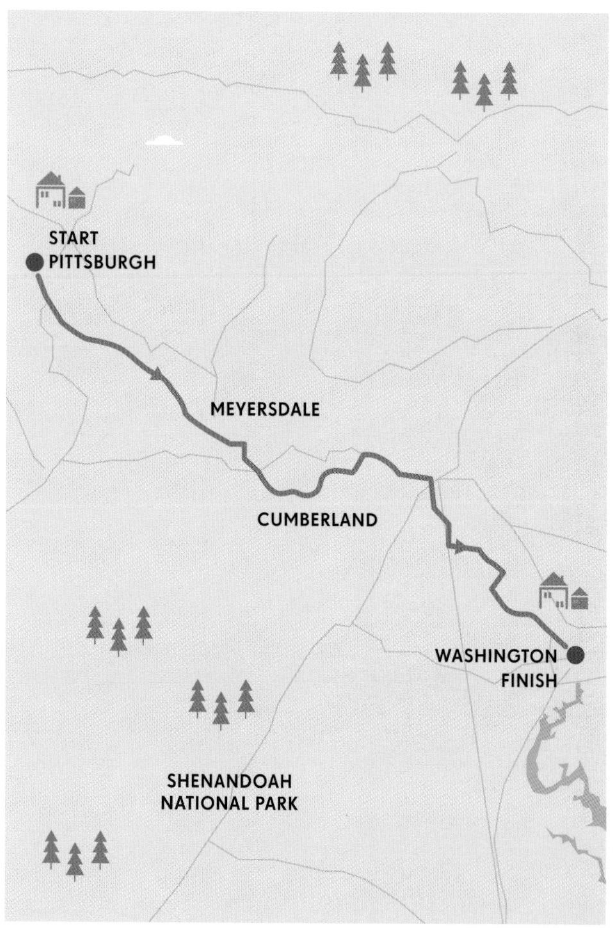

Logistics dictated the starting point for our GAP-C&O journey: We live in Chicago – a roughly eight-hour drive to Pittsburgh. From there, we left our car, hooked our panniers to our racks and set out for six days of cycling, staying along the way in B&Bs we'd reserved weeks in advance. The goal was to end up in the nation's capital, where we'd rent a minivan to drive back to the Steel City. (Amtrak is an option, but the limited number of bike spaces on the train had filled up fast.) Along the way, we'd encounter all kinds of cyclists, from hard-core adventurers who camped every night to easygoing folks who rented their bikes and hired shuttles to schlep their luggage from town to town.

The GAP's western terminus, Point State Park – where the Allegheny, Monongahela and Ohio rivers converge – gives way to a paved trail that leads past historic bridges, warehouses-turned-tech offices and the 12 towering smokestacks left from Homestead Works, once the world's largest steel-producing plant and now a shopping center. From there, the trail turns to crushed limestone, much of it pristinely maintained by volunteers.

On the first day of our mid-June trip, the Mon/Yough Trail Council – a group that oversees a 15-mile section of the GAP – treated dozens of riders, including us, to a free 'Trail Appreciation Day' hot dog lunch in Boston, 20 miles down the trail from Pittsburgh. We climbed gradually over the next three days on the old rail trail toward the Eastern Continental Divide, often hearing trains, but not seeing them, like ghosts of the past, amid the lush green landscape. In Ohiopyle State Park, we lingered on the long bridges over the Youghiogheny River, admiring the kayakers and white-water rafters taking on the river's rapids.

The highlight of our trip? Our shortest day, in which we rode 34 miles – most of them downhill – from Meyersdale, Pennsylvania, over the Eastern Continental Divide (water at this point flows to the Gulf of Mexico on one side and the Atlantic Ocean on the other), through Big Savage tunnel (at 3295ft long, the name fits) and then past the Mason-Dixon Line to Cumberland, Maryland.

Cumberland – home of the Whiskey Rebellion that gave President George Washington fits in the 1790s – marks the transition point from rail trail limestone to the dirt-and-rock buffet that is the C&O, maintained by the National Park Service. While the surface makes for rougher going, the scenery and wildlife don't disappoint; we saw turtles of all sizes, deer, herons and even an owl. The ride through Paw Paw tunnel, *only* 3118ft long, is truly a 'light at the end' experience, with a paradise of waterfalls, greenery and crystal blue skies greeting us once we emerged.

The C&O follows the Potomac, as well as the borders of West Virginia and Virginia, en route to Washington, DC. We spent the

"In Ohiopyle State Park, we lingered on bridges over the Youghiogheny River, admiring the kayakers"

penultimate night of our journey in Harpers Ferry, West Virginia – the midway point of the Appalachian Trail – in a B&B where Major Gen. Thomas 'Stonewall' Jackson holed up during the Civil War.

Speaking of war, that journey to Harpers Ferry came on the day with the aforementioned flat tires and mosquitoes.

After walking the kid's bike into Williamsport, we spotted the tiny, sharp rock that had ripped the hole in his tube and Kevlar-lined tire. Problem identified, we patched things up, bought another tube from a friendly cyclist (no bike shop in town) and made our way to Shepherdstown (a handsome historic town that's worth a few hours of your time in any case) to get things fixed for good.

When we pulled into Georgetown on day six, we splurged on a historic row house B&B not far from mile marker 0, which is tucked a short distance away from where the path ends. It took watching a YouTube video for us to find it – but there wasn't a mosquito in sight. **CF**

FALLINGWATER

One of Frank Lloyd Wright's architectural gems, Fallingwater was completed in 1939, and lies four miles off the GAP, near Ohiopyle. But visiting the famous house – which, yes, is built over a waterfall – takes some advance planning. Reservations to tour the place are highly recommended, but the road there is steep and narrow. For tour information, go to www.fallingwater.org. Wilderness Voyagers, just off the trail in Ohiopyle, shuttles cyclists up to Fallingwater for a fee.

Left to right: Fallingwater by Frank Lloyd Wright; bridge over the Youghiogheny River; Civil War cannons on Doubleday Hill; a rail trail bridge on the GAP. Previous page: riding the GAP through Pennsylvania

TOOLKIT

Start // Pittsburgh
End // Washington, DC
Distance // 335 miles (539km)
Getting there // Drive, fly or take Amtrak to Pittsburgh. We found free street parking and left our car there without incident. For a more secure option, use a parking garage.
Where to stay // Campsites abound along both trails, including 30 free first-come, first-served hiker-biker sites on the C&O. We opted for B&Bs and inns in Connellsville and Meyersdale in Pennsylvania; Cumberland and Hancock in Maryland, and Harpers Ferry, West Virginia.
What to read // The 240-page GAP-C&O 'TrailGuide,' which includes a pull-out map of both paths and information about bike rentals and tours. Get it at www.gaptrailstore.org.

Opposite: the NKP-765 locomotive on the Cuyahoga Valley Scenic Railroad

MORE LIKE THIS CANAL RIDES

ERIE CANALWAY TRAIL, NEW YORK

Want a GAP and C&O-like experience in the Empire State? The Erie Canalway fits that bill, though cyclists have to do a little road riding to complete the full trip between Albany and Buffalo; more than three-quarters of this 365-mile (587km) ride are on trails, most of them crushed stone, with the rest on streets. Built in the 1820s, the canal connects the Hudson River to Lake Erie, which made it a catalyst for America's westward expansion. Scenic highlights include the section between Syracuse and Little Falls, sandwiched between the Adirondack Mountains to the north and the Catskill Mountains to the south. Historical stop offs include Seneca Falls, birthplace of the women's rights movement.

Start // Albany
End // Buffalo
Distance // 365 miles (587km)
Info // www.eriecanalway.org, ptny.org/cycle-the-erie-canal

OHIO & ERIE CANAL TOWPATH TRAIL, OHIO

Constructed between 1825 and 1832, the Ohio & Erie is credited with opening up Ohio to the rest of the eastern US by connecting Cleveland, along Lake Erie, to Portsmouth, along the Ohio River. Today, this 101-mile (163km) trail through the Cuyahoga River Valley – 87 miles (140km) of it on dedicated pathways, 14 miles (23km) on roads – takes cyclists through a mix of forests, fields and wetlands. Want to experience a section of the trail two different ways? Ride it one way and return by train using the Cuyahoga Valley Scenic Railroad's 'Bike Aboard' service. For train information, visit www.cvsr.com.

Start // Cleveland
End // New Philadelphia
Distance // 101 miles (163km)
Info // www.ohioanderiecanalway.com/activities/biking/

I&M CANAL TRAIL, ILLINOIS

The Illinois & Michigan Canal created the first water route between the East Coast and Gulf of Mexico by connecting Lake Michigan to the Illinois and Mississippi rivers. The trail next to it begins on pavement in the Chicago area and turns to crushed limestone further southwest. If you're staying in downtown Chicago, take a Metra Heritage Corridor train to Willow Springs to begin the ride, then use both the I&M and Centennial trails to pass through the Waterfall Glen Forest Preserve and under the towering Veterans Memorial Tollway bridge. In Lockport, visit the Gaylord Building, a restored limestone warehouse from the 1830s. Continuing south, pass through the Joliet Iron Works Historic Site and follow roads through the city of Joliet. After that, it's 61 miles (98km) of mostly smooth, state-maintained towpath along the canal. Camping and lodging are available at towns along the way, including Ottawa, home of the first of the famous debates between Abraham Lincoln and Stephen Douglas as they vied for the Senate seat of Illinois.

Start // Willow Springs
End // LaSalle-Peru
Distance // 85 miles (137km)
Info // www.dnr.illinois.gov/recreation/greenwaysandtrails/Pages/IMCanal.aspx

765
765
765

THE MINUTEMAN BIKEWAY

Play Paul Revere on a ride from Boston's northern outskirts to Lexington – scene of the first battle of America's Revolutionary War – along the Minuteman Bikeway.

It's not every day you come face to face with a national hero. But in suburban Massachusetts I eyeballed two of them, just a hop and a skip apart. Or, more accurately a push and a pedal – because cycling's the way to do it.

There's a clue to the heritage of my route in the name. The Minuteman Bikeway snakes 11 miles between the outskirts of Boston and a disused railroad depot at Bedford, tracing – roughly speaking – the route taken by Paul Revere on his famous night ride of 18 April 1775. But though patriotically named for the best-trained Colonial militia – ready at a moment's notice to take arms against oppressive British redcoats – this isn't a Disney-fied tourist route, but a popular commuter cycle path. It's also the perfect way to access some of the most important historic sites in the area during a Boston city break, so I rented a bike and grabbed a map for the relaxing half-day ride.

Having braved the city's morning rush hour, at Boston Common I joined the blissfully traffic-free cycle path west along the Charles River, the shouts of coxes berating college rowing crews drifting across the water. Through Harvard Sq and on to Belmont I zigzagged through quiet back roads and among the beautifully restored wetlands of the Alewife Brook Reservation to northern Cambridge.

A granite column marking the bikeway's terminus is etched with alewifes, reflecting this spot's traditional name. I felt a pang of disappointment: I'd pictured an exuberant tavern-keeper's partner, sloshing foaming flagons. But no: an alewife – pronounced more like 'all-wuff' – is a tiny fish found in the nearby Mystic River. No matter. The road to independence beckoned.

In fact, the bikeway's genesis was revolutionary in more ways than one. This tarmac ribbon replaced the former Boston–Lexington railroad; after it was mothballed in the late 1970s, local activists battled to transform the route into today's cycle trail, opened in 1992. The Minuteman project was at the vanguard of the Rails-to-Trails Conservancy, a movement formally created in 1986 that backs communities across the US working to convert disused lines.

As I trundled past the monolithic milepost I thought of Revere and his nocturnal mission to warn Lexington and Concord's rebel militia of the arrival of the British. And almost immediately a reminder of another, less well-known episode of that crucial night appeared at Spy Pond. In the 19th century, before modern

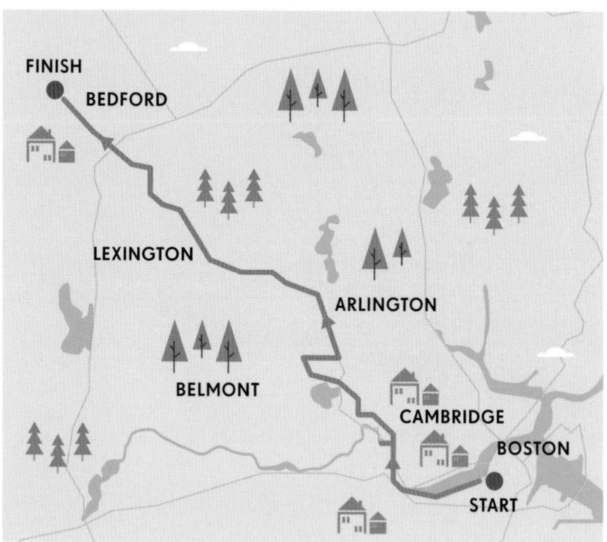

Scenes from the American Revolutionary War, clockwise from right: Captain William Smith's home on Battle Rd between Lexington and Concord; a reenactment with Redcoats in Lexington; the statue of Paul Revere in Lexington

refrigeration, ice was harvested commercially here, and today it's a popular ice-skating venue. But on 19 April 1775 it was just a country lake, where Mother Batherwick was out gathering dandelions – or so a signboard here proclaims – when she spotted British soldiers retreating from Lexington. Far from fleeing, the bumptious old woman took them prisoner – quite how, the board doesn't say. But among the clapboard houses and swaying trees shedding their autumn foliage, it added fascinating detail to my burgeoning picture of that momentous day.

Just a couple more minutes' pedaling brought me to Arlington and the steely – or, rather, bronze-y – gaze of Hero Number One: Uncle Sam. Yes, the Uncle Sam, or so his hometown claims: Samuel Wilson, a merchant born here in Arlington, won renown supplying the US army during another war against the British in 1812. His statue doesn't look much like the goateed fellow on the recruitment posters – but then it's debatable whether he truly was the inspiration for the national figurehead.

I doffed my bike helmet respectfully, just in case, and scooted onwards, past the brown timber walls of the Old Schwamb Mill – the country's oldest continuously operating mill site, where wood has been shaped since around 1650 – and on to Arlington's Great Meadows, roughly halfway along the trail. Pausing in the shade of a tree bedecked with flaming fall hues, I listened to a cricket chirping its final song of summer. Boston – and thoughts of war – seemed a long way distant.

The bikeway skirts around the centre of Lexington, and I decided to save that treat for later, pushing on for another half hour to Bedford. At the official end of the Minuteman sits gleaming railcar No 6211, a restored 1950s relic of the Boston and Maine Railroad and a reminder of the web of railway lines that once radiated out from Boston. Today most are silent – except, on some at least, for the whirr of pedals and bike chains.

Content to have completed the trail, I returned to Lexington to delve a little more into the events of 1775. For a spot with such a momentous historic legacy, Lexington is a pleasantly understated town. I scooted past vintage houses studding its wide streets, spotting the Buckman Tavern, mustering point of the militia on that memorable April morning, and the 1698 Hancock-Clarke Parsonage, where Revere warned Samuel Adams of the approaching British regulars.

At Battle Green, site of the fateful skirmish, I stood in the shadow of Hero Number Two: Captain John Parker, tall on his rocky plinth, clasping his rifle ready to defend his hometown. It was Parker who led the local militia in their stand, losing his cousin and seven other rebels to redcoat arms in the first battle of the American Revolutionary War.

There's something apt about arriving at Lexington, like Revere, on a saddle rather than a car or bus seat. It might not be the most dramatic ride, nor the most challenging, but the Minuteman provides a journey into the past – an exhilarating way to explore the history of Massachusetts' insurrectionary forebears. **PB**

WHERE DID WAR REALLY START?

Ralph Waldo Emerson claimed the shot signalling the start of America's Revolutionary War was fired at the North Bridge in Concord. Residents of Lexington, 6 miles east, counter it was earlier, on their Battle Green, when militia briefly fought British regulars. Consider both sides: cycle to Concord along the unsealed Battle Road Trail from Lexington (or the Reformatory Branch Trail from Bedford), or catch the Liberty Ride trolleybus.

Previous page: Harvard University in Cambridge, Massachusetts

TOOLKIT

Start // Alewife Station, North Cambridge, Massachusetts
End // Bedford Depot Park/South St, Massachusetts
Distance // 10.5 miles (17km)
Getting there // Alewife 'T' Station is on the red subway line. www.mbta.com
Bike rental // Urban Adventours (www.urbanadventours.com) rents out hybrid bikes. Lexington's Ride Studio Cafe (www.ridestudiocafe.com) provides bikes, parts, advice and great coffee.
Where to stay // The Inn at Hastings Park (www.innathastingspark.com) is a boutique hotel with terrific food, close to Lexington's Battle Green.
When to ride // The trail is open year-round; it's snow-ploughed in winters.
More information // www.minutemanbikeway.org

Opposite: the Kelly Creek Trestle Bridge on the Route of the Hiawatha

MORE LIKE THIS
HISTORY TRAILS

LEWIS AND CLARK TRAIL

Nobody expects you to ride the full 3000 miles (4828km) of the path taken by the pioneer Captains Meriwether Lewis and William Clark. After all, it took their expedition more than two years to get from Illinois to Oregon: they didn't have the benefit of the Adventure Cycling Association's superbly plotted route guide and navigational resources. This route for bike riders follows the expedition's route as closely as possible, bearing in mind Lewis and Clark paddled along the Missouri, Columbia and Yellowstone Rivers. Due to the desire for historical accuracy, the route has some challenging sections, including roads without shoulders, unsurfaced tracks and sometimes more than 100 miles (160km) between stops. May to September is the best time to ride and it could take up to three months in total. The reward will be experiencing this historic journey and stopping at such sites as the Lewis and Clark National Historic Trail Interpretative Center in Great Falls, Montana.
Start // Hartford, Illinois
End // Seaside, Oregon
Distance // 3126 miles (5030km)
Info // www.adventurecycling.org

ROUTE OF THE HIAWATHA

Mind the bears! In winter this 15 mile (24km) rail trail closes because hibernating bears hole up in the tunnels. With 10 long tunnels, including the 1.6-mile (2.5km) Taft Tunnel, this family-friendly rail trail through the Bitterroot Mountains between Idaho and Montana is the perfect habitat for the cantankerous mammals. The Route of the Hiawatha is one of America's most scenic and historic rail trails, and features not only tunnels, but seven trestle bridges along its downhill route from the East Portal trailhead. Pair this excursion with the 73-mile (117km) rail trail the Coeur d'Alenes, which follows the route of the Union Pacific railroad across northern Idaho from Mullan, a mining town on the mountainous Montana border, to Plummer near the Washington border.
Start // Shuttles operate from the Lookout Pass Ski Area
End // The Coeur d'Alenes concludes at Plummer
Distance // 88 miles (142km)
Info // www.ridethehiawatha.com; www.friendsofcdatrails.org

THE UNDERGROUND RAILROAD

For African American slaves in the 19th century, the Underground Railroad was a ticket out of the slave-owning states of the South, bound north to the free states or what is now Canada. Although not one single route but rather a collection of sympathizers and safe houses, the Adventure Cycling Association has endeavored to memorialize the network by plotting a cycling trail that travels 2000 miles (3230km) from Mobile, Alabama, the port where many enslaved people first set foot on America, to Owen Sound, Ontario, once a rowdy port known as 'Little Liverpool.' The route passes by historic Civil War locations, before crossing the Ohio River, once regarded as the South's border with the free states to the north. You'll want to break the journey into sections because there are so many places to visit (in particular the National Underground Railroad Freedom Center in Cinncinnati) and so much to absorb.
Start // Mobile, Alabama
End // Owen Sound, Ontario
Distance // 2007 miles (3229km)
Info // www.adventurecycling.org

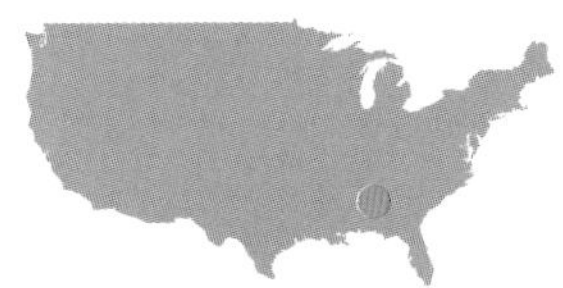

THE NATCHEZ TRACE PARKWAY

The Natchez Trace coasts through three southern states of America, with thousands of years of history beneath your wheels and the sounds of Elvis in your ears.

At the northern terminus of the Natchez Trace Parkway, a milepost sticks up like a thumb on the side of the road. For many bikers, the brown sign represents the final lap, an exclamation point punctuating a two-wheeled odyssey that started two states away in Mississippi. For southbound cyclists like me, however, the marker is just the beginning. 'Mile one,' I exclaim ceremoniously, translating the sign's three digits.

Over 10 days, I will pedal 444 miles from Nashville to Natchez, with a small wedge of Alabama in between. During my journey on the National Park Service road, I will roll through thousands of years of history, and not necessarily in order. I will follow in the footsteps of prehistoric giant sloths and Chickasaw tribes, Kaintucks (Ohio River farmers and boaters) and Elvis, and Civil War soldiers and Oprah.

During hours-long rides, I will share the two-lane paved road with a handful of cars and motorcycles (the maximum speed limit of 50mph deters rushed drivers), kindred spirits in padded shorts and helmets (peak season is autumn) and countless critters, including armadillos both dead and alive. And in and out of my saddle, I will experience southern traditions that touch all aspects of life, from grits to music to football.

The New Trace, a straight arrow that dates from 1936 and roughly parallels the original foot trail, is not as arduous as the Old Trace, a meandering dirt path studded with rocks and roots. Nor is it as perilous: the poisonous snakes, tribal attacks and bandits appear only in yellowed accounts.

But the communities are still dispersed like distant beacons. I have to watch the clock and my pace if I want to arrive at my

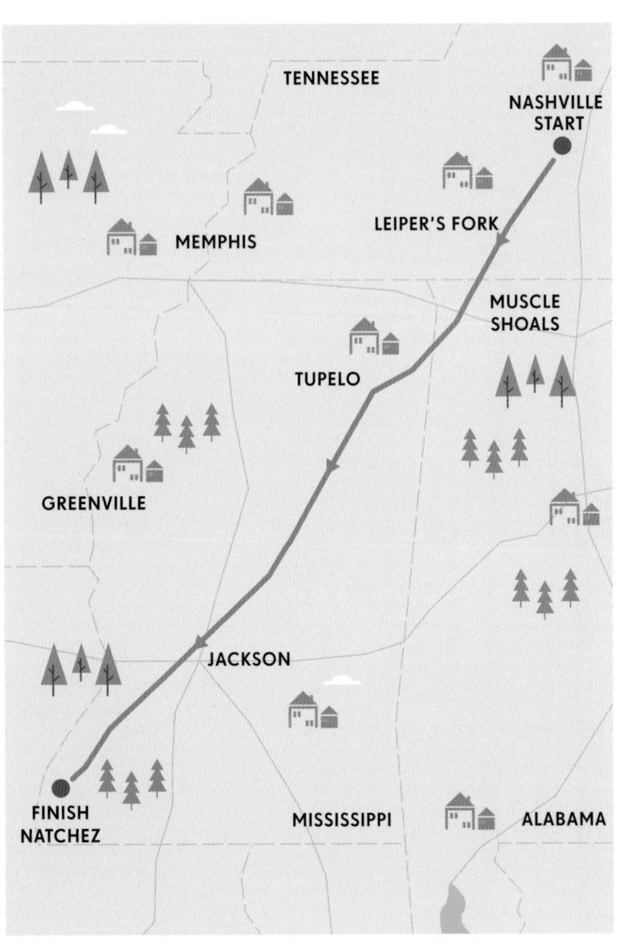

BETTY
BOOTS
BROADWAY
BREWHOUSE
&
MOJO

lodging before nightfall – or, in the case of Leiper's Fork, to catch open mic night at Puckett's Grocery & Restaurant.

The 19th-century village, about 15 miles from the Trace entrance in Tennessee, is a darling among Nashville stars (the Judds, Carrie Underwood) and troubadour musicians seeking an impromptu jam (Aerosmith bandmates). When I enter Puckett's, two young guitarists are electrifying the crowd with a Jimi Hendrix cover. I'm introduced to the unofficial mayor of Leiper's Fork, a towering gray-haired man in a baseball cap, named Goose.

'This is one of the prettiest parts of the country, especially on the Trace,' Goose yells into my ear, mentioning the maple and oak trees lining the parkway. He then directs my gaze to the stage, pointing to the keyboardist, who plays with Neil Sedaka, and the guitarist, who tours with Ted Nugent. He widens his sweep to point out Naomi Judd's husband and a CIA agent who I am supposed to forget as soon as I see her.

I don't have much time to ease into the Trace. The longest distance – 72 miles – falls on the second day. The Tennessee portion is the hilliest, slowing my speed and stretching my energy reserves. Informational placards and historic sites further impede my progress. At the Meriwether Lewis National Monument, I meet a New Orleans–bound skateboarder tending to his injuries after a crash and the Nashville couple who have been cheering me on with fist pumps through their sunroof. We discuss the rumor that Lewis, the famed explorer, died of syphilis. But the National Park refuses to gossip. An interpretive sign by a stone memorial elusively explains that his life 'came tragically and mysteriously to a close.'

"At FAME Recording Studios, an employee invites me inside Studio A, where Aretha Franklin cut two hits"

In Florence, at Milepost 338, a group of motorcyclists huddle around Tom Hendrix to hear the emotional tale of his great-great-grandmother. As a Yuchi girl, he explains, she was forced to leave her tribal land in Alabama for Indian Territory in present-day Oklahoma. She was restless, however, and reversed course. She spent five years searching for her way back home.

In the 1980s, Tom started to collect millions of pounds of rocks and to build the 1.5-mile-long Te-lah-nay's Wall to honor her life and spirit. The eastern portion runs in a direct line and represents the Trail of Tears; the western section sprawls in many directions, symbolizing her meandering return route.

Muscle Shoals, about 20 miles off the Trace in Alabama, is

THE HOME OF ELVIS

The birthplace of Elvis is the B-side of Graceland. In Tupelo you can visit the 15-acre park complex that houses both his humble childhood home and a museum of memorabilia. There's also the legendary Tupelo Hardware Company, which still sells tools and instruments. Inside the store, stand on a black X that marks the spot where the future rock 'n' roll star picked out his first guitar.

Left to right: FAME recording studios in Muscle Shoals, Alabama; Elvis's birthplace in Tupelo, Mississippi; riding the Natchez Trace Parkway; hanging out at open mic night at Puckett's Grocery, Leiper's Fork. Previous page: Nashville, capital city of country music

where some of the biggest names up and down the radio dial have recorded, such as Otis Redding, Etta James, Paul Simon, Bob Dylan, the Rolling Stones, and Band of Horses. At Muscle Shoals Sound Studio, a museum guide encourages me to shake a pair of maracas in the booth where Mick Jagger and Keith Richards belted out three songs on *Sticky Fingers*. A German tourist ducks into a sacred but still-operating space: the bathroom where Richards wrote 'Wild Horses.'

At FAME Recording Studios, an employee invites me inside Studio A, where Aretha Franklin cut two hits and Alicia Keys played the piano for the 2013 documentary film, *Muscle Shoals*. In Studio B, he tells me that Duane Allman once slept and performed here. For the next 60-odd miles to Tupelo, I have southern rock stuck in my head.

For 361 miles, I have biked solo. But one morning, I unexpectedly become a duo. A French-Canadian in striped long underwear sidles up next to me and strikes up a conversation that endures for more than 80 miles. We become a trio when a former turkey farmer from North Carolina joins us.

We count down the final distance together, with the French-Canadian throwing up his arm at significant intervals. At the 3-mile mark, I start to feel a mix of elation and deflation. At the last mile of Natchez, I pedal slower, savoring it as much as I did the first mile in Nashville. **AS**

TOOLKIT

Start // Nashville, Tennessee
End // Natchez, Mississippi
Distance // 444 miles (714.5km)
Getting there // From Natchez, the airports aren't that close. Alexandria (Louisiana), is 70 miles (113km) away; Baton Rouge (Louisiana) is 90 miles (145km). Catch a Greyhound bus to the start of your ride or rent an airport shuttle. Nearby bike shops can box and ship your wheels.
Where to stay // For overnight options, cyclists can pitch a tent at more than a dozen campgrounds, including several bicycle-only sites, or pedal into Collinwood, Tennessee; Florence, Alabama; and Houston and Kosciusko in Mississippi.
Where to eat // The Trace does not provide any food concessions beyond the rare vending machine at a rest stop. Pack meals in panniers.
More info // www.natcheztracetravel.com

Opposite: fall foliage on the Blue Ridge Parkway, viewed from Waterrock Knob

MORE LIKE THIS
ALL-AMERICAN RIDES

RAGBRAI, IOWA

Short for the Register's Annual Great Bicycle Ride Across Iowa, RAGBRAI connects the dots of small towns stretching from the western shores of the Missouri River to the eastern banks of the Mississippi River. The ride, held during the last full week of July, started in 1973 as a six-day excursion, and every year the organizers plot a new route, shuffling the eight host communities procured for overnight stops. Despite the changes, several constants persist: the course distance and the direction from west to east, to avoid strong headwinds and biking into the sun. The landscape highlights country life, with red barns, silos, and fields carpeted in corn, wheat and sunflowers. And, contrary to pancake jokes, your legs will learn that Iowa is not flat. Read a first-hand account on p186.
Start/End // Changes annually, with the itinerary released in late January (www.ragbai.com)
Distance // On average 468 miles (753km)
Info // www.ragbrai.com

BLUE RIDGE PARKWAY, VIRGINIA TO NORTH CAROLINA

The iconic Blue Ridge Parkway rises and falls like a roller coaster track running from Virginia's Shenandoah National Park to North Carolina's Great Smoky Mountains National Park. Most bikers budget about 10 days to complete the 469-mile (755km) route, which crosses four national forests and features 176 bridges, more than two dozen tunnels and hundreds of historic sites. Riders will experience the America that inspires patriotic songs: uninterrupted forests, burbling rivers, splashy waterfalls, vibrant wildflowers or foliage (depending on the season), and mountains haloed in clouds. Roadside diversions abound, such as the Blue Ridge Music Center, Julian Price Memorial Park and Craggy Gardens. Time your visit to Waterrock Knob to coincide with the sun's aerial spectacle.
Start // Shenandoah National Park near Waynesboro, Virginia
End // Great Smoky Mountains National Park near Cherokee, North Carolina
Distance // 469 miles (755km)

GREAT ALLEGHENY PASSAGE (GAP), MARYLAND TO PENNSYLVANIA

The chirps of bike bells have replaced the toots of train whistles that once rang through the corridors of the Great Allegheny Passage (GAP). The 150-mile (241km) biking and hiking trail (no cars allowed) sprang from mostly abandoned railbeds laid between Cumberland, Maryland and Pittsburgh, Pennsylvania. The trail is flat and leisurely, and coasts by some remarkable landmarks. On the 13-mile (21km) Frostburg–Meyersdale leg, for example, the wow list includes the Mason–Dixon Line into Pennsylvania; the 3295ft-long (1015m) Big Savage Tunnel, which was named after the stranded 18th-century surveyor who had offered himself up as food to save his men; the Eastern Continental Divide, the trail's highest point at 2390ft (728m); and the curved Keystone Viaduct. Charming towns such as Confluence, on the Youghiogheny River, and Ohiopyle, a hyperactive hub of outdoor activities, entice bikers to hop off and stay awhile. See the story on p198.
Start // Cumberland, Maryland
End // Pittsburgh, Pennsylvania
Distance // 150 miles (241km)

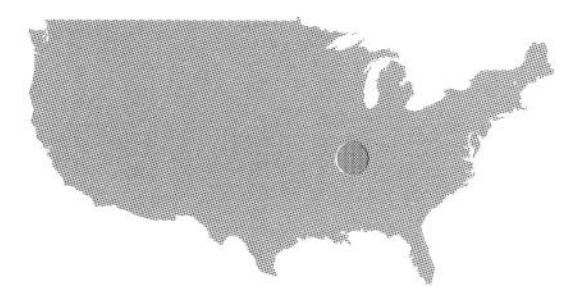

THE KATY TRAIL

Riverfront towns, limestone bluffs, and welcoming B&Bs greet cyclists in Lewis and Clark country on a week-long rails-to-trails journey through the middle of Missouri.

Our bikes' saddlebags stuffed with Spandex, sunscreen and other essentials, my husband and I ditched our car at the Amtrak parking lot in St Louis and pedaled to the Gateway Arch to start a week-long cycling trip heading west across Missouri's ample midriff.

As tourists craned their necks to marvel at the city's stainless steel landmark, we scanned the horizon searching for the St Louis Riverfront Trail. We knew that this ribbon of pavement skirting the Mississippi River would lead us to a patchwork of other paths that would eventually bring us to the real starting point of our two-wheeled adventure: the 238-mile-long Katy Trail, which is billed as the longest developed rail trail in the US.

Built on an abandoned stretch of the Missouri-Kansas-Texas (MKT) Railroad, aka the Katy, this car-free corridor passes through some of the Show-Me State's most show-off-worthy scenery. The trail bisects central Missouri as it weaves its way through Daniel Boone and Lewis and Clark country, past rolling farmland, forest, tallgrass prairie and a string of small towns that flourished during the railroad's glory days.

We biked the path for the first time in 2007 and liked it so much that we came back for seconds. But before we could officially embark on Katy 2.0, we had to get out of downtown St Louis to reach the trail proper.

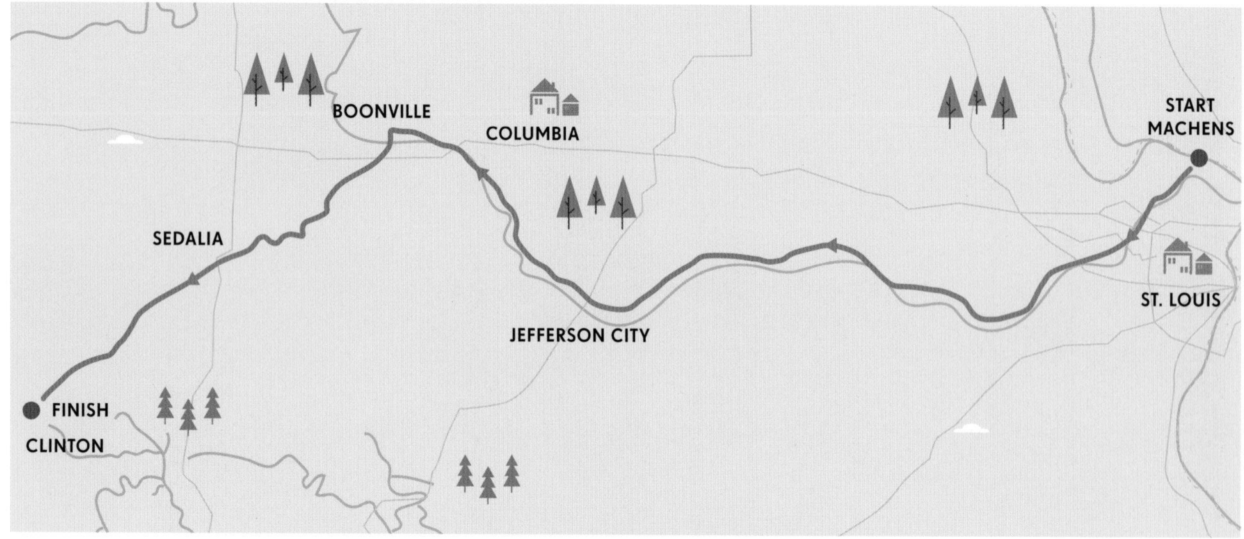

We asked a man standing in the Gateway Arch's shadow if he knew where we could find the riverfront path.

'Right there,' he said, pointing to the Mississippi, 'under the water.'

Turns out recent flooding had swallowed the trail – a problem that's since been remedied by new improvements to the Gateway Arch grounds. But this much-needed infrastructure fix was still in the future during our visit, forcing us to go off script and improvise a workaround to Mother Nature's monkey wrench.

Anyone who's taken enough long-distance bike rides knows that these kinds of hiccups – bad weather, flat tires and other unwelcome surprises – are part of the experience. They also know the experience is too rewarding to let a few roadblocks stand in their way, especially when it comes to something as special as the Katy.

The peaceful and bucolic trail largely follows the course of the Missouri River, with some of the most picturesque parts of the path flanked by massive limestone bluffs on one side and water on the other. Reminders of the once-almighty railroad are never far away, from the arched stone tunnel punched through the rock in the charming hamlet of Rocheport, to restored train depots that double as inviting pit stops.

The trail's crushed limestone surface is mostly flat, rendering it manageable for just about any cyclist. We met a seven-year-old and an octogenarian who were both tackling the entire route with their respective families.

The proximity of food and lodging along the Katy makes it ideal for a multi-day getaway, whether you're looking to camp (no thanks) or spend your nights in quaint B&Bs and historic hotels (yes please).

Cyclists constitute a good percentage of customers for the area's B&Bs, whose owners are used to dealing with their particular needs.

When we pulled up to the Lindenhof Bed & Breakfast in Augusta after a particularly hot day, the innkeeper greeted us with cold towels, ice water and a hose to clean our muddy bikes.

The owners of High Street Victorian B&B in Boonville helped do our laundry, fed us a breakfast big enough for the Tour de France peloton and sent us on our way with a bag full of homemade cookies.

We treated our tired muscles to a specially designed Katy Trail massage at Hermann Hill Vineyard Inn & Spa, perched on a bluff high above rows of Norton grapes.

In Sedalia, we stayed at the modest home of a grandmother named Maxine, who rents rooms in her house for $50 a night. Maxine did us a favor when we told her we were headed to dinner at Kehde's Barbeque (in a restored 1920 Pullman train car, and excellent) after 58 miles in the saddle. 'Take my car,' she insisted. 'I'm sure you don't want to get back on those bikes tonight.'

HEAD TO HERMANN

This quaint Missouri River town full of 19th-century brick buildings isn't on the Katy Trail but it's close enough – and cute enough – to merit a detour. Located about 3 miles from the trailhead in McKittrick (mile marker 100.8), Hermann has German heritage that's on display during its annual Oktoberfest celebration. But it's wine, not beer, that the area is best known for. Sample some along the Hermann Wine Trail.

Left to right: the Katy Trail runs between fields near Pilot Grove, Missouri; Hermann Hill Vineyard Inn & Spa; art by Catharine Magel adorns the St Louis Riverfront Trail. Previous page: the Missouri forest canopy above the Katy Trail

On our first go at the Katy in 2007, it took us four days to bike the entire trail. Rookie mistake. This time we tacked on an extra three days for more sightseeing and the aforementioned Mother Nature monkey wrenches, which came in the form of a washed-out section of trail and an obstacle course of fallen trees. As in St Louis, we dealt with these setbacks by finding alternative routes on the road.

Those extra few days also came in handy because Katy had grown since the last time we saw her. A 13-mile (21km) extension added in 2011 bumped the eastern terminus from the historic city of St Charles to a hard-to-find trailhead in rural Machens, roughly 30 miles north of St Louis' Gateway Arch (where we started riding). Unless you're a purist who insists on doing the whole trail nose-to-tail, you're better off sticking to the 190-mile stretch between St Charles and Sedalia, Amtrak's westernmost stop on the Katy.

I happen to be one of those annoying purists, which is why our last day of biking took us 39 miles southwest of Sedalia all the way to the end of the trail in Clinton, where we snapped a few selfies before doubling back to Sedalia.

After 357 miles of cycling over seven days, we wheeled our bikes aboard Amtrak's Missouri River Runner and rode the rails back to our waiting car in St Louis, content to give our legs a rest and let the train do the work. **LR**

TOOLKIT

Start // Machens, Missouri
End // Clinton, Missouri
Distance // 238 miles (383km)
Getting there // Fly, drive or take an Amtrak train to St Louis. From downtown, you can either bike or arrange for a shuttle to the trailhead in Machens (or nearby St Charles, which has more amenities). See www.bikekatytrail.com.
When to ride // Shoot for spring or fall; summer heat and humidity can be brutal.
Where to stay // Bed down in Rocheport (mile marker 178.3) in The Schoolhouse Bed and Breakfast, a 1914 school building that's now a listed 11-room B&B.
Go with a group // Missouri State Parks organizes a five-day Katy Trail Ride each June that includes most meals, camping sites, hot showers, luggage transport and other support for up to 350 participants; www.mostateparks.com.

Opposite: the statue of Ben Bikin' in Sparta, Wisconsin, proclaiming the town to be the 'Bicycling Capital of America'

MORE LIKE THIS MIDWEST RAIL-TRAIL RIDES

ELROY TO SPARTA, WISCONSIN

With a trio of rock tunnels, bucolic scenery and welcoming towns along the way, this path in southwest Wisconsin makes for an easily doable day's ride. In the world of rail trails, Elroy–Sparta ranks as an OG, an original gangster that claims to be the country's first rail trail. Its western terminus, Sparta, also claims to be the 'Bicycling Capital of America,' bragging rights that stem from the town's enviable location at the center of 101 miles (162km) of connected state trails. Three railroad tunnels, each dating to the 19th century, add some excitement to the journey. Inside, they're pitch-black and cool, even on the hottest of days. Bring a flashlight and jacket; you'll use both. The tunnels near the towns of Kendall and Wilton are about a quarter-mile long, but the one near Sparta spans nearly three-quarters of a mile. Don't feel like riding the trail twice? Shuttle service is available at both ends.

Start // Elroy
End // Sparta
Distance // 32 miles (51.5km)

ILLINOIS PRAIRIE PATH

Widely credited with getting the nation's rails-to-trails movement rolling, this pioneering path started with a humble letter to the editor that ran in the *Chicago Tribune* in 1963. Retired naturalist May Theilgaard Watts penned a proposal to turn the abandoned Chicago, Aurora and Elgin Railroad right of way into a nature path. That seed blossomed into what is now a Y-shaped trail network that feels worlds away from nearby Chicago. The bulk of the path stretches across DuPage County, where it passes through forest preserves and some charming suburbs like Glen Ellyn, brimming with boutiques, restaurants and cafes. Centrally located Wheaton is a good base to get on your bike and cruise along the mostly crushed-limestone path, taking one of the spurs west to the Fox River or all the way east to Forest Park.

Start // Wheaton
End // Aurora, Elgin or Forest Park
Distance // 62 miles (100km)

PERE MARQUETTE, MICHIGAN

This 30-mile (48km) stretch of smooth pavement in the middle of the mitten-shaped Lower Peninsula traces an old rail route from 1870 (not to be confused with the Pere Marquette State, but you can connect the two – see below). A quarter century ago, it was reborn as a recreational path measuring a roomy 14ft (4m) wide. Pine forests, farms and parks flank segments of the trail, dotted with former sawmill towns that thrived during the region's lumber boom. Make a stop at Sanford, where you can fuel up at one of the local eateries and get a taste of what life was like back in the day at the schoolhouse-turned-history museum. Want to keep pedaling? At the trail's west end in Clare, on-road bike lanes through town funnel you to the trailhead for Pere Marquette State Trail. This 53-mile (85km) expanse of asphalt and crushed stone goes all the way to Baldwin, an ideal base for canoeing and fishing.

Start // Midland
End // Clare
Distance // 30 miles (48km)

WELCOME TO SPARTA, WISCONSIN

GLACIER NATIONAL PARK LOOP

If you want wild, look no further: a four-day adventure into bear country, to crystal-clear lakes, all beneath the last remaining glaciers of the Northern Rocky Mountains.

It is not every day you can ride a 20-mile car-free dirt road through a National Park wilderness, to be rewarded with a Huckleberry Bear Claw pastry from a world-renowned bakery and a cooling swim in a glacial lake. These attractions, along with many others of the Glacier National Park Loop, keep luring me back to northern Montana.

The Glacier National Park Loop starts and ends in the town of Whitefish, Montana. With a rich history of timber and logging, Whitefish today serves as an adventure hub for those visiting its ski resort, the National Park, one of the many large lakes in the area, and more recently, the large network of flowing mountain-bike trails outside town. The Great Northern Railway runs through the center of Whitefish and, via Amtrak, delivers travelers from all over the country.

The loop follows gravel roads in the Whitefish Range, through the Kootenai and Flathead National Forests, as well as Glacier National Park. It's 105 miles (169km) and quite easygoing: I set aside four days and three nights, which allows time for a variety of scenic

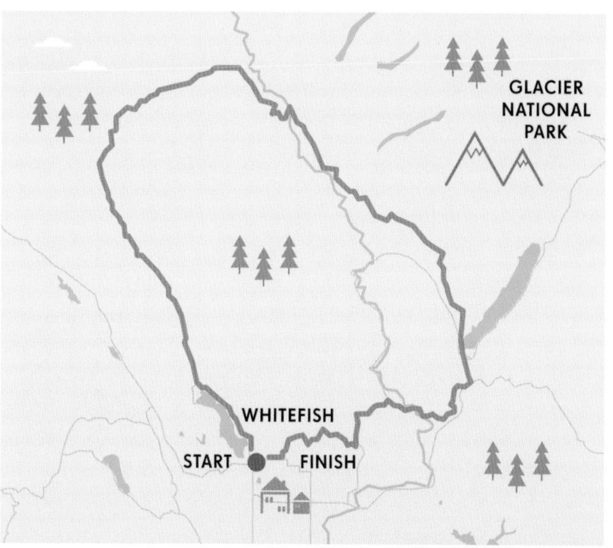

detours. Also consider the world-renowned climb up Going-to-the-Sun Road, about 60 miles round-trip from Apgar Campground: you'll ascend 4500ft over 30 miles, the reward being unparalleled views of the Rockies. (To keep traffic numbers manageable, the road is closed to cyclists at 11am so be sure to set off early – see p302.)

Having ridden this route in both directions, I prefer counter-clockwise, to enjoy the steep 30-mile descent from Red Meadow Pass down to Whitefish at the end of the ride. In this direction the route starts with a gradual transition from town to countryside and into the web of logging roads of the Flathead National Forest. From there the route drops into the North Fork Flathead River Valley before heading into Glacier National Park where cyclists can camp at one of the hiker-biker sites. Set up base camp and let the fun begin.

First essential task? A leap off the dock into the icy blue waters of Lake McDonald, at over 9 miles in length, the park's largest. There are no showers in the campgrounds so the lake is my bath – even though the water is shockingly cold, it's incredibly refreshing and the view of the surrounding Rocky Mountain peaks sure beats the one from my bath back home. What's next? A Huckleberry milkshake from the ice cream shack.

Back en route I meander my way through the park's maze of bike paths, gravel roads, and a stretch of singletrack until I reach the trailhead for the Inside North Fork Rd. This gravel byway has long since surrendered to Mother Nature. As a result, the National Park only allows hikers and bikers along it. This is certainly one of the wildest places I have ridden a bike. I have seen black bears and a grizzly bear while riding Inside North Fork, so my bear spray is at

GOING, GOING...

There are currently 25 glaciers within the bounds of Glacier National Park, but there were 150 in the mid-19th century. To further dramatize the extent and rate of global warming, it's estimated that within 10 or 15 years, none of these spectacular features will grace the upper slopes of the park's peaks: the so-called Crown of the Continent will soon be robbed of its jewels. So see them while you still can.

Clockwise from above: dirt roads are free from traffic, mostly; a pitstop for baked goods at Polebridge Mercantile; Bowman Lake. Previous page: St Mary's Lake in Glacier National Park

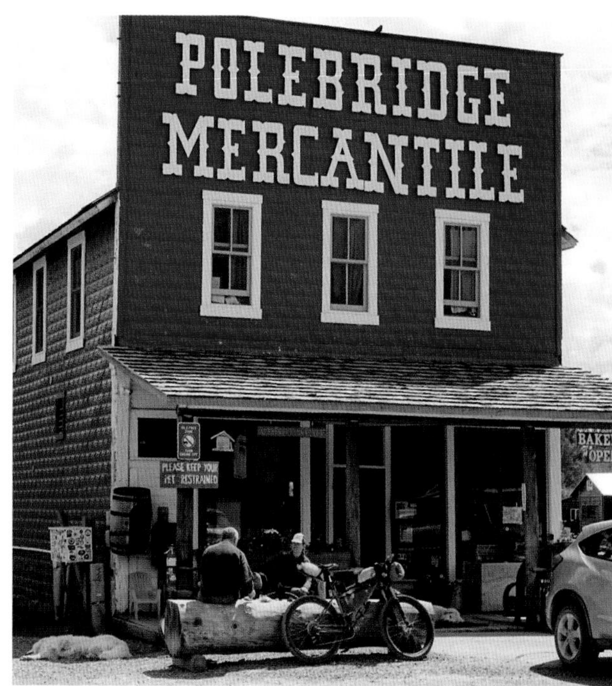

the ready and my portable Bluetooth stereo is busting out classic Cher. But any fear I have subsides as I settle into the rhythm and momentum of the rolling foothills through the old-growth ponderosa pine forests and watch new life emerge from the dead and burned ground. When the music isn't blasting, it's peaceful out here, and there are huckleberry, thimbleberry, and raspberry patches to be raided for roadside snacks. But I don't linger as any lush berry patches are bound to attract bigger, hairier visitors than me. Even through the gate at the end of the 20-mile wilderness stretch along the Inside North Fork Road, riding with the first cars I've seen in a while, I'm watching for bears.

But I don't let it worry me too much as I've a satellite mission to focus on, up to Bowman Lake. What awaits me? Yet another picture-postcard camping spot next to another bracingly cold, clear lake surrounded by imposing peaks. This park never fails to impress, and the following morning is one more reminder – where else can you awake in a wilderness and breakfast in a world-class bakery? In the morning I roll down to the 100-year old Polebridge Mercantile and take my time over one of their Huckleberry Bear Claws – and take one to go for the final climb and descent over Red Meadow Pass.

Although the climb is long, it is smooth and easy, offering grand views of the Northern Rocky Mountains. I know I'm at the top when I reach the Red Meadow Lake. I stop here to take in scenery that inspires paintings and one last swim before I make the final, fast 30-mile descent to town, clouds and rain rolling in behind me.

As I meander through a turn I stop dead in my tracks. A large white wolf is standing on the side of the road 20 yards ahead. I'm not scared – rather, it's a peaceful moment. Unfazed and in no hurry, the wolf walks into the trees and disappears into dense forest. **SS**

"A large white wolf is standing on the side of the road 20 yards ahead. I'm not scared – rather, it's a peaceful moment"

TOOLKIT

Start/End // Whitefish, Montana
Distance // 105 miles (169km)
Getting there // Kalispell City Airport is 20 miles (32km) from Whitefish; or take the Amtrak train to Whitefish.
What to take // GPS device, camping equipment, water filter, cookware, smell-proof bags, a battery charger, swimsuit, a bear bell, bug and bear spray.
Where to stay // Whitefish Hostel, camping in Glacier National Park and at Bowman Lake.
When to ride // mid-June through mid-October.
Permits // Call ahead for permits to pass through the Appleton-Whittell Research Ranch (+1-520-455-5522) and Babacomari Ranch (+1-520-455-5507).
More info // www.bikepacking.com/routes/red-meadow-pass

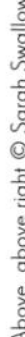
Above, above right © Sarah Swallow

Opposite: riding the Carriage Roads of Acadia National Park

MORE LIKE THIS NATIONAL PARK AND MONUMENT RIDES

GRAND STAIRCASE LOOP, UTAH

Take a trip two billion years into geological history and enjoy some of Southern Utah's most picturesque canyon country along the dirt roads of the Grand Staircase-Escalante National Monument and Glen Canyon National Recreation Area. Thanks to its sandstone cliffs and imposing rock monuments, the Grand Staircase Loop offers some of the most dynamic scenery in the American West. The loop is best completed clockwise during late fall and early spring. Being the high desert, expect warm sunny days and cold nights with the potential for strong winds. Do not attempt this route if rain is forecast: the porous dirt will turn to sodden clay within moments. There is one guaranteed water and food resupply at a gas station in Big Water (about halfway through the loop) so plan accordingly. Free permits are required to access the monument and can be attained at one of the many visitor centers surrounding the park.

Start/End // Escalante, Utah
Distance // 160 miles (257km)
Info // www.ridewithgps.com/routes/25324802

MT ST HELENS WEEKENDER, WASHINGTON

Mt St Helens is an active volcano located in southwest Washington that infamously erupted in 1980, leaving a barren wasteland in its wake. The Mt St Helens Epic Weekender is a 79-mile (127km) route that is best done in two to three days as it circumnavigates the volcano along a variety of mountain bike paths and singletrack trails, with a considerable amount of steep elevation gain. The loop starts and ends in Northwoods, Washington, a two-hour drive from Portland, Oregon or a three-hour drive from Seattle, Washington. On certain flanks of the volcano the devastation is still apparent, but there are both new growth and older forests to compensate, as well as scenic vistas of the Cascade Mountains, quiet alpine lakes, and refreshing waterfalls. Get the best out of the ride between mid-July and late September, or before snowfall. Mt St Helens is a National Monument and attracts many visitors during the summer months but riding this route you will hardly notice, as it follows paths the masses rarely reach.

Start/End // Northwoods, Washington
Distance // 79 miles (127km)
Info // www.ridewithgps.com/routes/15415625

ACADIA NATIONAL PARK, MAINE

The 27-mile (43km) Park Loop Road that circles Acadia National Park offers some of the most scenic interludes of any trip to the Northeast. The road was designed by landscape architect Frederick Law Olmsted Jr and built during the Great Depression of the 1930s by the Civilian Conservation Corps. Today it's a well surfaced but understandably busy route around the park. However, if you venture off the asphalt you'll discover Acadia's great gravel alternatives: the Carriage Roads, funded by philanthropist John D. Rockefeller and named for the horse-drawn carriages that would travel them. These sinuous routes lead to many of the park's ponds and lakes – top picks include the six-mile loop around the Eagle Lake and the climb up to Betty's Pond. Since the 1990s the Carriage Roads have been lovingly restored and, with bike rental readily available in Bar Harbor, they're a very accessible weekend of riding fun.

Distance // variable
Info // www.nps.gov

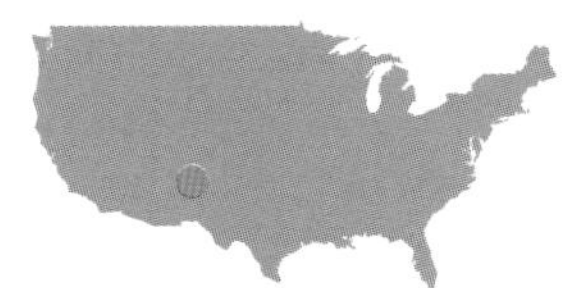

NEW MEXICO OFF-ROAD RUNNER

Running parallel to the Rio Grande, the New Mexico Off-Road Runner connects Santa Fe to Las Cruces via 500 history-packed miles of dirt, gravel, desert and paved roads.

New Mexico: the sun-patinated underdog to craggy, snow-capped Colorado. Or at least, that's how I've come to see it. Not that I mean to belittle it in any way, because New Mexico has a way of working its way under the skin. The mountains here are gentler. The high desert landscape softer. The light clearer. The border closer.

The Land of Enchantment, as it's so evocatively called, strikes a sublime blend of raw, natural beauty with historical intrigue, both of which take a touch more effort and imagination to unearth and unravel than in its neighbor. In doing so, a textured land is revealed, marked by both ponderosa forests and open desert, alligator junipers and prickly ocotillos, petroglyphs and ghost towns. Similarly, New Mexican history abounds in a multi-faceted way, be it Pueblo ruins, Navajo art, Colonial trading routes or Wild West drama, all of which are set beneath the state's expansive skies and starry nights. This sense of vast, sometimes overwhelming space taps into the desert wanderer within us all. A third larger than the UK, the state of New Mexico counts just two million residents; it's easy to cycle for days and barely see another soul.

Indeed, I discovered that riding the New Mexico Off-Road Runner touches on everything the state has to offer. The route begins in picture-perfect Santa Fe, the state's historic capital, a warren of adobe structures, art galleries and ancient cottonwoods. Initially heading east, I begin the 505-mile journey along a winding lattice of primitive dirt roads, getting a taste of classic high-desert riding.

Hopscotching from the Santa Fe National Forest to the Cibola, the Off-Road Runner then scouts a path through ranch-land to Moriarty, where little awaits me aside from a gas station, a dollar store and

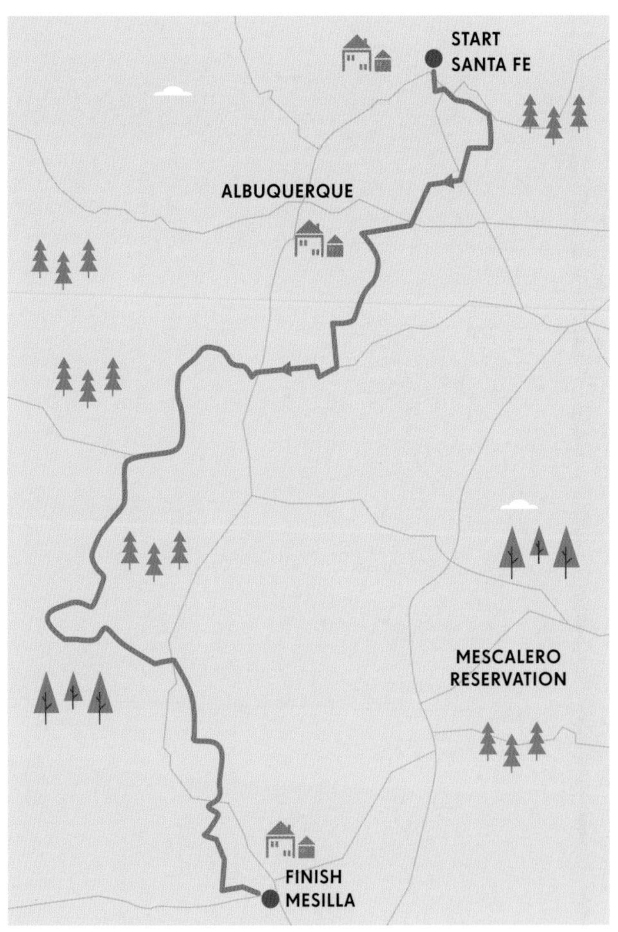

an excellent Mexican restaurant. Beyond, the terrain flits between quiet paved roads and established forest tracks that wend their way through the foothills of the overlooked, secluded Manzano Mountains. Following these, I pass a collection of small, traditional and quintessentially dishevelled New Mexican settlements. The sun-faded pickups, Hispanic churches, roadside shrines and abandoned adobe buildings here are part of the state's back-country charm, and wouldn't be out of place in northern Mexico itself.

Hurdling Abo Pass, a long and meditative paved stint across central New Mexico's open desert, I'm pointed toward the west side of the Rio Grande, set up for a circumnavigational dirt-road tour of Pico Ladrón. At 9209ft, it stands tall above the surrounding cholla-covered desert. This small range of rugged peaks, the Sierra Ladrones, was once home to both Anglo and Hispanic cattle rustlers, as well as Apache raiding parties. Hence its translation: the Mountain of Thieves. By way of further historical interest, the Off-Road Runner takes me past the once mineral-rich mining settlement of Riley; I spy one especially interesting gravestone marking an individual's untimely demise during a nearby mail-coach robbery in the late 19th century.

Beyond the historic, once thriving railhead town of Magdalena, I detour to the Very Large Array, a radio astronomy observatory. There, a number of 80ft-high radio dishes rotate in perfect symmetry, standing dramatically against typically brooding skies, tirelessly probing the furthest reaches of our universe.

Changes in vegetation are clues to a return to higher elevations, as cholla cacti give way to piñon and junipers once more. From the windswept, beautifully bleak plains of San Agustin, past a grove of rusting relics of old trucks, I leave the desert floor to climb high among the mighty ponderosas that line Bear Trap Canyon, reaching the highest point of the route at 9000ft; if conditions are clear, a detour to Withington Lookout is recommended for fine views across the San Mateo Mountains, the VLA and surrounding high desert. After passing by natural springs and plentiful prime camping real estate, I continue on a forest road toward the small settlement of Dusty. Further frontier history is in rich supply here too, if folklore is to be believed, for it's in the neighboring wilderness that the Apache Kid, the legendary renegade army scout, was said to have been hunted down and killed in 1894.

Dipping briefly into the Gila National Forest's Black Range, the ponderosa motif continues en route to Chloride Canyon, home to a series of spectacular, eroded rock formations, perfectly preserved petroglyphs and toe-drenching stream crossings. I bravely follow the signs to Truth or Consequences – the desert settlement once known as Hot Springs but renamed after a 1950s radio show (see sidebar). Once more, the Off-Road Runner crosses the Rio Grande,

DESERT SPA TOWN

Truth or Consequences – renamed after a 1950s radio quiz show in a nationwide competition – forms a welcome resupply point and chance to soothe aches in its hot springs. This area was frequented by Geronimo, the Apache leader who fought Mexican and American expansion. Most motels have their own private springs you can use. Given the brewery, food options and sheer character of the place, it's highly recommended.

Left to right: a posse of bikepackers on the Off-road Runner; camping for the night; roadside scenes. Previous page: racing the setting sun across the plains

passing by Elephant Butte dam, opened in 1916 and named after its elephant-shaped island. Turning south, I ride a roughly chiseled powerline road, leading to the eastern fringes of the mellow Caballo Mountains range. Here is open desert terrain, chunky two-track, prickly ocotillo and, come spring, carpets of wildflowers.

Where better to sample New Mexico's classic condiment than Hatch, the official Green Chile Capital of the World? Hatch also marks the meeting point of the Off-Road Runner and the Monumental Loop (see p124). The former traces its own, easier-going lattice of levy roads, gravel roads and desert doubletrack, guiding my now weary body through the folds of the Robledos Mountains to my final destination, Las Cruces.

In keeping with the Off-Road Runner's historical theme, my journey comes to an end in Mesilla, Las Cruces' photogenic old quarter, in the very plaza that once boasted such illustrious figures as Pancho Villa, Billy the Kid and Kit Carson among its eclectic visitors. Those who enjoy Wild West curios can finish off the ride with a trip to legendary lawman Pat Garrett's gravestone, in the nearby Masonic Cemetery, but I choose to hop on the Mexican bus that runs north from whence I came.

I'd already experienced enough to know that if you take the time to soak up New Mexico and its subtleties, you'll see how the Land of Enchantment lives up to its name. **CG**

TOOLKIT

Start // Santa Fe
End // Mesilla
Distance // 505 miles (813km). Allow nine days.
Getting there // Both Santa Fe and Las Cruces have public transport options, including the Railrunner train line and the El Paso Limousine Express bus service. Domestic and international flights touch down in Albuquerque.
When to ride // Late autumn or early winter; check for storms and allow for the short days of midwinter.
How to ride // Either direction works but prevailing winds come out of the southwest. After rainfall, desert roads become unrideable. For the most part, they dry quickly after a few hours in the sun. Technically, there's nothing challenging about this ride, though a mountain bike will help conquer sandy stretches and smooth over corrugated sections.
Where to stay // Santa Fe is a great base; sample New Mexican cuisine and visit the art installation Meow Wolf.

Opposite: conquering the New Mexico section of the Great Divide Mountain Bike Route

MORE LIKE THIS RIDES WITH A MEXICAN FLAVOR

GREAT DIVIDE MOUNTAIN BIKE ROUTE, NEW MEXICO

The New Mexico portion of the classic Great Divide Mountain Bike Route runs for over 600 miles (965km) from near the Coloradan border to the very edge of Mexico. It's a fabulous section of this 3084-mile (4963km) route, which sees riders climb up and over the Jemez Mountains, traverse classic New Mexican high desert, feast on pies in Pie Town, and experience the beauty and hot springs of the Gila National Forest. This portion of the route must be ridden in autumn, after the monsoon season, to avoid impassable mud. Logistically speaking, the route can be connected to nearby Taos, which can be reached by public transportation from Santa Fe. Arrangements can be made for a shuttle service once you've reached the Mexican border. See www.adventurecycling.org for more information, and take maps (sections 5 and 6) and an up to date gpx file.
Start // Taos
End // Antelope Wells
Distance // 630 miles (1015km)

ANGELES NATIONAL FOREST, CALIFORNIA

Keeping to the Mexican theme – because LA is laced with Hispanic culture, complete with tasty tacos and burritos to fuel cyclists – a loop into the Angeles National Forest offers a remarkably remote experience despite proximity to the city. Make it an overnighter, and marvel at a sea-of-lights vista afforded by camping high above the City of Angels. The San Gabriel Mountains are a young range, so expect steep grades, broken paved roads and gravel, and views out to the Pacific from the Mount Wilson Observatory. En route, ride Switzer's Gabrielino Trail, past Redbox Ranger Station, and climb up to Mount Lukens, which, at 5074ft, marks the highest point in the city proper and a side to Los Angeles you never knew existed. The ride can be reached by bicycle from downtown, or hop on the Gold Line public transportation to Pasadena. As for those tacos, the barebones La Estrella taqueria, in South Pasadena, offers a slice of Mexico.
Start/End // Pasadena
Distance // 60 miles (97km)

THE OTHER SIDE OF NOWHERE, TEXAS

Further west lies Big Bend, so named for the enormous arc carved by the mighty Rio Grande on its journey to the Gulf of Mexico. Although the national park is well known for its grand vistas and dramatic canyons, the neighboring state park holds most interest for mountain bikers. Previously a working ranch, the area was acquired by the state in 1988, and is now laced with mile upon mile of roughly hewn dirt roads, as well as enough rock-strewn singletrack for several days of epic exploration. Big Bend State Park publishes an online biking guide with a number of loops, the longest being The Other Side of Nowhere, a ride that can be split into a three-day bikepacking trip. Combine your journey to far West Texas with a stopover in Marfa, where modern art dots the landscape, staying at the intriguing El Cosmico, which offers camping and accommodation in refurbished vintage trailers. Winter adventures only, due to scorching summer temperatures.
Start/End // Lajitas
Distance // 90 miles (145km)

HUDSON VALLEY ESCAPE

Escape from New York is not just a schlocky 1980s movie but a glorious bike ride up the Hudson valley, away from traffic and finishing up at a craft brewery.

For a city that now gets upward of 60 million visitors a year, there's no shortage of tourist guides to New York, but none of them will tell you about the hidden gem that is the Old Croton Aqueduct (OCA) trail. For most cyclists who want to get out of the city at the weekend, there is essentially one option: riding to the top of Manhattan and crossing the George Washington Bridge, and going north up the west side of the Hudson River.

The OCA trail on the east bank is better yet – though it doesn't give up its secret easily. Even the start of the route is tricky to find: a footpath along an old railway line that runs through Van Cortlandt Park in the Bronx. That name, by the way, is not the only sign you might encounter on this trip of the original Dutch colonizers who first settled New Amsterdam and the lower Hudson Valley.

The trail begins in earnest, but not promisingly, soon after the Bronx middle-class enclave of Riverdale gives way to the grittier Westchester County town of Yonkers. It's easy to get 'Lost in Yonkers,' as the title of Neil Simon's 1990 Broadway comedy had it – though in the 1940s setting of that play, Yonkers was a white suburb; today, it's a near-majority African American and Latino town that was the scene of bitter battles over the desegregation of housing and schools as recently as the 1980s.

You ride through an empty parking lot that seems about to become someone's backyard, and suddenly, there you are – on the trail, high above the Hudson River, with views over to the Palisades, the west bank's basalt cliffs that were carved out by glaciers in the Ice Age. You're surrounded by hills but, remarkably, this ride is nearly flat as you head north up the valley. In fact, the path – sometimes gravel, sometimes dirt, but in most weather rideable on a road bike – rises at a steady gradient: 13in per mile, for some 40 miles.

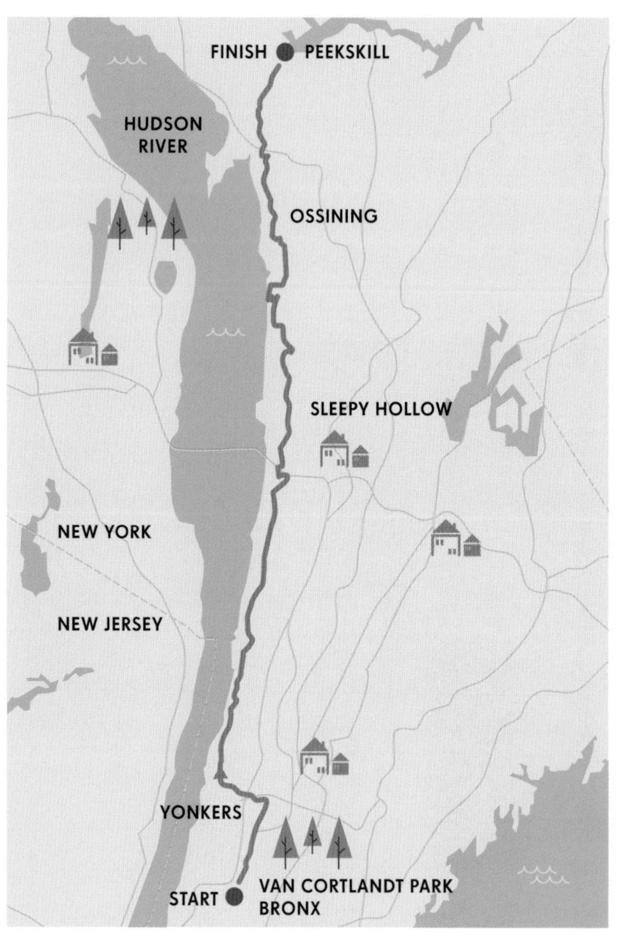

"Ossining is the civilian neighbor to a famous New York landmark: Sing Sing, the maximum security state prison"

I have not made up that statistic; it was what the aqueduct's engineers calculated in the late 1830s was necessary for gravity to carry fresh water from the Croton River above the town of Peekskill (the common suffix 'kill' hereabouts is the Dutch for stream) to the city. There, it filled two reservoirs – the disused one you can still see in the middle of Central Park, and another on Fifth Ave on the site of what later became the New York Public Library. This remarkable feat of civil construction, finished in 1842, brought respite to a metropolis that was dying for lack of water – its inhabitants literally so, given Lower Manhattan's disease-polluted wells.

Every few miles along the trail, you see little stone turrets about 10ft tall, ventilation valves rising from the buried brickwork of the tunnel that runs beneath your wheels. By 1890, even this conduit could not supply New York's needs, and it was supplemented by a larger tunnel to the east. But the old tunnel was not taken out of service until 1955, and the upper reaches are still in use. Today, Ossining, one of several towns en route that force a detour to get back on the aqueduct trail, is still supplied by water via the OCA.

Ossining is also the civilian neighbor to a famous New York landmark: Sing Sing, a maximum security state prison. Going 'up the river' was New York slang for doing time, and you may recall that the prison features in Truman Capote's novella *Breakfast at Tiffany's*, in which Holly Golightly is paid to visit 'a darling old man' for an hour's conversation each week, oblivious that she is acting as a courier for Salvatore 'Sally' Tomato whose anodyne remarks about the weather are coded instructions to his mob lieutenants.

By the time you reach Ossining, you have actually encountered all stations of society – though it may not be immediately apparent, as you slow down for the dog-walkers and joggers who share the trail. The route also passes through the grounds of several former grand estates, for before even the railway came to the Hudson Valley, New York high society set off here by boat to spend summers and weekends at their country seats.

Just before Tarrytown – and you can't miss Tarrytown because it's where the three-mile-long Tappan Zee Bridge crosses the river – the trail runs through the grounds of Lyndhurst Mansion, a vast Gothic Revival pile built in the 1830s for William Paulding, a former city mayor, and later owned by the railroad tycoon Jay Gould. Just south of that is the Sunnyside estate of Washington Irving, author of *Rip Van Winkle* and the *Sleepy Hollow* stories.

So there are plenty of reasons, besides coffee shops, to divert from the trail and stop off if you get tired and don't want to go the full distance to Peekskill, where the alehouse is just yards from the railway station. To get back, you can simply ride in reverse, but you can also bail at more or less any point – the Metro North train makes plenty of other stops along the way, and it's easy to see why these pretty towns of Irvington, Dobbs Ferry, and Hastings-on-Hudson, with their unspoiled main streets, have been repopulated by artists and rent-refugees from the city. For me, a day trip does it, but I never cease to marvel at the OCA escape – it's like finding a hidden portal into another world. **MS**

BIKE BRIDGE

In 2018, a new bridge across the Hudson opened to replace the Tappan Zee, built in the mid-1950s during the Eisenhower Interstate highway-building boom. By late 2019 or early 2020, the new bridge should get what the old one never had: a bike and walking path. This will be great news since it will connect the town of Nyack on the west bank and Tarrytown on the east, creating a new riding loop of around 50 miles out of the city.

Clockwise from left: the Van Cortlandt House Museum in the Bronx; the Highbridge Watertower; Croton Gorge Park. Previous page: the old dam across the Croton River that created a reservoir

TOOLKIT

Start // Van Cortlandt Park, The Bronx, New York City
End // Peekskill, New York
Distance // 40 miles (64km)
Where to stay // Downtown or midtown Manhattan are common preferences, but especially if you're Airbnb'ing, consider upper Manhattan neighborhoods like Washington Heights and Inwood: cheaper, closer to the good rides, and still only a short subway ride from the metropolis.
What to bring // The OCA trail is rideable with an ordinary road bike, but fatter, treaded tires are optimal. Carry your own pump, levers and tubes; bike shops are few and far between.
More info // Route-finding is quite technical. The Friends of the OCA publishes various maps (www.aqueduct.org); the conservancy group Rails-to-Trails provides a very practical map (www.traillink.com); but the most detailed and informative maps are available as pdfs from the New York Parks Department (www.parks.ny.gov).

Opposite: Belle Isle Park with MacArthur Bridge to the left

MORE LIKE THIS
RIDES INTO THE RUST BELT

THE GREATER NIAGARA CIRCLE ROUTE

This 87-mile (140km) loop, the great majority of it on dedicated paved bike trails, actually takes place on the Canadian side of the border formed by the Niagara River, which connects Lake Eerie to the south with Lake Ontario to the north. The river also forms the western end of the great Eerie Canal, the 310-mile (500km) waterway that essentially gave New York City trading access to the Great Lakes from the early 19th century. The bike route provides amazing views of the Niagara Gorge, and, of course, the Falls themselves, and takes you past the monumental hydropower plants named for Sir Adam Beck on the Canadian side and Robert Moses on the US side. On the eastern side of the loop, the route follows the Welland Canal, an engineering feat itself, taking sea-going ships through some eight locks and an elevation gain of over 300ft (91m).
Start/End // Niagara-on-the-Lake
Distance // 87 miles (140km)

BELLE ISLE LOOP, DETROIT

At the other end of Lake Eerie lies Detroit. Motown – capital of the US auto industry – might not seem like a promising place to ride a bike, but the local Greenways Coalition and Tour de Troit organization have done a great deal to change that. Funnily enough, the city actually has a far lower percentage of car ownership than the national average. From downtown Detroit, take the Riverwalk trail east along the Detroit river, over the MacArthur bridge on to Belle Isle, a 980-acre state park designed in the 1880s in part by the great landscape architect Frederick Law Olmsted. With his partner Calvert Vaux, Olmsted created Central Park and Prospect Park in New York City. The 6-mile (10km) loop is not physically challenging, but the views are picturesque – including that of the 60ft, marble-built Livingstone Memorial Lighthouse at the eastern end. The Isle itself will eventually be the terminus of an 800-mile (1287km) Iron Belle bike trail across the state of Michigan, now 70% complete.
Start/End // MacArthur Bridge
Distance // 6 miles (9km)

THE DIRTY DOZEN BIKE RACE, PITTSBURGH

Nominally a race, but for most the Dirty Dozen is a recreational ride that has taken place on the first Saturday after Thanksgiving for more than 35 years in this industrial city in northern Pennsylvania. Pittsburgh has made a remarkable recovery in recent decades – many of its old warehouses and mills converted to modern tech workspaces – but the Dirty Dozen Bike Race remains a gritty proposition. Only 55 miles (88km) in length, it includes more than 5000ft (1525m) of climbing up some thirteen (a baker's dozen) of the city's steepest climbs, some cobbled with Belgian block. The steepest gradient tops out at 37% – vertiginous enough to force much of the field to walk its 500ft (152m) distance. You may need to remind yourself that while it might look a bit like a Belgian Classics course, you're still in the foothills of Appalachia.
Start/End // Highland Park, Pittsburgh
Distance // 55 miles (88km)

A MANHATTAN CIRCUMNAVIGATION

An epic ride of America's most famed city that leaves behind the crowds to reveal waterside glimpses of hidden New York.

The bicycle renaissance is thriving in New York, which is a surprisingly rewarding cycling city. Locals reading that sentence may be tempted – in a very New York kind of way – to roll their eyes and mutter something about the rest of the world being behind the times. New York is very bike-friendly, from Central Park's wide-open boulevards, which are closed to cars for much of daylight hours, to an ever-increasing network of bike lanes crisscrossing iconic landmarks, and exhilarating bridge crossings. Visitors to the city only take partial advantage of this. Few make their way any further than the far end of the Brooklyn Bridge, which is a shame. There is more fun to be had on two wheels by setting your sights further.

The jewel in the crown of New York cycling is the Manhattan Waterfront Greenway. This path snakes its way around almost the entirety of Manhattan Island, rolling for 31 glorious miles. Looking at this ribbon of green on the map, I reasoned that this would be a suitable way to venture beyond the known city into places that tourists don't stray. To do so, I needed to take to two wheels. I wanted to roll through unknown neighborhoods, and explore the extremities of Manhattan. The interior, I figured, couldn't be comprehensively mapped without becoming a resident, but the perimeter could be fairly efficiently circumnavigated. So I joined those renting a bike, but set out with what I felt were grander ambitions.

As with any circular ride, there's no 'right' way to go, but the prevailing view seems to be to head up the west side to the far north of the island, then back down the east side and complete the loop via the southern tip of the city.

My bike rental location was near Union Sq, meaning I crossed Chelsea and the Meatpacking District as the morning rush petered

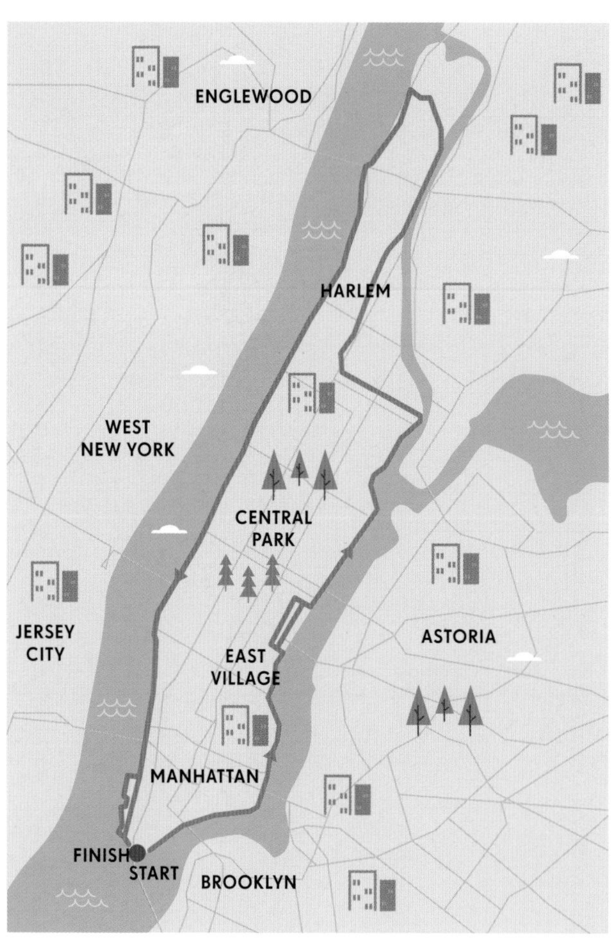

out, and I hit the Hudson bike path just south of the High Line. It was at this point that my perception of the city changed. Endless blocks of busy streets, stuffed with pedestrians and cars and honking taxis that made up the New York of my imagination was replaced by the broad Hudson River. A human scale emerged. It was more than a little strange to suddenly be away from the noise of the city, and instead be able to hear the grind of my wheels on the tarmac path, and the polite yet firm calls to attention from runners overtaking pedestrians. These warnings became more shrill and direct as we approached the cruise terminal and scores of bemused new arrivals found they were blocking the recreational route of speeding locals. Here was an instant reminder that I was still where I thought I was, in boisterous New York.

The Hudson Greenway, as this section is known, stretched on, and I found as I rode it that my sense of the topography of the city was shifting. Landmarks of northward progression – in particular Central Park – rolled past without notice. From the water I could tell I was leaving Midtown by the visible drop in the height of buildings I was riding parallel to. Fellow travelers on the route were thinning out too. Few tourists head out to lap the island, and on weekdays there aren't many commuters outside of peak times. I even experienced feelings of solitude while moving around the world's most famous city.

Fort Washington Park, which is marked by the Washington Bridge and the Little Red Lighthouse, felt like a signpost that I was leaving known areas behind and heading into unknown Manhattan. The far north of the island is stranger, and more

BRIDGE RIDES

The bridges connecting Manhattan with the outer boroughs and New York are landmarks on a circuit of the island. If you only ride one, the famous wooden boardwalk on Brooklyn Bridge should be it, but most can be cycled. The newest is also the oldest – the High Bridge connecting Harlem with the Bronx dates from 1848, when it was built as an aqueduct. Today it carries pedestrians and cyclists high above the Harlem River.

Clockwise from top: street scene in NYC; One World Trade Center; devour a pastrami on rye sandwich. Previous page: crossing Brooklyn Bridge. Overleaf: Queensboro Bridge

Left, above © Sivan Askayo

remote from the familiar parts of Brooklyn and Queens.

Fort Tryon Park is home to one of the city's most marvelous oddities: The Cloisters. This annex of the Metropolitan Museum of Art proved an ideal stop on my way, as much for the remarkable merging of five medieval abbeys into one whole, as for the works of art inside. Beyond here, shortly before Manhattan stops, cyclists dip inland through Inwood Hill, emerging on the east side of Manhattan for the first time on a path running along the Harlem Greenway. This was originally a horse-racing strip for weekending Manhattanites from which cyclists, ironically, were banned. Today a bike path follows it south until another detour takes you on a signed path through Harlem. This showed another side of the city. It was school graduation day and a happy, carefree atmosphere prevailed on the streets. Like so often on a bike, I pedaled through as an unnoticed observer.

Beyond a small diversion around the United Nations complex between 54th and 37th Streets, the Greenway then trundles happily down to Battery Park. South of the Williamsburg Bridge I started to pick up more cyclists, and couldn't resist a few additional miles across the Manhattan Bridge, racing subway trains crossing the water, and returning via the busy but exhilarating Brooklyn Bridge bike and pedestrian path.

Once I'd cleared the crowds at Battery Park it was a short pull back up the Hudson to complete the loop. Bike safely returned, I had one final problem: New York is too exciting a city to relax and put your feet up. I briefly puzzled as to how to fill the rest of the day. The answer came in the form of the Staten Island Ferry, leading to another of the city's boroughs – which looked like a good place for a bike ride itself, another day. **TH**

"I found as I rode the Hudson Greenway that my sense of the topography of the city was shifting"

TOOLKIT

Start/End // The beauty of Manhattan Waterfront Greenway is you can start the loop wherever you want.

Distance // 31 miles (50km)

When to ride // Spring and autumn are best to avoid the city's frigid winters and sticky summers, but if paths are clear and you've got suitable clothing it could be done anytime.

Bike rental // For quality hybrid- and road-bike rentals try Danny's Cycles (www.dannyscycles.com), which has several stores across New York, some now operated by Trek Bicycles.

More info // The New York City Bike Map (www.nyc.gov/html/dot/html/bicyclists/bikemaps.shtml) has details on cycle routes across Manhattan and beyond. A print copy is most useful and can be picked up in bike shops and tourist offices.

292.2807

Opposite: scenes from Bogotá's Ciclovía

MORE LIKE THIS
CITY RIDES

CICLOVÍA, BOGOTÁ

It's Sunday morning in the Colombian capital. Some 75 miles (120km) of the city's streets are being closed to cars and turned over to cyclists until 2pm. This is Ciclovía – both a revolution and, for the urbanites in this densely populated city, a liberation – and it has been happening every Sunday and holiday for 40 years. More than a million people take to two wheels every weekend and swoop gleefully down broad thoroughfares – children being free, adults being child-like for a few hours during otherwise routine weeks. There are two extra-long north-to-south bikeways (Carrera 7 and Avenida Boyacá) with a couple more shorter closed roads and several east–west traffic-free routes, so it's possible to cover much of the center of Bogotá on a bike. Highlights include the street art on Calle 26 and Avenida El Dorado.
Start/End // Wherever you like
Distance // 75 miles (120km)

MEXICO CITY

Megacities don't seem to offer much promise for anyone considering cycling. They have vast populations, strained transport networks and a sense of controlled chaos. Mexico City, however, is emerging as an exception to the rule, at the same time as its reputation as a city destination is growing. Here is a capital with millennia of history, reflected in dozens of museums and galleries, and the varied food and nightlife scene you'd expect when 21.2 million people come together. The major thoroughfares remain hard going, due to traffic and tarmac conditions, but, as with elsewhere in the world, bike tours exploring the city are popular with visitors and cover far more ground than you might on foot. With wheels you can explore some of the designated bike paths that crisscross the city, including one that runs from Bosque de Chapultepec to the Centro Historico.
Bike rental // Rent bikes for free for up to three hours at locations in the center. Ecobici (www.ecobici.df.gob.mx) is a commuter bike service that gives 45 minutes of free riding
When to ride // Sunday mornings, when several downtown streets are closed to traffic, opening up a 16-mile (26km) car-free route

BROOKLYN–QUEENS GREENWAY

The 40-mile (64km) Brooklyn–Queens Greenway offers another grand day out, running from Little Bay Park in Queens to Coney Island and linking such attractions as New York Aquarium, Brooklyn Museum and Brooklyn Botanic Garden. By tackling the route over a day or two you can further discover the outer boroughs and also explore the many parks and dedicated bike routes that demonstrate the continued growth of cycling in New York. Best time to try it? Avoid the sticky heat of midsummer in New York and the snow of deep winter.
Start // Little Bay Park, Queens
End // Coney Island
Distance // 40 miles (64km)

SMOKY MOUNTAINS CLIMB

Tennessee is well known for its whiskey and moonshine, but perhaps just as intoxicating are the winding, misty ridges of the Great Smoky Mountains. Especially when confronted on two wheels.

A few years ago, my road racing team and I traveled from the cornfields of Indianapolis, where we usually rode, to the tranquil ridges of Great Smoky Mountains National Park for a week of slow and steady climbing. We arrived a couple of days earlier to sneak in some extra riding. The six of us greeted the cool morning on the back balcony of our second-floor motel room. The murmur of the river below was soothing and loud, and rather than talk over it we drank our first cups of coffee in hushed anticipation. Our plan for the day was to summit Newfound Gap, the lowest drivable pass in the park, sitting at 5046ft.

We left our motel on the northern side of Gatlinburg mid-morning, stopping first at The Donut Friar for some extra fuel. This sweet old doughnut shop has been tucked into this busy mountain town since the '60s. I paid 99 cents (this place takes cash only) for the freshest, most perfectly crusty, handmade, sour-cream doughnut I have ever had. We sat in the upstairs loft while the smell of pastries swirled around us, tempting us to bin the ride and just stay put with our steamy coffee.

As we pedaled toward the start of the climb, I felt a zing of excitement (which might have just been a little sugar buzz). The 13-mile route winds up through the park at about a 5% grade, pitching up to 10% in some short sections, so we planned to regroup for the descent and head back to town for lunch together.

The six of us were all bike racers of varying calibre, and after a few minutes of steady pushing along we fell silent. The click of our shifters and the occasional utterances of astonishment were the only sounds we contributed to our picturesque surroundings.

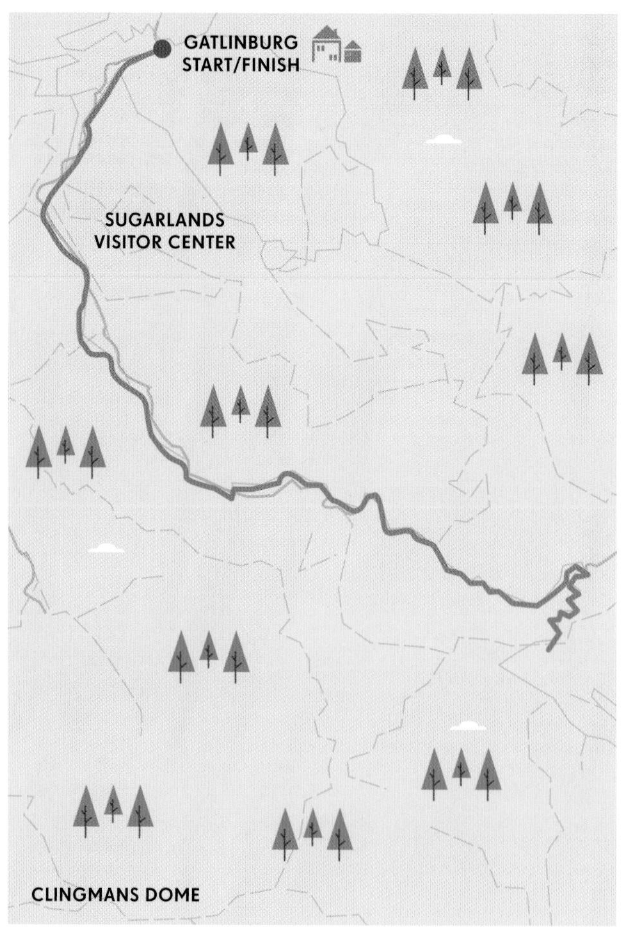

© Sean Pavone | Alamy Stock Photo

We wound through the Northern Hardwood forest, which was just beginning to bud with spring life. The air was misty and dew hung on the branches and rocks we passed, sparkling where the sun shone through the trees.

Eventually the steep pitch separated us and I was pedaling alone to the rhythm of my own breath. It was chilly, but a warm day for March. As I rode though sections of draughty mountain air and sun patches, I worked myself into a sweat and unzipped my long-sleeved jersey. The view from the road on the way up is gorgeous and expansive – and reveals a different side of the mountain to what you see from the overlook at the top, so it's worth the stop. I snaked higher up the mountain, winding my way round a few switchbacks and through a tunnel. The shadowy cliff walls were ensconced with icy drip sculptures, snowmelt refrozen as it rushed down the mountain.

About halfway up the climb is Chimney Tops Overlook (this sign just reads 'chimneys' so I thought maybe we were in for some log cabin ruins, but what's visible from the lookout is actually some uniquely tall and thin mountaintop rock features). Coming from the city, the air smelled fiercely fresh to me; it held a perpetual pleasant, earthy scent that I noticed on the breeze wafting up through the trees and gaps in the mountains.

As we neared the top, I could see the pass in the distance and how much mountain we had yet to climb, which looked a daunting amount. An effective consolation was looking out over the guardrail at how much I'd scaled so far. The steepest pitch is just before the top (isn't it always?), so I summited Newfound Gap with hardly anything left in the tank. I coasted over to the balcony where my friends Kyle and Conor were taking photos, unclipped, and plopped onto the low rock wall.

The parking lot was teeming with the tourists who had passed us in their cars on the way to see this lush overlook. A family expressed their amazement at our arduous summit, and offered to take our photo, which we gratefully accepted.

The mountaintop chill was already making our sweat-soaked bodies shiver, and we agreed to head back down as soon as we all were assembled.

The descent was as thrilling as it was quick. The hour and a half it took me to summit was a blur as we sailed to the bottom together in 30 minutes. With just a few switchbacks, it's a fast and chilly drop. I hunched behind the bike's handlebars and listened to the wind rush in my ears.

We showered back at the motel then sought out a burger and beer at Smoky Mountain Brewing, the oldest craft brewery in East Tennessee. We sat around the table, excited for the week ahead.

After a nap and a lazy afternoon at the hotel, we headed to dinner, and spent the rest of the night wandering the downtown strip of Gatlinburg, a strip which is as gaudy and outrageous as can be, with its neon T-shirt stores, samurai sword shop and Ripley's Believe It Or Not museum. So naturally it was loads of fun. There were enough distilleries offering free tastes that our dehydrated post-climb selves were properly tipsy after an hour of graciously accepting samples as we walked around.

We were strolling along when we heard live music coming from across the street. We wandered round a corner into a terrace, with a wooden balcony running along the building. A bluegrass band was jangling out a rendition of 'Rocky Top' and a group of smiling, elderly listeners were circled around in rocking chairs. After the song ended, the band welcomed us all to the Ole Smoky Moonshine Holler and invited anyone to dance as they started up their next song. Fueled by a lot of free samples, a few of us galloped into the middle and the kind old folks in their rocking chairs humored us by clapping along. We agreed to start tomorrow's ride a bit later, and continued dancing. **RM**

CLINGMANS DOME

If desired, you can continue to climb into the mountains for another 7 miles past Newfound Gap, all the way to Clingmans Dome. This is the highest point in the Great Smoky Mountains (and Tennessee) at 6643ft. From the observatory dome at the summit you can see as far as 100 miles on a clear day (bicycles are not permitted on the steep track to the dome, but the 360° views are worth the walk).

Left: the mountaintop observatory on Clingman's Dome. Previous page: the view from Gatlinburg Gap

TOOLKIT

Start/End // Gatlinburg, Tennessee
Distance // 26 miles (42km)
Total elevation gain // 3588ft (1094m)
Getting there // Fly into Knoxville, TN, from where it's an hour's drive to Gatlinburg.
Where to stay // Rocky Waters Motor Inn is my favorite in the Gatlinburg area.
When to ride // Be wary of planning a trip here during peak summer season – it's a popular destination, so the single road up to the gap will be busy with traffic. It's better to shoot for shoulder season, when traffic will be lighter and the leafless trees extend your vision around corners.
What to wear // A sweat-wicking base layer for the climb and a windproof jacket for the descent.
Tip // Stay a few days in Great Smoky Mountains National Park. There are tons of other great day-long rides and hikes.

Opposite: what goes up Mt Lemmon must come down

MORE LIKE THIS SHORT AND SCENIC CLIMBS

MT LEMMON, ARIZONA

The rocky-cliff-rimmed roads of Tucson wind up Mt Lemmon to a summit of 8200ft (2500m) above sea level. The dry desert landscape of saguaro cacti and mesquite trees gives way to evergreens near the top and, as you reach the peak, the gorgeous southwestern landscape spreads majestically to your left. There is a wide bike lane almost the entire way up, as well as five rest stops with water and bathrooms spaced along the route. The summit of Mt Lemmon is always much cooler than the base, which is a welcome reprieve from the sweltering summer heat in Arizona. You can stop at the top to refuel at Mt Lemmon Cookie Cabin with a giant cookie or slice of pizza. Designed for car traffic, Mt Lemmon is one of the most gradually climbing mountain passes, which makes for a smooth descent without hard braking.
Start/End // Tucson
Distance // 42 miles (68km)

PIKES PEAK, COLORADO

Right from the start at the park entry gate, the road is at a hard 5% grade, and after a few miles pitches up as far as 15%. The climb is relentless, with very little chance to spin and gather your bearings past the gift shop at Crystal Creek Reservoir. There isn't a bike lane, but the pavement is well maintained and traffic is generally sparse within the park. Regardless of what time of year it is, Pikes Peak is cold at the top and can dip to 5°C (40°F) even in July. At about 11,000ft you can peek over the guardrail and see the reservoir from an overlook. This is an incredible view (almost better than the view from the top!) so snag the Kodak moment while you've got it. The further you go up, the thinner the air gets and the road fills with switchbacks and increasingly steeper sections. If it's a clear day, the view is incredible. Descending is tricky, and you reach speeds of up to 50mph (80km/h). Bring snow gloves to keep your hands warm.
Start/End // Pikes Peak Park entrance ($10 fee; last entry to the park is 3pm)
Distance // 12.5 miles (20km) one-way

COLUMBIA RIVER GORGE, OREGON

This lovely ride along the Historic Columbia River Hwy is gentle in elevation and plentiful in natural beauty. From where you begin in Troutdale, a little town on a small tributary of the Columbia River, the grade is so subtle and the scenery so distractingly glorious that you only realize how much you've been ascending when you glance over and can see all the way down into the gorge. As you climb the mountain that lines the river deeper into the gorge, the road winds through rural farmland and evergreen forests. You take a slight descent towards the Vista House at Crown Point, and again climb up to the bulbous building. Definitely stop here to visit the observation deck, and ponder your insignificance in comparison with the vast, lush canyon that is the Columbia River Gorge. The turnaround point for the ride is about 8 miles (13km) further at the breathtaking Multnomah Falls, a 620ft (190m) double-drop waterfall with a pedestrian bridge over the second cliff.
Start/End// Troutdale
Distance // 67 miles (108 km)

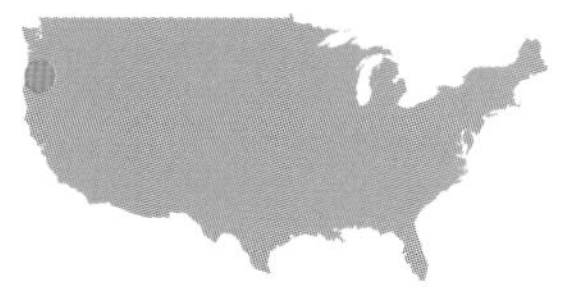

THE NESTUCCA RIVER SCENIC BYWAY

The legendary back route from Portland to Cape Lookout through some of the state's best wine country was once bike messenger classified material. Now, the secret's out...

For a long time, I had heard rumors about a better route from Portland to the coast than dueling with the logging trucks for 80 miles on Hwy 26. I learned that there was a back road along the Nestucca River Rd that connected Yamhill wine country to a secret camping spot near Pacific City. It was pre-smartphone era, so the directions were hazy and free from the burden of actual road names. I was a bike messenger at the time, and fellow messengers traded tales of Nestucca as more of a legend passed down through generations than a practical set of directions – a guarded secret that had to be earned, not Googled. Eventually I shook a co-worker down for more specifics and handed her a pen and piece of paper. This is how I came to own what looked like an ancient treasure map of the Willamette Valley, with an X marking the real fortune: a hidden place to (illicitly) set up tents on the beach.

So I packed my road bike with a tent and panniers, and set out for the ocean with a friend. We started in the suburb of Hillsboro, but the real ride didn't start until we reached Carlton, a small community sandwiched between Oregon vineyards and bordered by mountains to the west. The route's first half would be long and weary, 48 miles with no services according to the sketch on my map: a block of Swiss cheese with a line through it, next to a

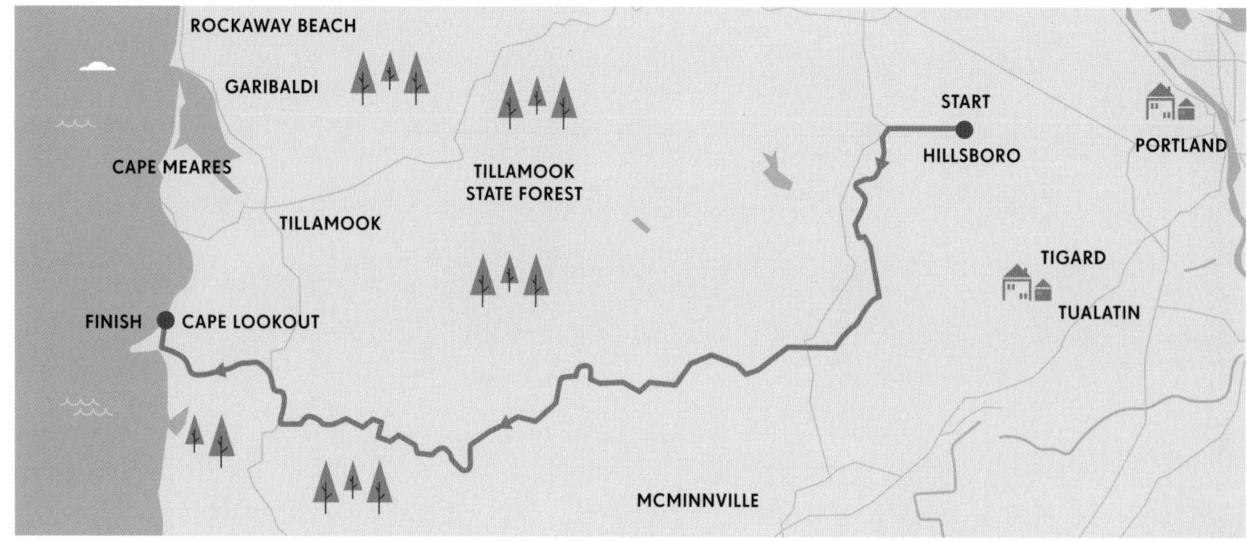

© Jason Borum

frowny face. No need to tell me twice – we loaded up on food and water at the Carlton Market general store, right at the turn on Nestucca.

As we started off down the Nestucca River Scenic Byway, to give it its correct name, the road pitched up and opened a gap between my friend and me, which gave me time to pick wild blackberries from trees lining the corner of every curve. We pedaled out of farm country up into forestland, passing only the occasional house. Not a single logging truck rumbled by, though their proximity was evident from the partially clear-cut forests. All was quiet for a while under a canopy of Douglas fir.

Just as we entered the steep final part of the 20-mile climb, my friend felt one of those snaps every cyclist dreads and discovered her freewheel had broken off and was just spinning. This was beyond my roadside repair level. We stood together, looking at her bike, desperately willing it to somehow regain gears. Despair gave way to stress-eating energy bars. Eventually we pushed our bikes until we spotted a shaded, mossy camping spot next to the river.

In the morning, two bowhunters gave us a ride back to Carlton in the back of a pickup truck. Few words were exchanged, but they were friendly enough, despite full camouflage face paint and a stockpile of weaponry. Shivering in the darkness of thick

"Threaded alongside the river was a gravel section that kicked up dust and exacted a toll of one flat bike tube for passage"

trees overhead, we huddled down in the truck bed with our bikes, wondering if we would be bounced over the side. I've never been so grateful for such an uncomfortable, chilly ride.

Weeks later, back in Portland, I was haunted still by our failure. The road had been perfect. Shaded, rolling, winding, free from cars, with scenic overlooks aplenty – the more I dwelled on it, the more I built Nestucca up to be the universe's finest stretch of pavement. I knew I had to clear a weekend to squeeze in another attempt before Portland's long rainy season.

Barely able to read the smeared writing on what was left of my original map, I once again set out for Pacific City on my bike – alone. (By the way, for your own ride you might prefer to cut down on the city riding and save yourself a few miles – if so, take the MAX light-rail blue line from downtown Portland to its last stop in Hillsboro.) I hit the turn into Nestucca Rd and began huffing up the long climb. A dog gave chase for the equivalent of a city block, but I didn't see any other humans or

PINOT ON POINT

The Yamhill County wine scene has exploded in the past 15 years, and Carlton is right at the heart of it. Before you hit the climb – or better yet, on your round-trip back home – stop by Carlton Cellars for a sample of local pinot noir. Opened in 2007, the small winery offers laid-back tastings and informative tours of the winemaking process. If the winery is closed when you arrive, check out yamhillcarlton.org/wineries for regional vineyards.

Left to right: the Nestucca River Rd offers scenic Oregon vistas whether ridden solo; or with company; Pacific Hwy views; deep in the Oregon woods Previous page: road cycling through the state

animals for miles. Threaded alongside the river was a miles-long gravel section that kicked up dust and exacted a toll of one flat bike tube for passage. The full climb was longer than I had remembered, with about 2500ft of elevation gain – and a descent that ripped tears out of the corners of my eyes and probably added years to my life.

Finally I burst out into the town of Beaver in Tillamook County, where I connected to Hwy 101 South on the Pacific Coast Bike Route from Canada to Mexico. Success! I had completed my quest to ride from the city to the beach, free from that stream of 18-wheeled reminders of my own mortality. It would be the first of many trips along this quintessentially Oregon scenic byway. (Note: unless you've organized a shuttle or car ride back to Portland, the best way back is to reverse the route.)

In the years since, I've discovered that organized riders who have mapped out the once-fabled route along the Nestucca River Rd head north a dozen miles or so from Beaver to camp at Cape Lookout State Park (take your pick from yurts, tents or cabins). On the record, I'd have to recommend that route. But off the record? I'll stick to my trusty, weathered map with its smeared outlines of roads and sketches of stick people riding bicycles – and that still-clandestine little camping spot near Pacific City where I've buried all my treasure. **CG**

TOOLKIT

Start // Hillsboro, Portland or Oregon Pacific City for a hotel stay, Camp Lookout State Park for camping

End // Cape Lookout, Oregon

Distance // 90 miles (145km) one way from Hillsboro MAX station to Pacific City (twice that if you ride back to Portland).

Getting there // Train to Portland Amtrak or fly in to Portland International Airport..

When to ride // September for dry, cooler weather, but pack a rain jacket no matter when you go.

What to take // Plenty of food and water – there are no services between Carlton and Beaver, though you can fill bottles at a campsite. Camping and cooking equipment.

Where to stay // Camp Lookout State Park hiker-biker camp. Or The Inn at Cape Kiwanda in Pacific City (luxury); the Anchorage Motel in Pacific City (budget). To break the ride, the Alder Glen or Rocky Creek campgrounds in federal forests.

Opposite: the Multnomah Falls can be viewed on Oregon's Bridge of the Gods loop

MORE LIKE THIS
THREE UNMISSABLE PORTLAND LOOPS

THE BRIDGE OF THE GODS

This can't-miss ride takes you on a clockwise loop through the Columbia Gorge between Washington and Oregon and over a metal grate bridge that gives you a stunning (if terrifying) view down at the Columbia River. You'll ride out on the shady, winding Washougal River Rd, where summer swimming holes abound, climb up to Beacon Rock State Park, and then cross the most aptly named bridge in the west. Your trip home is a cruise past the legendary Multnomah Falls and a crank up to the Crown Point State Scenic Corridor for an unforgettable vista of the Gorge. It's an all-day effort that condenses several of the most famous tourist attractions of the Pacific Northwest.

Start/End // Mt Tabor Park, SE Salmon St, Portland
Distance // 89 miles (143km)
Info // www.gpsies.com

LARCH MOUNTAIN

If you're looking for one monster climb with a breathtaking view, Larch Mountain is 6378ft (1944m) of vertical gain, fun and gasping for air. This counter clockwise loop takes you to the top of an extinct volcano, where you'll be rewarded with a 360-degree view of all the major peaks in the area. Just remember to pack a light jacket so you can take time to enjoy the view up top and refill your bottles at the store in Corbett – it'll be your last chance for services before you hunker down and start the 14.5-mile (23km) climb. The descent is one of those glorious, gradual downhills that requires easy pedaling but makes you feel like a superhero.

Start/End // Mt Tabor Park, SE Salmon St, Portland
Distance // 70 miles (113km)
Info // www.gpsies.com

CANBY FERRY CROSSING

Pack a few extra bucks in your jersey pocket – you'll need it for the quick ferry ride across the Willamette River that serves as a little rest stop toward the middle of this rolling loop through the small communities just south of Portland. Far from a disruption to your pedaling, the chance to ride a ferry is one of the best reasons to do this ride, which starts and ends right on the eastside bike path near downtown Portland. Throughout the ride, you'll find plenty of spots to stop and take in views of the city's bridges, as well as opportunities to load up on snacks at stores and cafes. Try the Singer Hill Cafe in Oregon City for a coffee or lunch break.

Start/End // Eastside Esplanade across the river from downtown Portland
Distance // 53 miles (85km)
Info // www.gpsies.com

THE CENTRAL OREGON BACKCOUNTRY EXPLORER

Amid the old-growth forests and the geologic wonders of Central Oregon, keep an eye out for mountain lions – and goatheads...

Psssssss, 'there goes another one!' It was our eighth flat within a five-mile stretch of dirt road along the John Day River. A brief moment spent off-track to explore the remnants of a ghost town resulted in a plague of so-called goathead thorns wreaking havoc among the group. The goathead scourge limited our progress to 12 miles that day and we limped our way to the nearest town. There we were pleasantly surprised by an inviting bicycle traveler's hostel with all the home comforts and, most importantly, tools, a pump, even sealant for those of us running tubeless tires.

Such are the highs and lows of riding the Central Oregon Backcountry Explorer loop which does nicely as a short escape from Portland's rainy fall days. Three hours' drive from the city and sitting east of the Cascade Mountains, central Oregon has an arid, high desert climate. This 152-mile (245km) route follows paved and gravel roads as the landscape transforms from the grass meadows and old-growth ponderosa pine forests of the

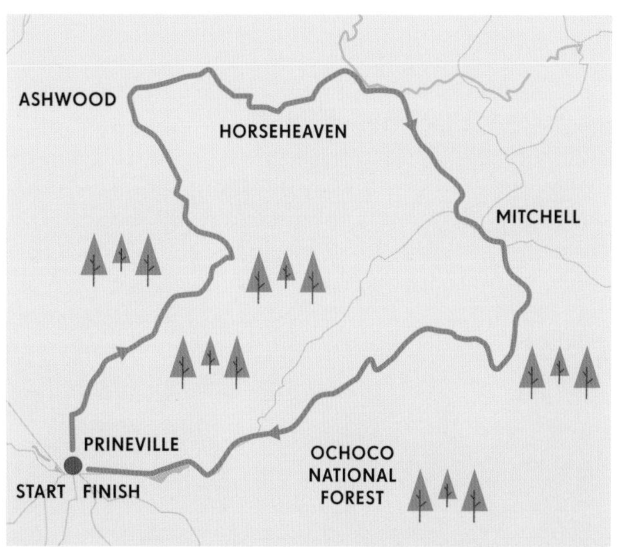

Ochoco Mountains, to the geological oddities of the juniper foothills in the John Day River Basin, while passing ranches, ghost towns, and vestiges of old mining operations. Apart from one night in a hostel, this is a camp-out, and we carry all our equipment, supplies and food with us, in an assortment of panniers on racks and bikepacking bags (the roads are smooth enough to allow for both).

The route begins in Prineville, whose early citizens knew the vital importance of a railway to their community's survival – they built their own to support the timber industry, and today the town is home to 10,000 residents.

Survival is on my mind, too. The hills of central Oregon are home to hardy species such as pronghorn antelope, mule deer, elk – and another impressive animal. Before we start our ride I mention to a grocery-store clerk where we're headed. 'Watch out for cougars up there,' he warns 'You can't see them, but they can see you.' I don't mention this exchange to my three friends, yet as we climb our way through the dense dark forests of the Ochoco Mountains I can't help but take a closer look at my surroundings – was that shadow in the corner of my eye an antelope, or a 200lb cat, stalking us?

At the top of the climb the pavement turns to dirt, and the road drops us into the John Day River Basin. Shady ponderosa pine forests give way to a volcanic landscape formed over 225 million years ago: a deserted expanse of conical hills, with sagebrush and juniper trees here and there.

There are also signs of the much more recent past. The town of Horse Heaven was established after an ore of mercury was discovered in the surrounding hills in 1933 – which is about when its luck ran out. After burning down, being rebuilt, and collapsing again, the community called it quits by 1958. The ghost town that remains of this civic hard-luck story does at least make for an evocative picnic stop.

Through a corridor of lava rock we spy the John Day River, named after an early 19th-century hunter and trapper who was robbed and stripped naked by Native Americans at the mouth of the river and forced to hike 80 miles to safety. Today, the watercourse is one of the longest undammed, free-flowing rivers in the US, teeming with wild Steelhead trout, Chinook salmon and many other species of fish. It's in this idyllic setting that our group hits a problem – not quite the problem that John Day himself faced, but still. Three flats out of our group of four, and one on its way. The perpetrator? A dried fruit from an invasive weed, bearing hard sharp spines, feared by cyclists and whose features give it its name: goatheads. Multiple tubes are replaced, patched, and then patched again. (All in all, those goatheads conspired to add an extra day to our planned four-day loop.)

Delayed and frustrated, we limp our way to the Painted Hills.

CULT FIGURES

In the 1980s, central Oregon was home to Rajneeshpuram, a commune housing 7000 followers of the Indian mystic, Bhagwan Shree Rajneesh (Osho). Known for their free-love ideology, the Rajneesh were controversial within the local communities for their attempts to expand and politically take over the nearby town of Antelope, as well as the county seat of the Dalles, and for their alleged involvement in a mass food-poisoning attack.

Left to right: the old pioneer town of Mitchell; snaking through the Oregon backcountry. Previous page: pedaling past ponderosa pines

Here at this extraordinary site, a national monument, our time worries are put into perspective by the climatic shift, from tropical to temperate over geological timescales, that have left the hills' ancient shale mounds ribboned with red and yellow.

All the same, it's good to reach the historic pioneer town of Mitchell by dusk. Seemingly preserved in aspic, this charming community offers camping in the town park, a general store, a brewery and a bicycle tourist hostel. Guests pay by voluntary donation at the Spoke'n Hostel which is built within a church and offers memory foam beds, showers, laundry, and a friendly atmosphere in which to share tales of woe with fellow bicycle travelers. (The hostel also sits on the Trans-America Trail, the paved coast-to-coast route that takes the intrepid all the way from Astoria, Oregon to Yorktown, Virginia.)

Refreshed and resupplied, we leave Mitchell the following morning and climb our way back over the Ochoco Mountains, and are rewarded for our efforts: through prairies and forests we spot wild horses and a bald eagle perched on a volcanic rock pillar emerging above the trees. We soak up the vista of central Oregon and marvel at the adventure of the past five days as we descend back into Prineville. Filled with wanderlust to return for more, we drive back to rainy Portland where we celebrate our record-breaking 12-flat fixes over some hefty burritos. **SS**

TOOLKIT

Start/End // Prineville, Oregon
Distance // 152 miles (245km)
Getting there // Redmond Municipal Airport, 19.5 miles (31km) away, Portland (three-hour drive), and Bend (50-minute drive).
What to take // GPS device, plenty of water storage and filter, camping equipment, cookware, clothes for the change in elevation, repair kit, extra sealant for tubeless tires (recommended!), spare tubes, and a spare battery pack, tires with at least 38mm width.
Where to stay // Spoke'n Hostel in Mitchell and camping on public lands.
When to ride // June through October.
More info // For the most up-to-date information and route version: www.bikepacking.com/routes/central-oregon-backcountry-explorer

Opposite: cacti and climbs on the Gila River Ramble

MORE LIKE THIS
ADVENTURES IN GEOLOGY

CEDAR MESA LOOP, UTAH

Following dirt roads and sandy washes, the Cedar Mesa Loop in southeast Utah makes a figure-of-eight over 152 miles (245km) through scenic canyons, cliffs, swooping rock formations and sandstone valleys, dominated by the Cedar Mesa. It's also a ride into the pre-history of North America: the archaeological record suggests that indigenous peoples inhabited this mesa, or plateau, for 13,000 years. Tucked into this striking red sandstone desert landscape are cliff dwellings of the Ancestral Puebloans, full of rock carvings and artifacts. Set aside time for the many opportunities to hike up to these sites (some require a permit). There is only one place to resupply water and food on this route, which requires a heavily weighted-down bike to traverse what is otherwise relatively easy terrain. Ride in late spring or fall. Avoid setting out after rain, as many of the roads on top of the mesa get muddy.
Start/End // Natural Bridges National Monument
Distance // 152 miles (245km)
Info // www.ridewithgps.com/routes/15239023

GILA RIVER RAMBLE, ARIZONA

The Gila River Ramble, southeast of Phoenix, is a multiday mountain-bike ride exploring the wondrous desert landscape of the Superstition Mountains. Be warned, this ride is hardly the casual stroll the name implies. The route traverses steep and rocky jeep tracks, exposed ridgelines, a river ford, and winding singletrack lined with grabby cholla cactus – more an epic desert adventure than a ramble. If that whets your appetite, then the payoff is a route that flows through a mesmerizing series of canyons linking abandoned mines, passing red rock buttes and mesas, winding through forests of towering saguaro sentinels and including amazing views of the craggy Superstition Mountains. It is recommended to ride this route counterclockwise through the cooler months from November to March, and to carefully plan your food and water. The only reliable resupply en route is at mile 40 in the archetypal Hollywood western town of Superior.
Start/End // Kelvin (east of Phoenix),
Distance // 112 miles (180km)
Info // www.ridewithgps.com/routes/7103080

CRATERS AND CINDER CONE LOOP, ARIZONA

To cycle through northern Arizona's San Francisco Volcanic field is to tiptoe your way through a minefield: the oldest of the 800 extinct volcanoes peppering the landscape here is just six million years of age, and the youngest, Sunset Crater, first appeared a thousand years ago – the blink of an eye in geological terms. The three to four day, 184-mile (296km) route begins and ends in Flagstaff, wending its way between these sleeping giants, the tallest of which tops out at over 12,600ft. The riding is not technical, and offers opportunities for numerous side trips to explore fire lookouts, Lava River Cave (a 0.5-mile-long lava tube), and SP Crater, (one of the most striking cinder cones in the area). There is only one resupply spot, at 60 miles (96km). Water can be scarce too: use water spigots at campgrounds and trailheads, and filter water from stock tanks if necessary.
Start/End // Flagstaff
Distance // 184 miles (296km)
Info // www.ridewithgps.com/routes/20986717

LU LACKA WYCO HUNDO

Are you ready for a leg-draining, 100-mile sentimental journey down some of Pennsylvania coal country's most challenging trails?

In a way, every ride tells a story of who we are, where we live, and the places in which we prefer to spend our time. If that's true, then Lu Lacka Wyco Hundo, an annual gravel adventure set in the bucolic back roads of Pennsylvania, is more like a coming-of-age novel.

The tongue-twister of a name references the regions it traverses: Luzerne, Lackawanna, and Wyoming counties, all historically important coal-mining areas in northern Pennsylvania. The route lies just west of the Poconos and south of the Endless Mountains, but make no mistake, the mountains do not end here. They roll through this region, coming at you one after another on a sea of green.

This is where the creator and organizer of Lu Lacka Wyco Hundo, Pat Engleman, spent his formative years and where he returns to escape inside himself for a while. His goal for the 100-plus mile LLWH is to share the story of his life by inviting us all to follow the same path – and surrender to the crashing waterfalls, grazing goats, glistening lakes, lily padded swamps, and immaculately tended farmlands that create the backdrop of this particular tale.

LLWH is held every spring, generally mid- to late April, usually on a 'shed your arm warmers by the first aid station' kind of day (I've completed each of the six rides and counting). It kicks off in a fire hall, as do many Pennsylvania weddings, funerals, and other gatherings of country life.

The ride starts with a police escort through downtown and then riders peel off to dash down a dead-end road, squeeze round a gate and on to the route proper. If you're in a hurry, get to the front for this part. Whatever your pace, it's time to relive Pat's (and maybe your own) childhood as you hit some rocky, rutted doubletrack before

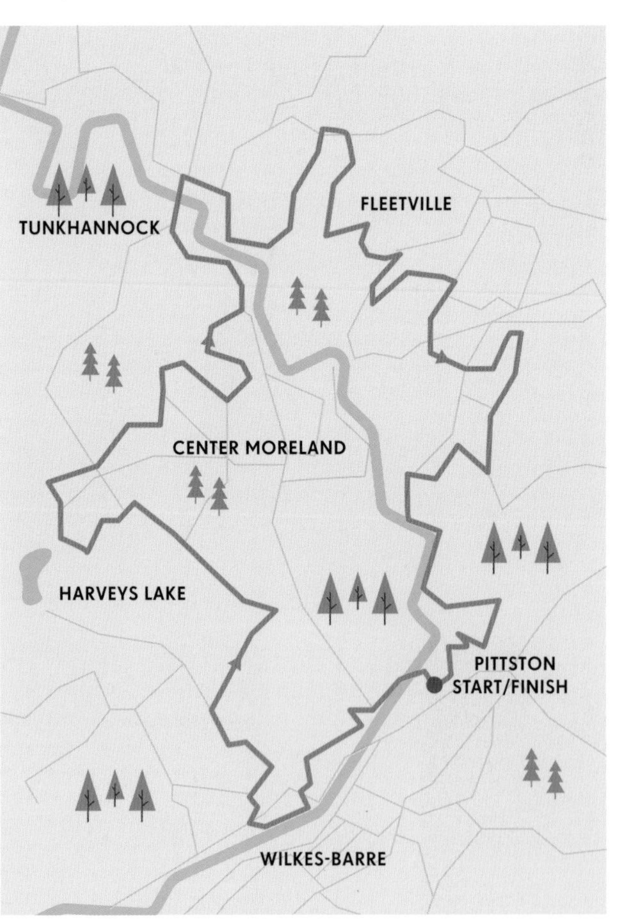

hanging a left at a long-abandoned vacuum cleaner and sweep through the leaf-strewn singletrack trails that Pat ripped around on his BMX bike as a kid. There will be crashing and walking and cursing and giggling as the pack weaves through this stand of woods, before riders pop out in the backyard of a church and crawl up an embankment of dense, slippery, dew-soaked grass, finally hucking off the curb and heading back out onto the road.

The singletrack section flies by in a blur, like childhood itself, perhaps. But you're not all grown-up yet – this adventure is all about what you find where the road builders stopped. Your tires are on gravel, hardpack dirt, abandoned rail beds, and otherwise off the beaten path for about 70% of your journey. About midway through this living picture-book of life in countryside America, you sweep down around shimmering Lake Winola, where Pat spent his summers, and pass by seasonal cabins and sketchy dive bars he undoubtedly tried to sneak into as a restless rural youth.

Improbable things will happen... the kind of stuff you'd experience with your friends growing up and recall wide-eyed at the dinner table, only to be admonished for exaggerating by the adults in the room. Like the time we were bee-lining it to the BMX part of the course and my friend Bernie got blindsided by a baby deer (they both trotted away). Or the time when a half dozen of us were silently willing our way up the steepest climb of the day – a 0.11 mile wall that averages over 17% incline – listening to the winds howling through the surrounding sycamore when, *CRACK*, a tree branch the size of a small maple fell and pinned my friend Doug to the ground. (We held our breath, fearing the worst, until he implored us to Instagram it.) Or the time I witnessed a rider double

BEWARE THE TACO

One of the LLWH's unexpected features is a makeshift taco stand (with cold beer!) at the summit of one of the longest, steepest stretches of road about halfway in. It's a delightfully terrible idea few can resist. None of this will help with what is inarguably the most arduous stretch to follow. I have watched grown men throw up their halfway-house tacos from the gut-churning exertion of cresting one more 10% climb than their stomachs could handle.

Clockwise from above: hitting gravel roads; the infamous taco stop and mid-ride refreshment; the author powering uphill. Previous page: red barns in Pennsylvania. Overleaf: descending

somersault off the side of a turn he'd overcooked, stick the landing Simone Biles–style, and soldier on.

Though you've already ridden through the stunning, pine-lined Dark Regions Climb, the real darkness falls during the 30-mile stretch between miles 57 and 87, when your eyes will gaze upward at every turn in disbelief that you are indeed still going upward. In the pre-ride meeting Pat half jokingly cautions riders to not engage the locals, as you'll be deep in some 'Don't Tread on Me' country. But whenever the locals have engaged us, it's been with bemusement, but respect. 'Ya might need some bourbon,' one gray-bearded bystander called from his drive at the foot of one climb, 'and you'll definitely need all your low gears... this one is long and real steep.'

Now is also about the time you might be wondering about your bike and tire choice. Though it's all perfectly doable on whatever bike you choose, lower gearing makes the nearly 9000ft of climbing easier on the legs, and wider tires make the sometimes mildly harrowing descending easier on the central nervous system.

For most of the ride, you have little sense of place, aside from 'out there.' But you know you're close to the end when you're directed to climb a series of railroad tie stairs to a long, rocky trail that drops you onto a bike path along the Susquehanna River Dyke. From there, you can gaze on the industrial skyline of Pittson, and its myriad church spires, houses of worship built by Pat's ancestors.

Full plates and pints await back at the fire hall, where riders sit for hours, with muscles too tired to move, yet just beneath the surface, brimming with the same childlike abandon you had when you began. The story is almost over, but it's also just beginning. **SY**

"There will be crashing and walking and cursing and giggling as the pack weaves through this stand of woods"

TOOLKIT

Start/End // Jenkins Township, Pittston, Pennsylvania
Distance // 105 miles (169km)
Getting there // Scranton International Airport is just a couple of miles away. New York City's JFK airport is 2½ hours' drive.
Where to stay // The Comfort Inn in Pittston is the closest major chain. Camping is also available in the region.
What to take // The roads are rough and fairly remote. Have two tubes, a patch kit, some cash for food and drink, and front and rear bike lights just in case it gets late.
When to ride // This route is best from mid-April (when the organized ride is held annually) to mid-October when you have ample daylight and the weather is warmer. Showers are always possible, so pack accordingly.
More info // www.cliffviewproductions.com/bike-rides

Opposite: the route of UnPAved goes deep into the woods

MORE LIKE THIS PENNSYLVANIA GRAVEL

UNPAVED

A relative newcomer on the gravel-grinding scene, unPAved of the Susquehanna River Valley boasts the tagline, 'Easy on the eyes. Hard on the legs.' And if you choose the 120-mile (193km) option, with nearly 10,000ft of climbing, endless vistas in the Bald Eagle State Forest, and ribbons of remote road in Pennsylvania Amish Country, you'll find both to be true. The start and finish are in Lewisburg, Pennsylvania, a hip little college town, and the route runs out along the Buffalo Valley Rail Trail where a gold mine of gravel roads awaits. The ride features fast hardpack dirt, gravel paths, an old tunnel, and, as it is held in peak PA foliage season, plenty of eye-popping fall color. If you're not up for the full distance, you can opt for 90-, 54-, or 30-mile alternate routes.

Start/End // Lewisburg
Distance // 120 miles (193km)
Info // www.unpavedpennsylvania.com

KEYSTONE GRAVEL

For those who like to push the limits of what a drop bar bike can do, Keystone Gravel, Pennsylvania's premiere 'gravelduro' is rife with off-road possibilities. Held mid-September in the mountainous Pine Creek Gorge region, Keystone Gravel is a 73-mile ride with more than 6000 vertical feet of climbing. It features grass, dirt, gravel, and a few paved roads. There are a half dozen or so timed Strava segments – up and down – that riders race each other on for prizes at the end of the day. But it's not so much a race as an adventure ride filled with waffles, cold brew coffee, tacos, and other aid station treats along the way. It's held on a jaw-droppingly gorgeous 300-acre farmstead, and the after party, which includes gourmet food, craft beer, and local live music, rivals the ride itself.

Start/End // Pine Creek Gorge
Distance // 73 miles (117km)
Info // www.keystonegravel.com

IRON CROSS

North America's Original UltraCross race, Iron Cross was originally held in the remote and rugged Michaux State Forest. It has recently moved to Williamsport, PA, but has stayed true to its roots, featuring not only gravel roads, but also a wide variety of challenging riding surfaces including singletrack, doubletrack, and a long, hard run that resembles rock climbing on Horse Path in the Tiadaghton State Forest. You won't want to miss Larry's Tavern, a beer stop late in the event that serves as a carrot for regulars who know that it's all downhill from there. Held in mid- to late October, the ride's weather is a bit of a gamble. It can be Indian summer sunny or cold with wet snowflakes falling from the sky. But it's all part of the great adventure known as Iron Cross.

Start/End // Williamsport
Distance // 50-plus miles (80-plus km)
Info // www.outdoorexperience.org/iron-cross

SRAM
131

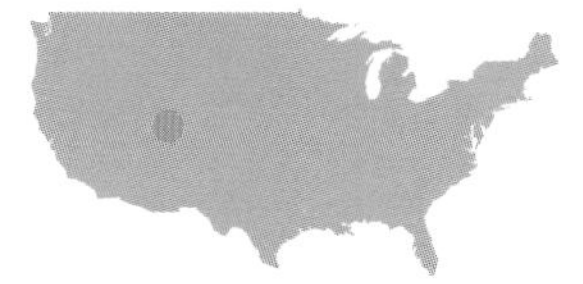

MOUNTAIN BIKING IN MOAB

Few places get mountain bikers as excited as Utah's Moab – a desert dreamscape of slickrock and singletrack revered for its riding culture and infamous 24-hour race.

When my riding partner dismounts and picks up his bike, I figure there's no shame in doing the same. I had a feeling that any attempt to ride this particular section of trail would end with me biting some dust, sprawled on my back with all the grace of an upended blister beetle – again – but I might have given it a stab.

That's if I weren't exploring Behind the Rocks with Mountain Bike Hall of Fame grandee John Stamstad, and if he considers something to be unrideable, then the argument is effectively over. Stamstad is the emperor of endurance cycling – a reputation he earned, in part, right here – on the route of the legendary 24 Hours of Moab cycle race that annually ran through the Utah desertscape from 1994 to 2012.

Having effectively invented solo 24-hour mountain-bike racing and pioneered the pursuit of Great Divide racing across America, Stamstad once set a world record by cycling a mountain bike across off-road terrain for 354.5 miles in 24 hours.

© Jordan Siemens | Getty Images

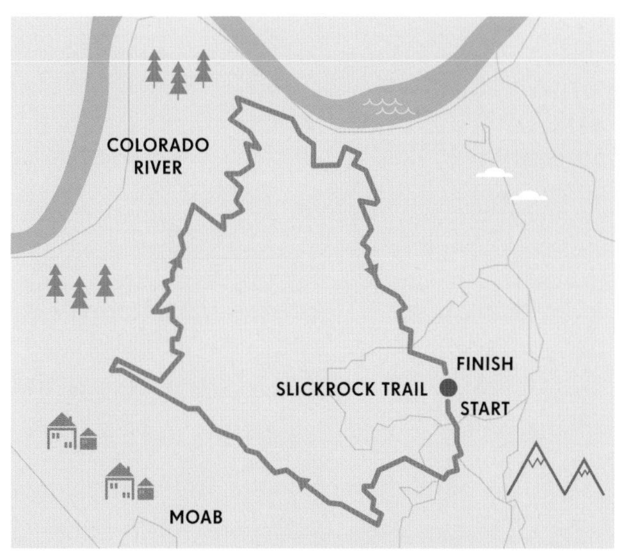

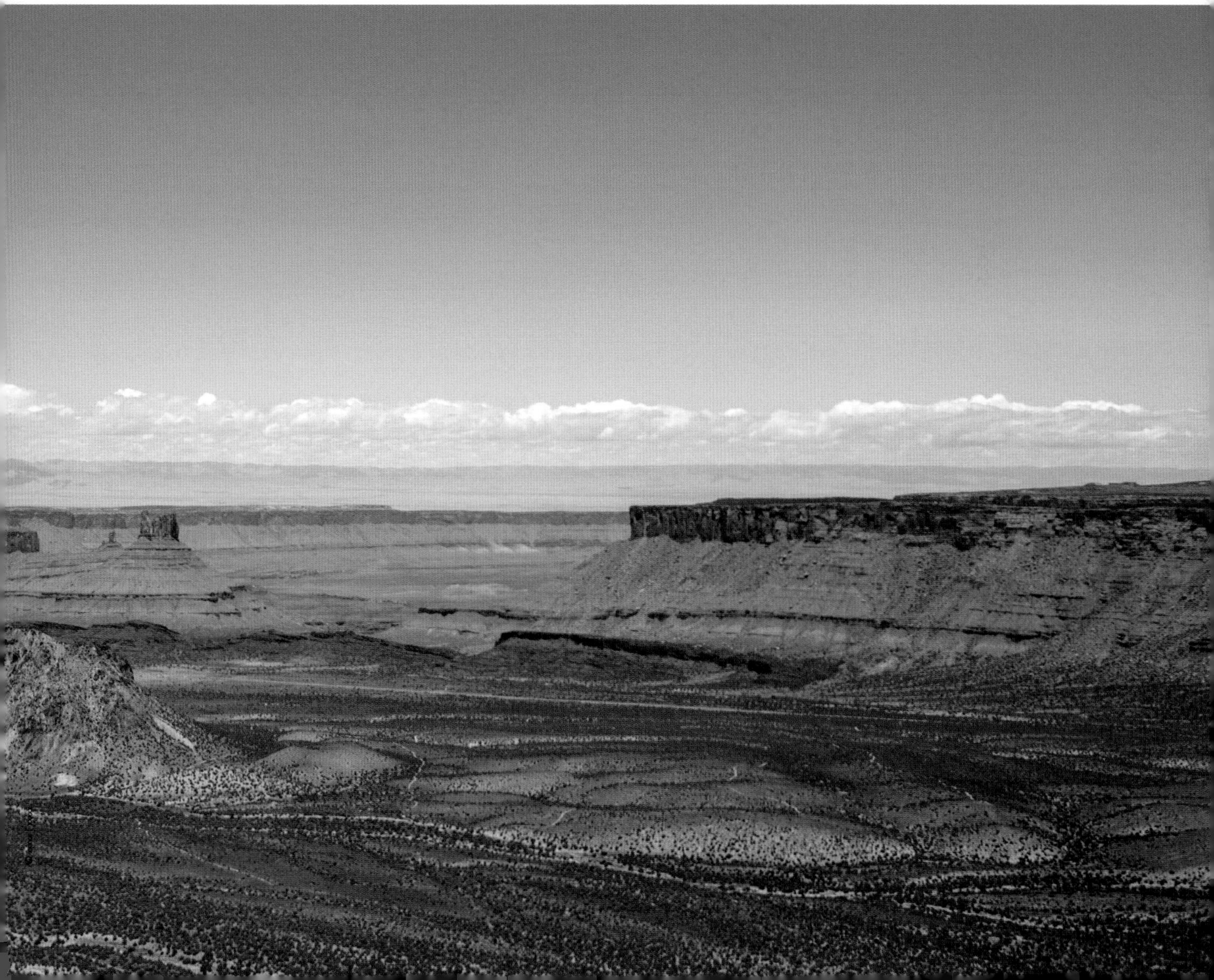

© ZUMA Press, Inc. / Alamy

Suffice to say, when he gets off his bike, it's for good reason. This spot is named Nose Dive, and bits of broken bicycles lie scattered in the dust all around – the bleached bones of the foolish few who have attempted to ride the dive. 'I used to be able to pick a line through here,' Stamstad laments. 'But the jeeps have destroyed it now. You can't ride out of it any more, so there's no point killing yourself on the descent.'

Stamstad never actually won the 24 Hours of Moab – not least because the last time he did it, he insisted on riding a single-speed bike (and still came second) – but he's done so many laps of the legendary circuit that he could ride it with his eyes shut (and very possibly has). The race route is a shortened version of the Behind the Rocks Lunatic Loop, a 28-mile (45km) trail that is probably Moab's least popular. A 'sandy sufferfest' is how the guy in Poison Spider Bicycles described it when he heard where we were heading.

But I'm desperate to experience the epic course, and now the event is in hiatus, this is the only way. My legs are eternally grateful that we only have to ride the route once, and the rest of me soon discovers that July is not a month when even Stamstad would want to be riding multiple loops for 24 hours on the trot. We're out early in the morning – long before the day comes to the boil, when temperatures in the rare shade simmer at around 100°F (38°C) – but perspiration quickly drenches my face and fills my eyes.

Stamstad shows me around every nook and cranny of the course, recounting tales from the trails as we roll. At one point I go sailing over the bars during a technical descent, and he thoughtfully attempts to spare my blushes by describing how he once passed the erstwhile race leader at this very place, as the guy lay on the ground with concussion. I'm obviously traveling somewhat slower, and it's only my pride that gets concussed.

I get back into the saddle and we continue, rounding a stunning golden edifice of almost Uluru proportions, which my companion grinningly informs me is known as Prostitute's Butte because of how it looks from the air. The trail then runs across a seductive section of Moab's iconic slickrock – smooth Navajo sandstone that appears sketchy, but actually grants knobbly tires an uncanny amount of traction, allowing riders to roll over the most unlikely gradients while remaining rubber side down.

The 15-mile (24km) race circuit finishes shortly afterwards and we seek shelter from the inferno of the midday sun. At a diner in town, the menu includes an 'All-day Mountain Bikers' Breakfast,' which delivers a carb-laden load that would keep most riders fueled for the duration of a 24-hour race.

Once the worst of the heat has passed, we explore the more popular routes that slither across the slickrock and skim the rim of the canyon, making Moab a hallowed haunt for mountain bikers, irrespective of the race. Incredibly, these classic tracks were laid down during the Jurassic period, and no human intervention has been required to make or maintain them as perfect MTB trails.

That said, the mega-popular, world-renowned 10-mile Slickrock Trail itself follows a series of white dots painted onto the rocks, which do jolt you out of the amber-tinted ambience of the natural surrounds somewhat, so Stamstad takes me on the wilder Amasa Back Trailhead route instead.

This adventure, another 10-miler, sees us ascend over 1000ft, climbing across sandstone all the way to a magical mesa top, with an astonishing vista across the Colorado River and Kane Creek. Beyond the rust-coloured desert, the La Sal Mountains on the horizon still have a dusting of snow, which seems almost impossible from the furnace of the canyon.

Numerous drop-offs, technical climbs and steep descents keep us on our game throughout this return route, and rolling around close to the canyon rim – which plunges away with hair-raising severity – demands serious concentration, but it's not just the elevation that gives me goosebumps here.

Riding back to the trailhead, as thunder rumbles in the distance and fork-tongued lightning licks the distant range, it feels like I've ascended some sort of higher plane of mountain biking. And then I'm bounced out of my whimsical reverie by a red rock that has waited 200 million years just to throw me over the bars of my bike and bring me back to earth. **PK**

24-HOUR MOUNTAIN-BIKE RACING

Another Mountain Bike Hall of Famer, Laird Knight, created 24-hour MTB racing – where riders attempt as many loops of a technical off-road course in 24 hours as possible – as a team pursuit. In 1996 Stamstad entered a 24-hour race in Canaan as a team, but all four names on the sheet were a variation of his own. He did the event solo, beat most of the field and invented a new form of endurance racing.

Left: navigating the sandstone Amasa Back trail. Previous page: looking out over the mesas around Moab

TOOLKIT

Start/End // Behind the Rocks/24-Hours of Moab route: US-191, just beyond Kane Springs Picnic Area; Amasa Back Trailhead: Amasa Back car park; Slickrock Trail: Sand Flats Rd.

Distance // Behind the Rocks: 15 miles (24km); Amasa Back Trailhead: 10 miles (16km); Slickrock Trail: 10 miles (16km).

What to ride // A dual-suspension mountain bike.

Tour // Ride independently, or consult the experts at Poison Spider Bicycles (www.poisonspiderbicycles.com) for guidance, or to arrange a spot on the Porcupine Shuttle, which leaves daily, taking bikers to do the epic 32-mile (51km) 'Whole Enchilada.'

When to ride // Spring and autumn deliver ideal conditions.

More info // www.utahmountainbiking.com

Opposite: racing the dual slalom at the Sea Otter Classic

MORE LIKE THIS MOUNTAIN BIKE RACES

SQ'AKW'US 50, BRITISH COLUMBIA, CANADA

For 20 years the Test of Metal mountain-bike race attracted hundreds of racers and thousands of their friends and family to Squamish, a logging town on the Pacific coast of British Columbia midway between Vancouver and Whistler. The reputation of Squamish singletrack – tough, challenging trails through dark, root-laced forests and down steep granite slabs – matches those of its renowned neighbors. In 2017 the mantle of the must-ride local race was handed over to the Sq'akw'us 50, a weekend-long summer festival of fat tires, fresh ales and hard riding. Two races of different lengths ensure there's something for everybody, with the longest route taking riders up trails such as 50 Shades of Green and down some black diamond-graded stretches. It's guaranteed to whet your appetite for the feast of mountain biking in this corner of BC – and send your skills up a notch too.
Start/End // Squamish
Distance // 31 miles (50km)
Info // www.spakwus50.com

SEA OTTER CLASSIC, CALIFORNIA

Each spring, 70,000 cycling fans and up to 10,000 bike racers of all types migrate to Monterey for a four-day cycling festival. The event at Laguna Seca Raceway is part trade show – with the latest kit on show from global brands – and part festival of bike racing. Whatever you're into there will be an event to enter: cross-country, enduro, dual slalom or downhill mountain biking; road, criterium or circuit racing. UCI-sanctioned pro races provide further entertainment for spectators. The cross-country mountain bike race uses the trails of Fort Ord Monument, also the venue for a Gravel Grind. The roads of the surrounding wine country host the 91-mile (146km) Gran Fondo Carmelo or ride 49 miles (79km) along the coast on the Gran Fondo Pacifico, watching for furry sea otters bobbing in the bay below. Whatever flavor of two-wheel fun you're into, the Sea Otter Classic covers it.
Start/End // Various, usually from Laguna Seca Raceway
Distance // Various
Info // www.seaotterclassic.com

24 HOURS OF FLATHEAD, MONTANA

The 12 and 24 Hours of Flathead is notable for two things. One, it's Montana's only 24-hour mountain bike race. And two, and more importantly, entries are open to individuals living with paralysis and other life-altering disabilities. In fact, so supportive is the race organization that all of the proceeds of the race go towards a grant that funds adaptive sports equipment to help people explore and enjoy the outdoors. There are two courses: a 2-mile (3km) route suitable for adaptive hand cycles and an 8-mile (12km) course for cyclists, which features 1400ft (427m) of ascent. Both start from Herron Park, just outside the town of Kalispell. Competitors can race solo or in teams for 12 or 24 hours. And, this being Montana, there's some great scenery to explore in Flathead Valley once race day (and night) is done.
Start/End // Herron Park, Kalispell
Distance // 8 miles (12km) or 2 miles (3km)
Info // www.24hoursofflathead.org

100%

THE TRANS-AMERICA TRAIL

A few years ago, no one had cycled this route. Today, the off-road Trans-America Trail, a 5273-mile backcountry odyssey from east to west coast, is fast becoming a once-in-a-lifetime classic.

If people have heard about the Trans-America Trail at all, they picture the classic Adventure Cycling Association route that follows paved roads from Astoria, Oregon to Yorktown, Virginia. But the only thing in common with the Trans-America Trail described here is the name: this TAT follows dirt roads, gravel roads, forest roads, jeep trails, and paved back roads. Yes, there is a dirtroad route from east to west across the US, and it's nearly double the length of the Great Divide Mountain Bike Route that takes trail riders from Canada to the Mexican border.

Don't be surprised if you haven't heard of it; this route was initially designed by and for adventure motorcyclists and 4WD enthusiasts. Then, in the summer of 2015, my partner and I cycled the route in its entirety. It has since been ridden by many others and adapted into an ultra-endurance event called the American Trail Race that begins in May every year.

The numbers tell one story: a distance of over 5000 miles and 300,000ft of elevation gain (more than 10 times the height of Mt Everest) through some of the most remote stretches of the US. The journey tells another, of an America less seen, a country that can be experienced free from the stresses of big cities, cars, and tourists. From east to west the route grows more remote with each pedal stroke. Eventually, you might be pedaling 120, even 140 miles

before the next small town (finding and carrying enough water is the biggest challenge for TAT riders). While the entire journey can take up to four months at a casual pace, the highlights of the TAT can also be enjoyed in individual sections.

As soon as I discovered that there was a dirt road route across the US I was all-in. My partner and I marked a departure date on the calendar and spent a year planning the ride and arranging our personal lives for a three-month hiatus. We would be leaving in August in order to beat the snowfall in the Rocky Mountains and to enjoy cooler temperatures by the time we reached the desert of central Utah and the Great Basin. This meant dealing with the heat and humidity of the southeastern US in the peak of summer.

Following primarily dirt roads, and ways less traveled, we began our journey in the Outer Banks of North Carolina and traveled west across coastal Carolina and over the Great Smoky Mountain Range. From the Smoky Mountains the route follows the back roads of the lush, humid river valleys and forests of the central US through southern Tennessee and northern Mississippi. It then crosses over the Mississippi River into the rugged Ozark Mountains of Arkansas before it begins the gradual, straight ascent through the prairie grasslands of northern Oklahoma and the no-man's-land of the state's remote panhandle. For 100 miles, the trail travels through northeast New Mexico before navigating northwest into the Rocky

"From the Smoky Mountains the route follows the back roads of the river valleys and forests of Tennessee and Mississippi"

Mountains and over the rugged high alpine passes of the San Juan mountains. The red rocks of Moab are the route's introduction to a long stretch across the high desert of Utah, the Great Basin of Nevada, and eastern Oregon. Following the footsteps of the early pioneers of the California Gold Rush, the TAT finally leaves the desert and drops into the greener land of Surprise Valley, California and over the Cascade Mountains of Oregon where the water begins to flow in the creek beds again. The route comes to an end on Battle Rock Beach in the moody coastal town of Port Orford, Oregon.

As this was our first bike tour of this scale, we stumbled our way through. We ran out of water, got stuck in the mud, hid from thunderstorms, slept with bugs, and rode with a crosswind for over 600 miles. We did without, snuck water from private property, pushed our bikes for miles, and sprinted from aggressive dogs. We were awe-struck by the natural beauty unfolding in front of us, food tasted better than it ever had, we've never slept so well, and our encounters with fellow humans were spontaneous and authentic.

THE MAN BEHIND THE TAT

Sam Correro, a passionate adventure motorcyclist from Tennessee, developed the Trans-America Trail over 15 years as a way to cross the country off-pavement with his motorcycle, completing the route in 1996. He has since launched a website as a resource to purchase up-to-date maps and information for the route. These days, the TAT attracts hundreds of travelers from all over the world.

Left to right: the east side of Imogene Pass, Ouray, Colorado; a common sign from North Carolina through Mississippi; No-Man's-Land, Oklahoma; roadside menu in Cass, Arkansas. Previous page: conquering the west side of Imogene Pass in Telluride, Colorado

It was rewarding. We did hard things and they were good for us. All our senses and emotions were heightened, and eventually we found a natural rhythm, pace, and ease of living on the TAT.

By Oklahoma, the creek beds were dry, forcing us to rely on windmill pumps and the kindness of people who still lived on the land for water. Occasionally, several days would go by before we encountered another person. There was solitude during our time between towns. It was just us and our surroundings, whether that was at the top of a 13,000ft mountain pass, or hiding from a torrential downpour in our tent in a church parking lot, or bathing peacefully by a cool running stream. Like the early settlers of the West, each mile we traveled revealed a new experience in terms of scenery, terrain, food, culture, and climate. The country unfolded in front of our eyes fast enough for the change to be dramatic, but at a pace slow enough that we were immersed in the landscape of that moment.

The TAT was a wild journey that changed my life. I decided to close my bicycle shop in Ohio and pursue a life of travel, adventure cycling, route development, and writing. Not all who follow this path will perhaps have their lives altered. But those willing to make the pilgrimage are bound to learn a little more about themselves, this extraordinary land, and the people who live here. **SS**

TOOLKIT

Start // Cape Lookout, North Carolina
End // Port Orford, Oregon
Distance // 5273 miles (8486km)
Getting there // Delta and American Airlines fly into Coastal Regional Airport. From there it's 65 miles by taxi or shuttle to Beaufort, and then ferry to Cape Lookout.
What to take // GPS device, water filter, camping equipment, cookware, clothes for the change in climates, extra battery charger.
Where to stay // 30–50 miles typically separate towns in the eastern US, 70–140 miles out West. Most towns have motels and hotels. Enquire for city park camping at any police or fire station. Churches are also very accommodating to through-travelers and will allow you to camp in their yard. In the West, enjoy wild free camping on public lands.
When to ride // Start on the East Coast from May to August.
More info // www.transamtrail.com

Opposite: tropical scenery on the Baja Peninsula

MORE LIKE THIS
COAST-TO-COAST ADVENTURES

COAST-TO-COAST ACROSS CENTRAL BAJA, MEXICO

This route is one of the most challenging, diverse sections of the infamous Baja Divide (the 1700-mile/2736km, off-pavement bikepacking route that runs down the length of the Baja Peninsula, Mexico). Connecting the Pacific Ocean with the Sea of Cortez, the route heads south-west toward the Pacific coast from the peaceful fresh-water oasis of San Ignacio, along a lagoon popular with whale watchers, across dry lakebeds, through canyons, to the oasis of Mulegé, on the east of the peninsula. From the harbor, hire a fisherman to take you and your bicycle across the bay to Los Hornitos in a *panga* then ride the remote shoreline tracks to El Rosarita, where you can catch the bus to your next destination or continue on the Baja Divide. Mountain bikes with 3in tires are recommended.

Start // San Ignacio
End // El Rosarito
Distance // 224 miles (360km)
Info // www.ridewithgps.com/routes/29034934

MICHIGAN COAST-TO-COAST

The Michigan Coast-to-Coast is a new, epic 210-mile (334km) gravel grinder that takes places in mid-June. The course heads west across the state of Michigan from Lake Huron to Lake Michigan through farmlands, wetlands, uplands, and majestic forests on hardpacked gravel roads, sandy doubletrack and snowmobile trails (a 45mm-width tire is advisable). There are resupply checkpoints every 50 miles/80km (the Dublin General Store, the final checkpoint, offers locally made jerky from rabbit, pheasant, and ostrich to name a few). NB: there are few services in Au Gres, but come race's end in Ludington you can enjoy a dip in the lake followed by a good meal and a microbrew from one of the many local pubs. For more information about the event and course details visit: www.micoasttocoast.com

Start // Au Gres, Michigan
End // Ludington, Michigan
Distance // 210 miles (334km)
Info // www.ridewithgps.com/routes/28418676

LA RUTA DE LOS CONQUISTADORES, COSTA RICA

La Ruta De Los Conquistadores is famously known as Costa Rica's premier mountain-bike stage race, named after the paths created by Spanish conquistadors. Whereas the stage race, held each November, covers the 161-mile (260km)course over three gruelling days, the route, ridden as a week-long bike tour, is much more enjoyable (yet still challenging), allowing time to soak up the cultural flavor and geologic, ecological, and climatic diversity of Costa Rica. La Ruta crosses the Central American landmass from the Pacific to the Atlantic Coast, through tropical rainforests, banana plantations, and small farming villages, over volcanoes, suspended bridges over deep river gorges, and along breezy coastlines. The route follows a plethora of surfaces and paths from singletrack, fire, gravel, and paved roads to deep mud, sand, volcano ash. The dry season is December through April and is the best time to enjoy the ride. (Each year the race route is updated – visit www.larutadelosconquistadores.org.)

Start // Jaco
End // Limón
Distance // 161 miles (259km)

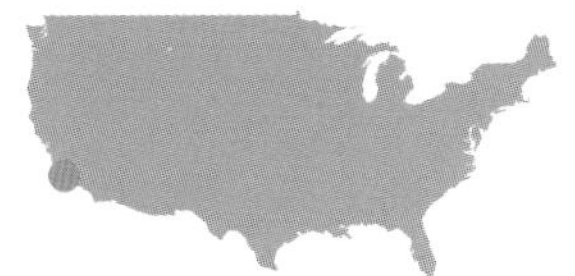

COAST TO COAST VIA THE SOUTHERN TIER

The quickest coast-to-coast ride knocks over a thousand miles off the standard route – and also serves up the best food along the way.

Most riders with cross-country wanderlust probably gaze out an office window and dream about the Trans-America bike trail, the quintessential 4228-mile route from Virginia to Oregon mapped out by the Adventure Cycling Association during 1976's Bikecentennial summer (not to be confused with the more recently developed off-road trail of the same name). But for those of us who can only get a month or two off work to pedal from one ocean to the other? The 3055-mile Southern Tier Bicycle Route from San Diego to St Augustine, Florida, is the ultimate coast-to-coast, escape-your-life adventure.

The first time I rode the Southern Tier, I wasn't exactly looking to escape my life, but I was looking to escape the Pacific Northwest rainy season. One of the many advantages of riding from California to Florida is that you're not limited by snowed-in mountain passes like you would be further north, so you can start your journey as early as February. Another is the food – but we'll get to that a little later.

After buying a set of maps from the Adventure Cycling Association, my friend Claire and I took Amtrak down the west coast to start our trip in early March. The ride started auspiciously enough – I woke on the first day to a boot nudging

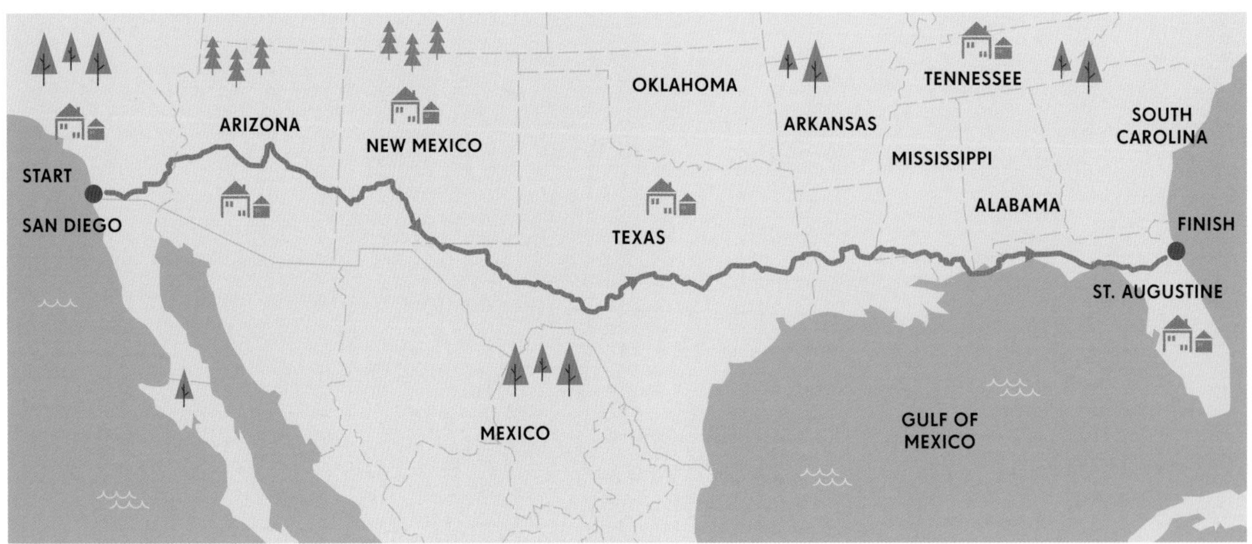

my face and a police officer's flashlight pointed into my eyes. We had ridden from the train to the route's start at midnight and passed out in sleeping bags under a tree in a public park. Now, it was 4am and we had all the motivation we needed to start pedaling east. And we needed it. Turns out one of the biggest climbs on the Southern Tier, In-Ko-Pah Pass, is within 40 miles of leaving San Diego.

Riding across the South at a pace of 70 miles a day means getting acquainted with a lot of RV parks, which might feel dispiriting if not for an abundance of friendly locals. As Claire and I pedaled our way across the desert, we made a point to stop in every little watering hole we could for a drink. And for the most part, the bar regulars were happy to see two unfamiliar faces. The only time the landscape became truly demoralizing was a long, no-services stretch along California's Imperial County that looked as sandy and desolate as the *Star Wars* planet of Tatooine. But once we started zigzagging through the busy suburbs of Phoenix, Arizona, we missed those quiet back roads populated solely by ranch horses and Saguaro cacti.

In New Mexico, we took on the biggest climb on the route: Emory Pass, the Southern Tier's 8828ft high point. I still remember the look of shock from a car passenger headed in the opposite direction as she spotted me cranking up the pass at 4mph on my fully loaded bike. But that wasn't the part of the state that left the biggest impression. We also visited the Gila Cliff Dwellings National Monument, in particular those of the Mogollon people, thousand-year-old homes built into caves along the Gila River. It was a fascinating reminder of the rich histories of the areas we passed through, from early indigenous nomads to the Spanish and Mexican cultural influences seen in every town. No surprise that, for lovers of Mexican food, this was one of the best culinary segments of the trip.

"As we hit the Atlantic, I thought of all the landscapes, cultures, and people we'd seen. Did we ride across only one country?"

After New Mexico, we 'messed with Texas' for three weeks, pedaling from El Paso on the Rio Grande to the state's eastern border. (Yes, you read that right – it took us three weeks to cross the Lone Star State.) Everything is bigger in Texas, including the roads – we were startled to be riding on massive, multi-lane interstates. Thankfully the shoulders were relatively smooth and usually generous enough to put some distance between us and the 18-wheelers.

After crisscrossing the Guadalupe River through the wildflower-rich Texas Hill Country, we reached Austin, where we took a weeklong break from the road to enjoy the city's famous barbecue and music scene. Austin isn't just a convenient halfway

point for the route – it also serves as a dividing line between cultures and climates. To the west, at our backs, lay empty deserts and wide-open vistas. To the east, we cruised into lush, humid Cajun Country.

Mark my words: the only way to see the southeast is on a bike. For starters, you'll need a big, road-weary appetite to tackle hearty Cajun food like gumbo, muffuletta, and po'boys and still have room for seconds. You'll also get the chance to pass through unforgettable small towns – like the Zydeco capital of the world, Mamou, Louisiana – that drivers blow past because they're off the freeway. And when you roll into a popular beach vacation area like Gulf Shores, Alabama? No one can appreciate lounging all day on a white-sand beach like two cyclists with more than 2000 miles in their legs.

Finally, after thousands of miles and a shameful number of po'boys and tacos, we reached Florida, the flattest and wettest state of the trip. Our epic journey ended in the city of St Augustine, the oldest continuously European-occupied settlement in the US, colonized in 1565 by Spanish explorers. 'We made it!' I thought, as we dragged our bikes through the sand to look out at the Atlantic Ocean. We rode across the country! And then I checked myself as I thought of all the landscapes and cultures and people we'd encountered. Did we ride across just the one country? It felt more like we rode across five. **CG**

A BIG EASY DETOUR

Although it's not on the Southern Tier main route, New Orleans is the ultimate spot for rest-day fun and debauchery (or as much debauchery as a tired cyclist has energy for). From Baton Rouge, take the alternative southern spur to the city of Mardi Gras. It's hard to go wrong in the home of Creole food and jazz. If nothing else, take an easy day to just wander the French Quarter and enjoy the architecture around Jackson Square.

Left to right: entering the Texan town of Alpine; on the open road from Alpine to Marathon, Texas. Previous page: Southern Tier cyclists riding from Fort Davis to Alpine, Texas

TOOLKIT

Start // San Diego, California

End // St Augustine, Florida

What to take // Panniers or a trailer, camping equipment. For a full packing list, check out ACA's 'What to Take' guide: www.adventurecycling.org/resources/how-to-department/bicycle-travel-basics/what-to-take-and-how-to-pack

Where to stay // You'll find forest service campsites, RV parks, and motels 60–70 miles (97–113km) apart across the Southern Tier. ACA maps list all options: www.adventurecycling.org/cyclosource-store/route-maps/southern-tier-route

More info // The entire route is available in the form of print maps, GPS files, and even an app from ACA. Get more info here: www.adventurecycling.org/resources/blog/meet-the-new-southern-tier-map-app-from-adventure-cycling

Opposite: the Niagara Falls is one of the many awe-inspiring sights along the Northern Tier's 4000 miles

MORE LIKE THIS
LONG-DISTANCE ODYSSEYS

PACIFIC COAST

Touring the Pacific coast is an experience like no other, with unforgettable vistas overlooking rugged beaches and corridors of massive redwoods to pedal, which later give way to sunny beaches that look as if they're straight out of a film set. Expect plenty of climbing and long, curvy descents as you work your way south from Canada to the border of Mexico and leave the rocky shorelines and picturesque lighthouses of the Pacific Northwest for the sand and bike paths of Southern California. Give yourself a couple months and take your time to see everything. This is the ideal tour if you love majestic ocean views and meeting other cyclists – you'll rarely find yourself alone at the forest service hiker-biker campgrounds along this beloved route.
Start // Vancouver, British Columbia
End // Imperial Beach, California
Distance // 1848 miles (2974km)
Info // www.adventurecycling.org/routes-and-maps/adventure-cycling-route-network/pacific-coast

TRANSAMERICA TRAIL

There are lots of reasons this 4000-mile (6400km) road route between the coasts of Virginia and Oregon (not to be confused with the off-road route on p280) serves as the epitome of a cross-country American tour – it passes through 10 states, cinches the midsection of the country, traverses a multitude of diverse ecosystems and terrains, and follows a general trajectory of European settlement in the US. It was also the first cross-country bicycle route across the US, mapped out back in the big Bikecentennial celebration of 1976 by a group of young travelers who formed the Adventure Cycling Association. Start in historic Yorktown and pedal through the Appalachian mountains of Kentucky, to the Kansas Plains, over the Rockies, through Yellowstone National Park, and up into Pacific Northwestern forestland. Though the route doesn't pass through any big cities, you'll see many of the small towns and best parts of America you never knew you were missing out on.
Start // Yorktown, Virginia
End // Astoria, Oregon
Distance // About 4228 miles (6804km)
Info // www.adventurecycling.org/routes-and-maps/adventure-cycling-route-network/transamerica-trail

NORTHERN TIER

The best argument for quitting your job to ride this stunning band across the northern US is the opportunity to pedal up Going-to-the-Sun Road in Glacier National Park before climate change melts the last of the glaciers. But that's just one of the route's many highlights, which takes you from the Cascade Mountains across the Rockies and into the Plains before ending on Cadillac Mountain in Bar Harbor. You'll ride through green Minnesota farmland, the quaint small villages of Vermont, and even cross the Peace Bridge into Canada to see Niagara Falls. Although a tour of the Northern Tier is slightly more tricky to time – some of the National Parks out west are only open on certain dates – there's no more challenging and rewarding place to spend your summer.
Start // Anacortes, Washington
End // Bar Harbor, Maine
Distance // 4246 miles (6833km)
Info // www.adventurecycling.org/routes-and-maps/adventure-cycling-route-network/northern-tier

THE COVERED BRIDGES OF VERMONT

Drink in the flaming fall foliage – and gallons of gloopy maple syrup – on a cycling circuit between a handful of the US Northeast's most winsome towns.

The flaming fall foliage in Vermont is a knockout. Quite literally – it left me sparked out, flat on my back and gasping for breath.

Cycling along the leafy back lanes of Addison County, I was savoring the gentle burn in my calves on the short ascents, then the whispered kiss of the September breeze on my face as I freewheeled down. Alternately puffing and purring, I was happily drinking in the ubiquitous wood-scapes of crimson and incandescent amber when suddenly it seemed I'd been drinking a little too deeply. Concentration broken by the vistas while pelting joyfully downhill, I turned a corner to be faced with an unexpected T-junction. On jammed the brakes. The bike stopped dead. I didn't – and flew over the handlebars, with just time to think: so this is what they mean by fall in New England...

Fortunately, both the bike and I survived pretty much unscathed – only my reverie had been punctured. Dusting off my bike, I vowed to focus more on the road and less on the scenery.

That's easier said than done in these parts. Riding through central Vermont in autumn is like cycling through a succession of mesmerizing screen savers. Forested hillsides glow with traffic-light hues, red and amber and vibrant green. Red Dutch-gabled barns rise from cornfields, wooden covered bridges span serene waterways and pumpkins are piled at roadsides. It's idealized New England turned up to 11 – and biking heaven.

That comical tumble came just a couple of hours into a 100-mile triangular ride between three of the most charming burgs in the Champlain Valley, midway from Massachusetts to Montréal. This broad, undulating dale, bounded by the Green Mountains to the east and New York State's Adirondacks to the west, is becoming

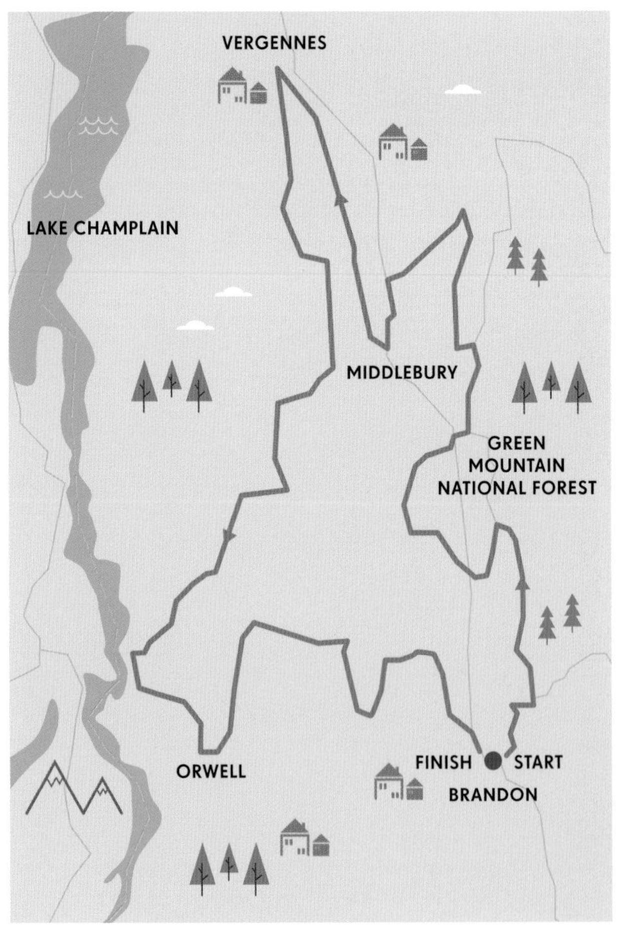

LEGAL LOAD
LIMIT
8
TONS
TWO DOLLARS FINE
to drive on this bridge
FASTER THAN A WALK.

renowned for inn-to-inn cycling tours, as is Vermont in general – with good reason.

For starters, it's predominantly rural – only Wyoming has a smaller population than Vermont, and the state's tallest building is only 11 storeys – and most of its roads are wide, quiet and eminently bike-friendly. The food's terrific, all artisan this and that, craft beers and, well, oceans of maple syrup. And it's breathtakingly beautiful.

My three-day jaunt began in Brandon, an artsy little settlement of clapboard houses where wicker chairs rock on shady verandas. I'd timed my trip well. A handful of chilly nights had kick-started the leaf-peeping season, so when I saddled up on a crisp September morning, the hilltops were already smoldering with fall colors.

I tootled languidly along Park St and out past traditional farmsteads, glancing at the map to confirm my deliberately tortuous path. The plan was to pedal about four hours each day, covering 30 or 40 miles – but the blue line marking my route staggered across the page like a drunken spider, partly to avoid busy roads, partly to take in the most scenic patches.

A speedy pace was impossible anyway, because photo calls came thick and fast. I'd no sooner pack away the camera after one viewpoint than another materialized. First came the Falls of Lana, cascading 60ft or so down the forested hillside. Then I skirted Lake Dunmore, wooden jetties jutting into placid waters. I might manage half a mile, then be waylaid for 10 minutes snapping grazing cows, hayfields and grain silos, or a barn-cum-antiques-store from which spilled toy cars, rusty signs, vintage hoes and whirligigs.

"I made a circuitous loop north, waylaid by whimsical road names demanding to be checked out"

It was mid-afternoon when I meandered into that night's halt, Middlebury. The archetypal Vermont college town (Robert Frost lectured here), it's blessed with white-spired churches, galleries, cafes and views over the burbling Otter River. I strolled along its brick-built main street and explored the Henry Sheldon Museum – 'Bringing Vermont History to Life since 1882' – and Vermont Folklife Center, showcasing local arts and crafts.

Next morning I fueled up at the farmers' market, its stalls laden with breads, cheeses, goat's milk soap, and mountains of pumpkins the glowing ochre shade of late afternoon sun. Not to mention maple syrup. Bottles and jugs and flasks and flagons of maple syrup.

Loaded with portable calories, I pedaled back into the countryside en route to Shoreham, 10 miles or so from Middlebury.

FROM SAP TO SYRUP

Vermont produces more maple syrup than any other US state. Native American peoples taught settlers how to tap maple trunks in late winter (late February/early March) to collect the sap that oozes out as it rises in the morning and falls at night. To make syrup, they'd throw hot rocks into hollowed-out logs filled with sap; today, wood-fired evaporators are used. Forty gallons of sap produce just one gallon of syrup.

Left to right: Lake Champlain; Middlebury College; maple syrup; Halloween scene. Previous page: one of Vermont's famed covered bridges

But why go direct when you can enjoy the even-more-scenic route? Instead of heading directly west, I made a circuitous loop north via Vergennes, waylaid periodically by whimsical road names demanding to be checked out: Lemon Fair Rd, Bittersweet Falls Rd, Snake Mountain Rd. The latter traced a ridge providing panoramic views across the broad sweep of the Champlain Valley, Middlebury's college and steeples rising from a sea of autumn colors to my left.

Bolstered by a breakfast mountain of blueberry pancakes in Shoreham, on my final morning I pedaled through a murky pea-souper and whizzed past the turn off for Larrabee Point, where a ferry crosses Lake Champlain to New York State and historic Fort Ticonderoga, then halted to investigate a roadside army of painted wooden creatures. In the adjacent barn I found the gallery of sculptor Norton Latourelle, who has carved a Noah's ark of dogs, birds and rabbits – plus a curious long-necked beast labeled 'Champ.'

'He was first seen long before your Loch Ness Monster,' Norton grinned. 'The early French explorer Samuel de Champlain described him as a "20ft serpent, thick as a barrel and with the head of a horse."'

A tall tale, to be sure. But a search for a mysterious water creature might provide just the excuse to return and pedal some more of Vermont's snaking, sensational byways. **PB**

TOOLKIT

Start/End // Brandon, Vermont
Distance // About 99 miles (160km) Brandon–Middlebury–(Vergennes)–Shoreham–Brandon
Getting there // Rutland Airport is 22 miles (35km) south of Brandon. Cape Air (www.capeair.com) flies from Boston Logan.
Tour // Inn to Inn (www.inntoinn.com) offers a four-night package, including half-board accommodation, maps, route notes, bike rental and baggage transfers.
Bike rental // Green Mountain Bikes (www.greenmountainbikes.com) rents bikes that can be delivered to inns.
When to ride // April to October. Foliage season is mid-September to mid-October, when rates rise and accommodation gets booked out.

Opposite: the Kancamagus Hwy climbs its way through the White Mountains

MORE LIKE THIS FALLING LEAVES RIDES

SONOMA COUNTY, USA

Sonoma County is where California's velo and vino cultures collide in a happy claret splatter every autumn. For a classic Wine Country ride, leave the hub town of Healdsburg, ride along Westside and turn right onto West Dry Creek Rd, an undulating 9-mile (14km) avenue that's one of California's most popular cycling roads. At Yoakim Bridge Rd, cross the valley to Dry Creek Rd, hang a left and climb Canyon Rd before enjoying the descent into Alexander Valley. Turn right, roll through Geyserville, cross Russian River and take Hwy 128, Red Winery and Pine Flat roads back towards Healdsburg, via Jimtown, with valley-hugging vineyards to the right and hills ablaze with autumnal colors on your left.

Start/End // Healdsburg
Distance // 32 miles (51km)

KANCAMAGUS HWY, NEW HAMPSHIRE

Continue your leaf-peeping pilgrimage in one of the best US states for fall foliage: New Hampshire. The Kancamagus Scenic Byway is the eastern portion of New Hampshire Rte 112 and it climbs through the White Mountains – in September and October the route is a popular drive with leaf-peepers but due to the low speeds it's a fairly comfortable experience sharing the road (weekends are more crowded). Starting from Conway it's a long, steady climb westward up to the pass but it steepens the further you go. The reward will be views of Mt Washington – savor them and the colors of the surrounding forest because you won't want to take your eyes off the road on the fast descent as you drop the 2000ft you just earned.

Start // Conway
End // Lincoln
Distance // 32 miles (51km)

PETIT-TÉMIS INTERPROVINCIAL TRAIL, CANADA

On this rail trail, riders not only enjoy an autumnal display of russet foliage but also cross between two Canadian provinces. The trail – also part of the Trans-Canada Trail – sets out from Rivière-du-Loup in Québec and meanders east through the Témiscouata to New Brunswick. You can hop on a ferry at Témiscouata-sur-le-Lac to cross into Parc National du Lac Témiscouata or continue along the southern shore to finish the trail at Edmunston. It's a family-friendly, traffic-free and relatively level trail that shows off the best of Québec's forests and waterways and there are several campgrounds along the way if you decide to linger among the fall leaves. Note that bicycle helmets are compulsory in New Brunswick.

Start // Rivière-du-Loup
End // Edmunston
Distance // 84 miles (134km)
Info // www.petit-témis.ca

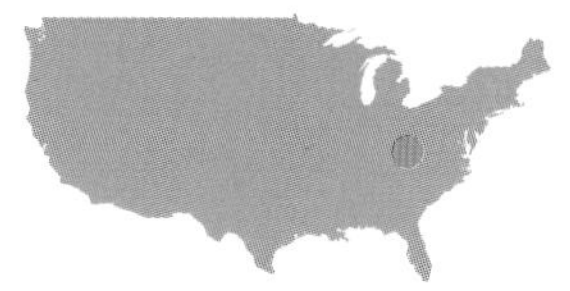

SHENANDOAH'S SKYLINE DRIVE

From the depths of the Depression rose this demanding ridgetop ride through the heart of Virginia's Appalachian nature. Fortunately those hardy builders ensured there are plenty of picturesque stop offs.

Six miles beyond and more than 1500ft higher than the Front Royal Entrance Station at the north end of Shenandoah National Park, I knew I was in for a challenge. Ahead lay lots more: 99 miles and 8000-plus cumulative feet of climbing on the appropriately named Skyline Drive, the famous ridgetop road that runs the length of this Appalachian park in Virginia.

I'd already been warned, of course. About the dozen or so categorized climbs, the two narrow lanes with no shoulders, the blind curves, impatient drivers and changeable weather. Even the bears! But the rhapsodies were just as rich. The eye-tearing descents, canopy-shaded corridors of tall oaks and pines, slow speed limit of 35mph and the dozens of overlooks with views of the Blue Ridge and Allegheny mountains and flanking valleys, sometimes shrouded in mist or, in autumn, speckled bright with seasonal color. And yes, the bears and other wildlife too, moving freely, sometimes across the road right in front of you. I felt ready for this mix of good and not-so-good that every cyclist expects.

The first hard miles on the Skyline Drive, however, were an important reality check. And the first good place to regather my hill-frayed wits was the Dickey Ridge Visitor Center, just 5 miles into the park. Fortunately, the historic building was exactly what I needed: a chance to reckon with the avenue ahead through a small but useful nature exhibit, scale model of Shenandoah, introductory video and ranger talk about bears and bear safety. The paper maps and other information available at the front desk also came in handy, as did the water tap and bathrooms, which I knew were not in abundant supply along the drive.

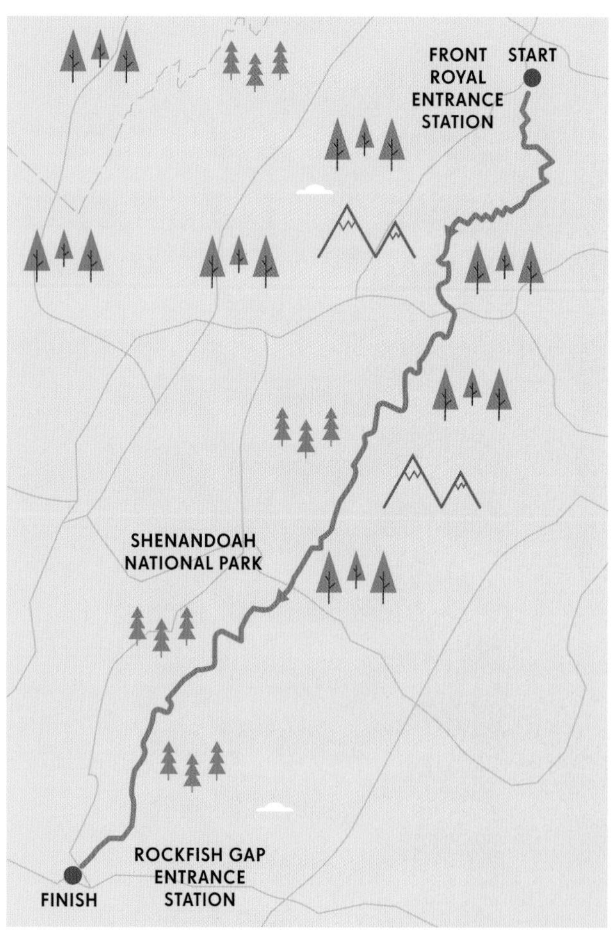

> *"The greatest ride hazards on the Skyline Drive were entirely natural – variable weather and wildlife. I was always on the alert for bears"*

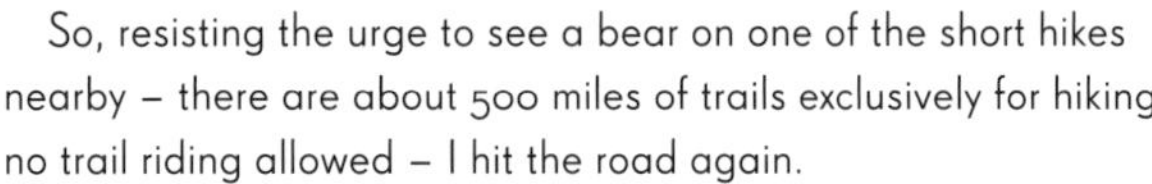

So, resisting the urge to see a bear on one of the short hikes nearby – there are about 500 miles of trails exclusively for hiking; no trail riding allowed – I hit the road again.

With the arduous ascent behind me, the longest and steepest I would face, the relief of a 2-mile descent was very welcome, even though the road continued to roller coaster, which I learned was typical of the Skyline Drive. The next three climbs of only a few miles each received only short downhill rewards, the last one interrupted after milepost 17 at the Range View Overlook, reputed to have the best views in the northern section of the park.

Truth told, my gaze had already repeatedly wandered to the expansive panoramas, on both sides of the ridge, at the pull-offs, of which there are more than 75 along the Skyline's full length. Throughout my ride, even when I didn't get out of the saddle, these sidings never palled, both for the visual feast they offered and the relief from the road.

Finally, a tick beyond milepost 21, right after the Hogback Overlook, a glorious 1000ft plummet began, giving my legs an extended break and my brain a chance to consider what I had learned and seen about my surroundings. I was able to settle into a riding rhythm that would carry me through the two allotted days. I'd quickly determined that although Skyline Drive was designed for cars – made additionally obvious by warnings to cyclists published in all of the park literature – the pedaling was truly glorious.

In fact, the greatest ride hazards were entirely natural: variable weather and wildlife. Up in the mountains, storms and thick fog can blow in quite unexpectedly. As a result, reflective gear is highly recommended, and strong front and rear lights are required. With wildlife, though I saw many smaller animals like deer and groundhogs, I was always on alert for bears, but never crossed any.

I didn't cross much at all, really. I was visiting in shoulder season (highly recommended!), so the roads were not busy and the drivers usually respectful. Even better, the pavement was consistently excellent. And with time and calm enough to appreciate an environment alive with birds, butterflies and flowers, I felt at ease and the ride blurred into a tree-lined haze of long, but not steep, climbs and fast descents.

IRON MIKE

In 1933, faced with the Great Depression, 10 Civilian Conservation Corps camps were established in the Shenandoah area so that 10,000 unemployed men participating in this major public work relief program could build the trails, picnic grounds, and stone guard walls that made the park's visitor infrastructure viable. At the Big Meadows visitor center, 'Iron Mike' is a bronze statue commemorating their work.

Left to right: black bears are present in the park; spring sunshine; a local warbler; cycle-touring the Skyline Drive. Previous page: sunset over Shenandoah National Park

At Elkwallow (milepost 24), I experienced the first of three 'waysides.' The other two are at Big Meadows (milepost 51) and Loft Mountain (milepost 81). (There's also water at Panorama, milepost 31; and Pinnacles, milepost 35.) These service areas are crucial for cyclists, complete with running water, bathrooms, camp stores, lunch counters and even permanent, 24-hour bike repair stations with a built-in pump (Schrader valves only) and a basic kit of tools permanently affixed by cables to a bike workstand. A QR code pulls up rudimentary bike-repair videos.

Shenandoah's biggest service center, and the most likely place to divide a park ride over two days, is Big Meadows, a rare high-elevation wetland located at milepost 51, roughly halfway through the park. It is also the location of one of the park's four campgrounds, one of its two full-service lodges, which I stayed in, and the large Byrd Visitor Center, with an excellent exhibit about the controversial creation of the park, largely by the Depression-era Civilian Conservation Corps.

By the end of the Skyline Drive, I was bursting with a real sense of cycling accomplishment. Perhaps next time I won't stop at Shenandoah's southern boundary where it segues directly into another meandering highway: the Blue Ridge Parkway carries on for another 469 miles to Great Smoky Mountains National Park in North Carolina. **EG**

TOOLKIT

Start // Front Royal Entrance Station, Shenandoah National Park
End // Rockfish Gap Entrance Station, Shenandoah National Park
Distance // 105 miles (169km)
Getting there // Washington, DC's well-served airports (Washington Dulles International and Reagan National) are about 75 miles (120km) east of Front Royal. Amtrak trains and Greyhound buses run to Charlottesville, also site of Charlottesville-Albemarle Airport, approximately 25 miles (40km) east of Rockfish Gap.
Where to stay/eat // Inside the park, there are good-quality campgrounds, lodges and 'waysides' with gift shops and food.
When to ride // Mid-April through mid-October are best, though from mid-June to mid-August it can be quite hot and humid. Peak fall foliage season is very popular.
More info // www.nps.gov/shen

Opposite: Wizard Island in Crater Lake, part of Oregon's Crater Lake National Park

MORE LIKE THIS
NATIONAL PARK RIDGE RIDES

RIM DRIVE, CRATER LAKE NATIONAL PARK, OREGON

In southwest Oregon, the deep blue of Crater Lake glistens in the sun, ringed by the caldera of a volcano that erupted thousands of years ago. Snaking along its perimeter rim is a scenic highway called, appropriately, Rim Drive. For strong cyclists, this is a dream road, with wide shoulders, a speed limit of 35mph (56km/h), a minimum elevation of 6450ft (1966m) and steep grades that rise and fall through four peaks over 7350ft (2240m) and eight main viewing areas with breathtaking vistas. A few days each year, the eastern two thirds of the Rim Drive are open only to cyclists and hikers. One of those days is called Ride the Rim, a free event that provides full support and park admission.
Start/End // Rim Village Visitor Centre
Distance // 33 miles (53km)
Info // www.nps.gov/crla/ and ridetherimoregon.com

GOING-TO-THE-SUN ROAD, GLACIER NATIONAL PARK, MONTANA

Traversing the mountains of northern Montana's Glacier National Park is this historic and engineering landmark: a narrow and winding, but shoulder-less, two-lane road chiseled through awe-inspiring alpine country, including a tough but spectacular 12-mile (19km), 3300ft (1000m) climb over the 6646ft (2025m) Logan Pass, followed by a seven-mile (11km) descent. Given the high elevation, mountainous terrain and heavy snowfall, the full Going-to-the-Sun Road may only be passable from late June to mid-October, so it is critical to check ahead. Also, from mid-June to Labor Day there are restrictions on cyclists' midday access to parts of the road. But where else can two-wheelers turn for sharp curves that open on to sweeping panoramas complete with grazing mountain goats and bighorn sheep?
Start // Apgar Visitor Center
End // Saint Mary Visitor Center
Distance // 50 miles (80km)
Info // www.nps.gov/glac

TRAIL RIDGE ROAD, ROCKY MOUNTAIN NATIONAL PARK, COLORADO

This 'Highway to the Sky' is the highest continuous paved road in the US, topping out at 12,183ft (3713m), and with more than 10 miles (16km) above the tree line. A scenic and historic byway beloved by hill-hungry bikers, it eases across the Rockies and over the Continental Divide, rising more than 4300ft (1,310m) in about 20 miles (32km) before plunging back down 3500ft (1067m) in 22 miles (35km). As the road was engineered to maintain a grade of usually less than 5%, it isn't particularly steep. But the air is thin! The breathtaking overlooks should certainly not be overlooked, especially when the weather is clear. The full road is usually only open from Memorial Day to Columbus Day.
Start // Fall River Visitor Center (Estes Park)
End // Kawuneeche Visitor Center (Grand Lake)
Distance // 42 miles (68km)
Info // www.nps.gov/romo

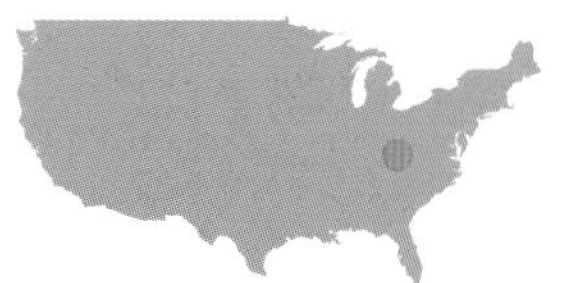

THE VIRGINIA CREEPER TRAIL

Pin your ears back for a 35-mile downhill spin – and the bygone sounds that once made the Appalachian Mountains the folk-music center of the US.

Down in the valley it's a balmy March morning, but up here, on the thickly forested slopes of Whitetop Mountain, the snow stands a foot deep. The van that brought us and our bikes here has left, and we stand looking at each other, the silence heavy. Can we ride through the snow? On *these* battered, rental mountain bikes?

My husband and I are here in the Appalachian Mountains at the southwestern most corner of Virginia, to ride the Virginia Creeper Trail, a 35-mile (56km) rail trail. In the 19th and early 20th century this path was the Norfolk & Western Railway's Abingdon Line, hauling timber from Whitetop Mountain to the mill in the town of Damascus. Locals nicknamed the service the 'Virginia Creeper' for its plodding pace; it was said to be so slow that workers could walk alongside the train picking berries.

We're not moving much faster as we start out, even going downhill. While you can ride the trail in either direction, we've chosen the popular option of being ferried up the mountain from Damascus by a local bike-rental service and ending in the Great Appalachian Valley town of Abingdon, where we'll be picked up and taken to our car. But in heavy, wet snow, we find ourselves walking the bikes for the first several miles.

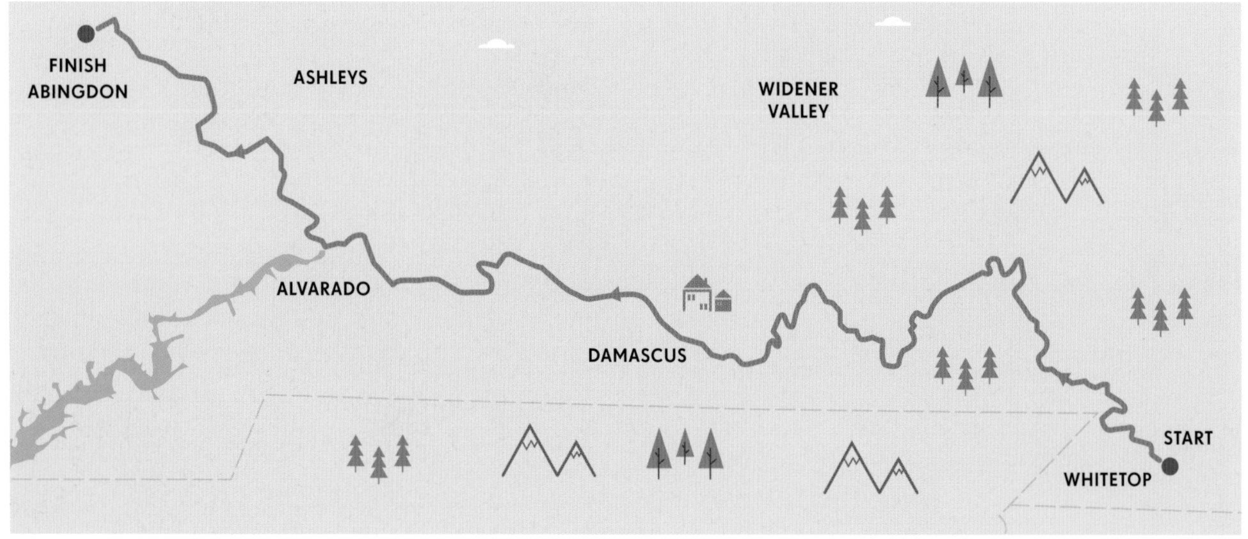

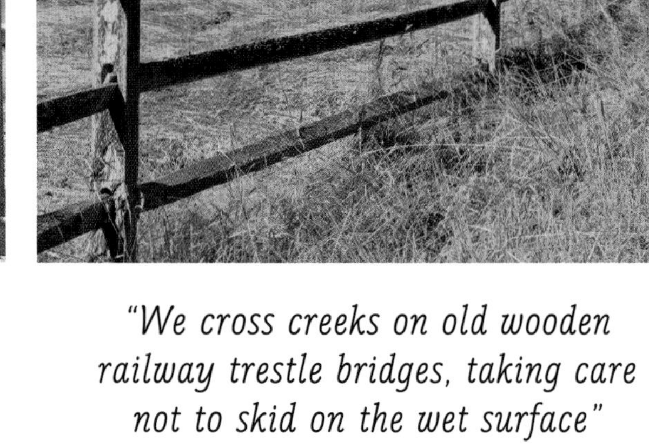

Though not what we'd intended, it's a stunning walk. We pass beneath wintry branches waving like skeletons in the pale gray sky, the trees occasionally parting to reveal rolling farmland thick with mist, dotted with barns that look like they've been standing since the days when the train still chugged up the hill. Though on warm spring and summer weekends the trail can see hundreds, if not thousands, of riders, today we're nearly alone. (Later, I'll ride the trail again in early summer, when it's a tunnel of green and the hills explode with mountain laurel, rhododendron and fire pinks.)

After an hour or so the snow thins out and we're able to hop on our bikes. We ride over old wooden railway trestles, taking care not to skid on the wet surface, crossing creeks and passing through a narrow gorge whose sides sparkle with a curtain of icicles. The creeks, snow-melt-engorged, rumble angrily past, spewing white foam.

After 17 miles of downhill through forests of white pine and red maple we come to the town of Damascus, population approximately 800. Once home to a thriving lumber mill, today Damascus trades on its location at the crossroads of four trails: the Virginia Creeper, the Appalachian Trail, US Bicycle Route 76 and the Iron Mountain Trail. In May, 20,000 or more hikers converge on the town for the Appalachian Trail Days Festival, with music, outdoor gear sales, a parade and more. Today, however, the single main street is quiet, though lights twinkle invitingly inside several cyclist-oriented cafes. But we've brought our own lunch, so we hunker down by the cherry-red train caboose on display in the empty town park to eat our apples and peanut butter sandwiches.

"We cross creeks on old wooden railway trestle bridges, taking care not to skid on the wet surface"

Many riders end here in Damascus, but we're pressing on to Abingdon. From Damascus onward, the trail is more or less flat. We ride through pastureland and alongside a river, watching cows graze and birds wheel overhead. Down here it's warm enough for me to finally take off my jacket, and the cool spring air feels good on my arms. My stomach is just starting to rumble again when, in less than two hours, we arrive at the trailhead in Abingdon.

That evening, after washing the mud and sweat off in the Comfort Inn (for those, unlike me, who think ahead, there are plenty of delightful family-run inns and B&Bs in the area) and head into Abingdon. I've booked us dinner at The Tavern, built in 1779. This creaky building has played host to figures such as president Andrew Jackson, served as a Civil War hospital, and held the first post office in the western Blue Ridge Mountains. We devour

Above (both images) © Pat & Chuck Blackley | Alamy Stock Photo

RAILS TO TRAILS

Since the 1980s, rail trails have become a popular way of rehabbing abandoned railways. Some trails, like the Virginia Creeper, help preserve rural landscapes scarred by mining and forestry. Others are more urban, keeping otherwise underutilized parts of cities alive, and encouraging bike commuters. Today there are more than 2000 rail trails in the US, offering more than 23,000 miles of riding, with hundreds more in the works.

Left to right: the Old Alvarado Station on the Virginia Creeper rail trail; Green Cove and red barns; family fun on Trestle 46; Virginia's fall colours. Previous page: the Watauga trestle bridge, no.12

platter-sized *Wienerschnitzel* by candlelight in the sloping second-floor dining room, picturing ourselves as stagecoach travelers passing through these mountains centuries ago.

After dinner, we wander down the postcard-pretty brick Main St to the Barter Theater. Opened in 1933, it's the oldest running professional theater in America. Depression-strapped locals were once allowed to pay their ticket fees in food – carrots, jam, country ham – hence the theater's name. We're out of country ham so pay the 21st-century way – online, with a credit card – for tonight's show, a postmodern exploration of technology that's as good as any performance I've seen, though a bit strange amid the charmingly rural environs.

Despite its remoteness, the area's cultural routes run deep. Fiddles and banjos have long rung out in the hollows of these mountains, and by the early 20th century the hills of southwest Virginia were famous for their Appalachian folk music. In the 1930s, Whitetop Mountain was home to the legendary White Top Folk Festival, a gathering of old time musicians prominent enough to attract the likes of Eleanor Roosevelt.

In the morning, our legs are sore, but not so sore we don't drive back to the trailhead, coffees in hand, for a quick stroll along the trail. Our car will be muddy for the drive back, but it's worth it for those last glimpses of tranquil Appalachian countryside. **EM**

TOOLKIT

Start // Whitetop Station, Virginia
End // Abingdon, Virginia (or vice versa)
Distance // 35 miles (56km)
Getting there // The nearest commercial airport is the Tri-Cities Airport nearly 30 miles across the state line in Tennessee. A car is essential for visiting the area.
Where to stay // There are a handful of chain motels around Abingdon; more charming is the White Birches Inn (www.whitebirchesinn.com) in the town's historic district.
When to ride // Spring is abloom with wildflowers, summer is lusciously green and fall colorful with foliage.
Bike services // There are nearly a dozen bike rental shops in the area, mostly in Damascus. Most provide a shuttle service to the top of the trail as well.
More info // www.vacreepertrail.org

Opposite: the historic residences and leafy streets of Washington DC's Georgetown neighborhood

MORE LIKE THIS SOUTHERN RAIL TRAILS

THE AMERICAN TOBACCO TRAIL, NORTH CAROLINA

Just a few decades ago, downtown Durham, North Carolina still smelled sweetly of tobacco leaves drying in brick warehouses. Today, the tobacco industry is gone, and the warehouses have been converted into hip apartments, galleries, breweries and restaurants. Visit this up-and-coming southern city by bike by hopping on the American Tobacco Trail, a 23-mile (37km) trail following the old American Tobacco Company freight line. The mostly-flat trail crosses fields and forests of Wake and Chatham Counties before hitting suburban Durham. The landscape gradually becomes more urban before terminating near downtown's Durham Bulls Athletic Park, home to the storied Triple-A baseball team. Refresh yourself with a microbrew, fusion tapas or artisanal ice cream, cruise the downtown galleries or drop in on a punk gig at a local bar before heading home.
Start // New Hill, Wake County
End // Downtown Durham
Distance // 23 miles (37km)
Info // www.triangletrails.org/american-tobacco-trail

CAPITAL CRESCENT TRAIL, WASHINGTON, DC

This 11-mile (18km) DC rail trail is not epic in distance, but it's a fun spin into the capital, and it's easy to see why it's popular with bike-commuting federal employees, stroller-pushing parents and the occasional ostentatiously jogging senator. The usual opening section, from Silver Spring, is currently closed; instead, begin in Bethesda, in suburban Maryland (shortening the ride by 3.5 miles/5.5km), and cruise the flat asphalt surface, tracing the old Georgetown Branch line of the Baltimore and Ohio Railroad, abandoned in the mid-1980s. Follow the Little Falls Branch tributary to the wide, cafe-au-lait-colored Potomac, passing the ruined battery of Civil War–era Fort Sumner. Following the Potomac into the city, you'll see historic boathouses and plenty of leafy, well-heeled neighborhoods before ending up in upmarket-funky Georgetown, with excellent shopping and tons of fun bars frequented by nearby university students. Wander the elite residential side streets to admire the historic townhouses – and see if you can glimpse any faces from the morning's *Washington Post*.
Start // Bethesda, Maryland
End // Georgetown, Washington, DC
Distance // 11 miles (18km), in shortened form 8 miles (13km)
Info // www.cctrail.org

GREENBRIER RIVER TRAIL, WEST VIRGINIA

Deep in old West Virginia logging country is the splendid Greenbrier River Trail, a 78-mile (126km) crushed limestone path following the old Chesapeake and Ohio Railway. The trains served the timber and mining industries here from the late 1800s before rumbling to a slow stop by mid-century. Today, some of the trail's most interesting draws are the industrial ghost towns along the way. At the northern trailhead is Cass, built by the West Virginia Pulp and Paper Company and largely abandoned when the mill closed in the early 1960s. Today you can get off your bike to visit the village's history museum or stay overnight in a refurbished worker's cottage. Ride on, following the Greenbrier River through a karst valley dense with old-growth trees, traversing mountain tunnels and crossing 35 bridges.
Start // Cass, West Virginia
End // North Caldwell, West Virginia (or vice versa)
Distance // 78 miles (126km)
Info // www.wvstateparks.com/park/greenbrier-river-trail

A CIRCUIT OF SAN JUAN ISLAND

A breezy half-day spin around San Juan Island passes fragrant lavender farms, groves of misty pines, gorgeous coastline, and pods of orcas.

Nestled between Seattle and the Canadian border in the postcard-perfect Puget Sound, San Juan Island is one of several that comprise the archipelago of San Juan Islands. Each of the islands are filled with stunning sights and quaint diversions that make a lovely escape for casual cyclists. Each island also has a particular appeal for people who love to travel with their bicycle – the laid-back cruising on Lopez Island versus the slightly more heart-racing terrain of Orcas Island – but the picturesque San Juan Island is just right, offering maximum views and a taste of adventure that is approachable for a wide range of riders.

I discovered the bicycle-friendly roads that circle San Juan Island offer something new around every bend – rocky outcrops that plunge into sparkling waves, lofty groves of Douglas fir, migratory birdlife, bucolic farms and miles of coast. But this 35-mile ride has just as many excuses to get off the bike, including a pair

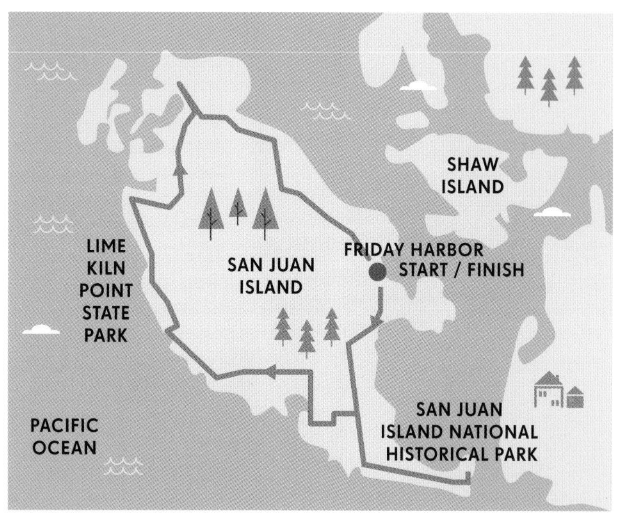

of pretty harbor towns, roadside farm stands, and historic sites that speak to the region's colorful past. The biodiversity of such a small island is fascinating – from dense conifer forest and open farmlands to beautiful beaches. Modestly rolling terrain, 247 annual days of sunshine, and breathtaking scenery makes it an ideal destination to ride.

My partner and I began at the island's main port, Friday Harbor, connected by a frequent ferry service to Washington. After fueling up on breakfast at one of the harborside cafes we were on our way.

Heading south out of town on Argyle Rd, we followed the signs to the American Camp visitor center, one of the two former 19th-century military camps that make up the San Juan Island National Historical Park. A ranger was on hand answering questions about the so-called Pig War, an 1859 boundary skirmish between the British and the US. The conflict owes its colorful name to the incident that sparked it: a dispute between an American farmer and an employee of the Hudson's Bay Company who owned an unruly pig. Fortunately, the pig was the only casualty.

A few more miles south and we reached South Beach, which has incredible views across the Strait of Juan de Fuca to the snow-capped drama of the Olympic Mountain range. We continued south to the Cattle Point Lighthouse along a steep bluff and paused at pull-offs for mesmerizing views of Vancouver Island, Olympic National Park and Port Angeles.

Continuing west and north we made our way to Lime Kiln Point

"Volunteer whale watchers scan the waves for orcas and other species of whales that include gray, humpback and minke"

State Park – known to the locals as Whale Watch Park – which is one of the island's most popular spots for a picnic. If you're here in the summer, you have a good chance of spotting a pod of orca whales. There are volunteer whale watchers at the most popular overlooks, scanning the waves for orcas and other species of whales that include gray, humpback, and minke. This is a good excuse to park the bike, as the area is great to explore on foot. We wandered around an historic lighthouse, an interpretive centre with hands-on exhibits and displays about the orcas, and an ancient lime kiln. This is where you should top up your water as well, as the slightly more vigorous riding is about to begin.

Leaving Lime Kiln Point, the road gains a couple of hundred feet of elevation, passing some of the most spectacular coastal sights on the entire ride. Over the hill, we cruised down to San Juan County Park. If you missed the whales at the first stop, try again; the unfortunately named Smallpox Bay is another prime spot to look for the pods. This part of the island is home to all kinds of other wildlife as well, including deer and bald eagles. Turning left on West Valley Rd, we rolled past the curious gang at the Krystal

THE ORCAS OF SAN JUAN ISLANDS

The San Juan Islands host three resident pods of black and white orcas – a population of just over 80 whales, many of whom are known on a first-name basis by the locals. The orcas call these waters home between May and October. If you want to see them up close, consider a kayaking excursion – but your chances are just as good to spot them as they swim near the shore.

Left to right: the San Juan Islands have three pods of resident orcas; Roche Harbor and Lime Kiln Lighthouse on San Juan Island. Previous page: looking out over the San Juan archipelago with Mt Baker in the distance

Acres Alpaca Farm – which has a great gift shop of locally made goods – before seeing signs for English Camp. Situated on an open, grassy patch, this is another pleasant place for a rest.

As we continued down the road toward Roche Harbor, we started thinking about lunch. Locals recommended the Westcott Bay Shellfish Company, a small family farm that produces deliciously briny oysters and has no-frills picnic tables where you can enjoy the sun, and shuck your lunch. But we were in the mood for something a bit heartier, so headed into town.

Centered around a tidy port and the stately Hotel de Haro, the marina at Roche Harbor is a charming lunch stop. Lime production was a major industry here during the late 19th century, but these days the small harbor is a magnet for yachting retirees from the Pacific Northwest. Explore the lanes of the village before making your way to the San Juan Islands Sculpture Park, a 19-acre park with more than 150 works by local and international artists, including some amazing kinetic sculptures.

Back in the saddle, it was a straight shot back to Friday Harbor – just under 10 flat miles on Roche Harbor Rd. Halfway there, we passed the lovely Lakedale Resort – a lakeside hotel with some options for glamping – before arriving at the final diversion, San Juan Vineyards. We did a bit of tasting (we earned it!) before bringing a glass out to the patio and taking in the warm evening light. A quick three miles more brought us back to the start in Friday Harbor, for hot showers and an elegant dinner. **NC**

TOOLKIT

Start/End // Friday Harbor
Distance // 35 miles (56km).
Getting there // Take the Washington State Ferry from Anacortes (www.wsdot.com/ferries) or via Seattle's seasonal San Juan Clipper. Seasonal ferries also depart from Bellingham or Port Townsend.
Bike rental // There are plenty of bike-rental options in Friday Harbor, including high-end road bikes.
Where to eat/stay // Friday Harbor is San Juan Island's largest town, and has a host of dining and sleeping options. Romantic B&Bs are scattered all over the island.
When to ride // The best time of year for a visit is between late April and early September.
More info // For complete information on visiting the island, including cycling resources, see www.visitsanjuans.com.

Opposite: the Kinsol Trestle on the Cowichan Valley Trail

MORE LIKE THIS ISLAND RIDES

VIEQUES ISLAND, PUERTO RICO

Six miles off the southeastern coast of Puerto Rico, Vieques is a little strip of paradise – just 21 miles (34km) long and 4 miles (6km) wide. Much of this enchanted place was owned by the United States Navy until 2003, when two thirds of the island transitioned from a bombing range to lush nature reserve. Pedal down its long, dusty roads to find secluded beaches otherwise inaccessible by car. Many of the best of these have no names, but Red Beach is worth seeking out; the blonde crescent strip of sand lies beyond the cracked asphalt airstrip of the former Camp Garcia. Even during the high season (between late November and May) you'll have the place mostly to yourself.
Tour // Black Beard Sports (www.blackbeardsports.com) has rentals and leads tours

NANTUCKET ISLAND RIDE, USA

Filled with New England ambience, history, and fresh-air vistas, Nantucket is a relaxing destination that's perfect to explore by bike. The island is only 14 miles (22km) long and 3.5 miles (6km) wide, so a dedicated cyclist can spin around its entirety in one day, but you'll be better off to take some short rides around town and to the outlying beaches. Start with the boutiques and restaurants on the cobbled streets of historic Nantucket Harbor before navigating the network of smooth bike paths past ocean views, migratory birds, and windswept beaches. Refuel on bowls of chowder among the rows of neat gray-shingled cottages in the old fishing village of Saiconset.
Bike hire // The Island Bike Company (www.islandbike.com) has a range of bikes, including cruisers and roadies

COWICHAN VALLEY TRAIL, CANADA

Vancouver Island's beautifully rugged scenery lures all outdoor types, especially mountain bikers, but this easier gravel loop, which includes a wide, multiuse and largely level rail trail, is tailored for the more casual end of the spectrum and suitable for families with children. That said, its full 62-mile (100km) extent isn't to be underestimated for recreational riders. Cowichan Valley is on the southeast coast of Vancouver Island, about an hour's drive north of British Columbia's state capital, Victoria. This is (and was) an industrious region of farming and forestry but the last trains stopped running in the 1980s. What remain are several spectacular trestle bridges that you can cycle along today, such as the Kinsol Trestle. The main Cowichan Valley Trail forms the start of the Trans-Canada Trail, if you fancy continuing across the country; you can also cut the full loop short if preferred.
Start/End // Somenos Ball Park Fields, North Cowichan
Distance // 62 miles (100km)
Info // www.trailsbc.ca/loop/vancouver-island/cowichan-valley-c28ab

INDEX

A

B

C

N